Microsoft® Office Access™ 2007

ILLUSTRATED COURSE GUIDE

BASIC

Microsoft® Office Access™ 2007

ILLUSTRATED COURSE GUIDE

BASIC

Lisa Friedrichsen

Australia • Brazil • Japan • Korea • Mexico • Singapore • Spain • United Kingdom • United States

Illustrated Course Guide: Microsoft Office Access 2007 Basic

Lisa Friedrichsen

Senior Acquisitions Editor: Marjorie Hunt

Senior Product Manager: Christina Kling Garrett

Associate Product Manager: Rebecca Padrick

Editorial Assistant: Michelle Camisa

Marketing Coordinator: Jennifer Hankin

Contributing Author: Elizabeth Eisner Reding

Developmental Editor: Lisa Ruffolo

Content Project Manager: Jill Klaffky

Copy Editor: Gary Michael Spahl

QA Manuscript Reviewers: Nicole Ashton, Jeff Schwartz, Danielle Shaw, Teresa Storch, Susan Whalen

Cover Designer: Marissa Falco

Cover Artist: Mark Hunt

Composition: GEX Publishing Services

ISBN-13: 978-1-4239-0531-8

ISBN-10: 1-4239-0531-8

Course Technology
20 Channel Center Street
Boston, MA 02210
USA

Cengage Learning is a leading provider of customized learning solutions with office locations around the globe, including Singapore, the United Kingdom, Australia, Mexico, Brazil, and Japan. Locate your local office at:
international.cengage.com/region

Cengage Learning products are represented in Canada by Nelson Education, Ltd.

To learn more about Course Technology, visit **www.cengage.com/coursetechnology**

To learn more about Cengage Learning, visit **www.cengage.com.**

Purchase any of our products at your local college store or at our preferred online store **www.ichapters.com**

Printed in the United States of America
2 3 4 5 6 7 8 9 11 10 09

About The Illustrated Course Guides

Welcome to the Microsoft Office 2007 Illustrated Course Guides! The books in this series are ideally suited for a wide range of learners who need to gain skill proficiency at a particular level for Word, Excel, Access, PowerPoint, or Windows Vista. The highly visual and full-color lesson material is extremely approachable for learners of all levels, and the wealth of reinforcement exercises ensures skills retention. To maximize skills retention and measure proficiency, use Illustrated Course Guides in conjunction with SAM 2007, our robust assessment and training system.

As you probably have heard by now, Microsoft completely redesigned this latest version of Office from the ground up. No more menus! No more toolbars! The software changes Microsoft made were based on years of research during which they studied users' needs and work habits. The result is a phenomenal and powerful new version of the software that will make you and your learners more productive and help you get better results faster.

Before we started working on the Illustrated Course Guides for Microsoft Office 2007 we also conducted our own research. We reached out to nearly 100 instructors like you who have used previous editions of our Microsoft Office texts. Some of you responded to one of our surveys, others of you generously spent time with us on the phone, telling us your thoughts. Seven of you agreed to serve on our Advisory Board and guided our decisions.

As a result of all the feedback you gave us, we have preserved the features that you love, and made improvements that you suggested and requested. And of course we have covered all the key features of the new software. (For more details on what's new in this edition, please read the Preface.) We are confident that the Illustrated Course Guides for Microsoft Office 2007 and all their available resources will help any type of learner master Microsoft Office 2007.

Advisory Board

We thank our Advisory Board who enthusiastically gave us their opinions and guided our every decision on content and design from beginning to end. They are:

Kristen Callahan, Mercer County Community College
Paulette Comet, Assistant Professor, Community College of Baltimore County
Barbara Comfort, J. Sargeant Reynolds Community College
Margaret Cooksey, Tallahassee Community College
Rachelle Hall, Glendale Community College
Hazel Kates, Miami Dade College
Charles Lupico, Thomas Nelson Community College

Author Acknowledgments

Lisa Friedrichsen This book is dedicated to my learners, and all who are using this book to teach and learn about Access. Thank you. Also, thank you to all of the professionals who helped me create this book.

Preface

Welcome to *Illustrated Course Guide: Microsoft Office Access 2007 Basic.* If this is your first experience with the Illustrated Course Guides, you'll see that this book has a unique design: each skill is presented on two facing pages, with steps on the left and screens on the right. The layout makes it easy to digest a skill without having to read a lot of text and flip pages to see an illustration.

This book is an ideal learning tool for a wide range of learners—the "rookies" will find the clean design easy to follow and focused with only essential information presented, and the "hotshots" will appreciate being able to move quickly through the lessons to find the information they need without reading a lot of text. The design also makes this a great reference after the course is over! Note that the combined content in the Basic, Intermediate and Advanced Course Guides for Microsoft Office 2007 maps to the MCAS objectives, making the books an ideal preparation tool for the MCAS exam. See the illustration on the right to learn more about the pedagogical and design elements of a typical lesson.

What's New

We've made many changes and enhancements to the Microsoft Office 2007 Illustrated Course Guides. Here are some highlights of what's new:

- **New Getting Started with Microsoft® Office 2007 Unit**—This unit begins every Basic level Course Guide book and gets learners up to speed on features of Office 2007 that are common to all the applications, such as the Ribbon, the Office button, and the Quick Access toolbar.
- **Real Life Independent Challenge**—The new Real Life Independent Challenge exercises offer learners the opportunity to create projects that are meaningful to their lives, such as databases that track travel experiences, record geographic information, and maintain research on careers.

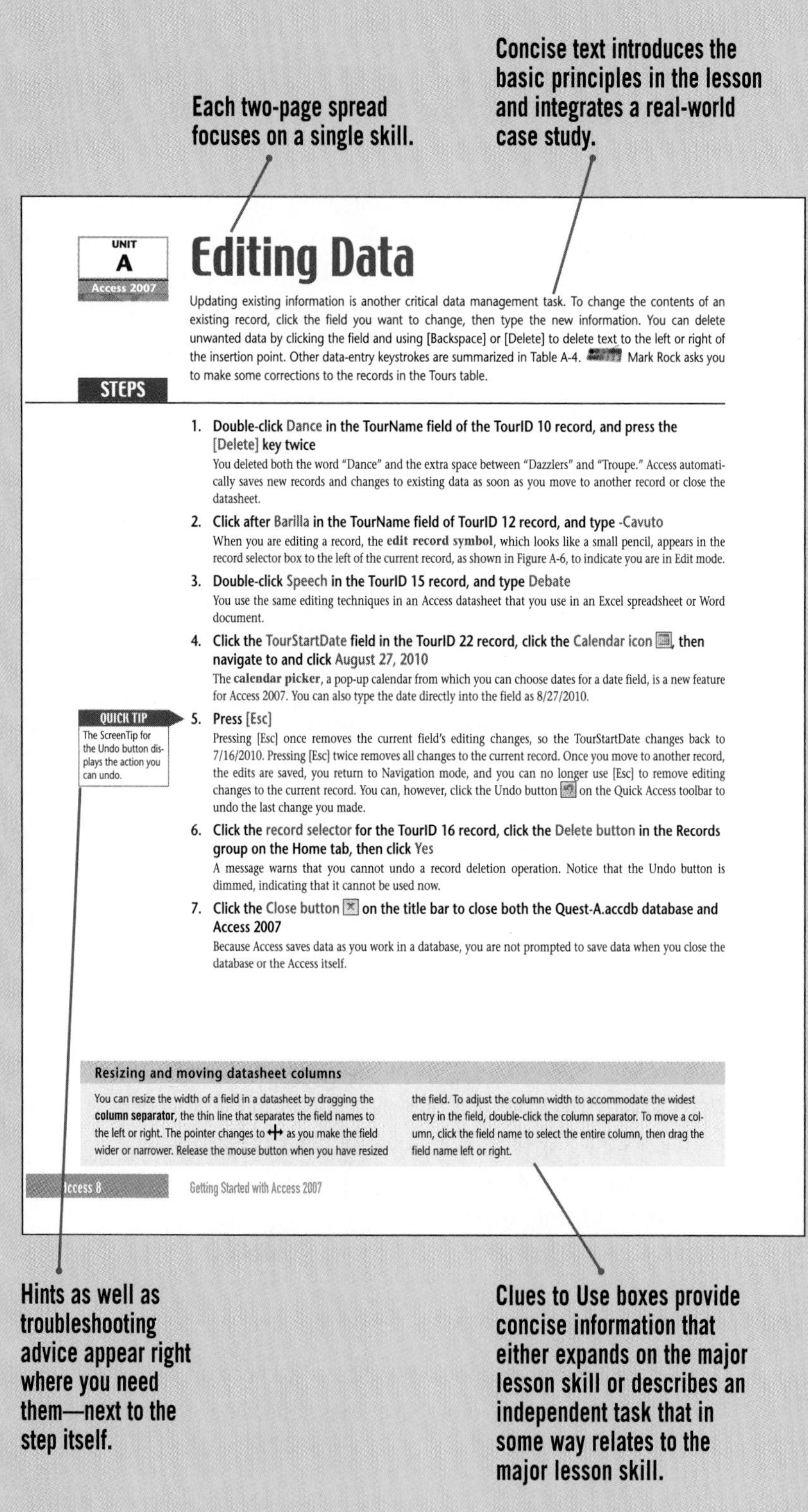
Each two-page spread focuses on a single skill.
Concise text introduces the basic principles in the lesson and integrates a real-world case study.
Hints as well as troubleshooting advice appear right where you need them—next to the step itself.
Clues to Use boxes provide concise information that either expands on the major lesson skill or describes an independent task that in some way relates to the major lesson skill.

UNIT A Access 2007

Editing Data

Updating existing information is another critical data management task. To change the contents of an existing record, click the field you want to change, then type the new information. You can delete unwanted data by clicking the field and using [Backspace] or [Delete] to delete text to the left or right of the insertion point. Other data-entry keystrokes are summarized in Table A-4. Mark Rock asks you to make some corrections to the records in the Tours table.

STEPS

1. **Double-click Dance in the TourName field of the TourID 10 record, and press the [Delete] key twice**
   You deleted both the word "Dance" and the extra space between "Dazzlers" and "Troupe." Access automatically saves new records and changes to existing data as soon as you move to another record or close the datasheet.
2. **Click after Barilla in the TourName field of TourID 12 record, and type -Cavuto**
   When you are editing a record, the **edit record symbol**, which looks like a small pencil, appears in the record selector box to the left of the current record, as shown in Figure A-6, to indicate you are in Edit mode.
3. **Double-click Speech in the TourID 15 record, and type Debate**
   You use the same editing techniques in an Access datasheet that you use in an Excel spreadsheet or Word document.
4. **Click the TourStartDate field in the TourID 22 record, click the Calendar icon, then navigate to and click August 27, 2010**
   The **calendar picker**, a pop-up calendar from which you can choose dates for a date field, is a new feature for Access 2007. You can also type the date directly into the field as 8/27/2010.
5. **Press [Esc]**
   Pressing [Esc] once removes the current field's editing changes, so the TourStartDate changes back to 7/16/2010. Pressing [Esc] twice removes all changes to the current record. Once you move to another record, the edits are saved, you return to Navigation mode, and you can no longer use [Esc] to remove editing changes to the current record. You can, however, click the Undo button on the Quick Access toolbar to undo the last change you made.
6. **Click the record selector for the TourID 16 record, click the Delete button in the Records group on the Home tab, then click Yes**
   A message warns that you cannot undo a record deletion operation. Notice that the Undo button is dimmed, indicating that it cannot be used now.
7. **Click the Close button on the title bar to close both the Quest-A.accdb database and Access 2007**
   Because Access saves data as you work in a database, you are not prompted to save data when you close the database or the Access itself.

QUICK TIP
The ScreenTip for the Undo button displays the action you can undo.

Resizing and moving datasheet columns

You can resize the width of a field in a datasheet by dragging the **column separator**, the thin line that separates the field names to the left or right. The pointer changes to ✛ as you make the field wider or narrower. Release the mouse button when you have resized the field. To adjust the column width to accommodate the widest entry in the field, double-click the column separator. To move a column, click the field name to select the entire column, then drag the field name left or right.

Access 8 Getting Started with Access 2007

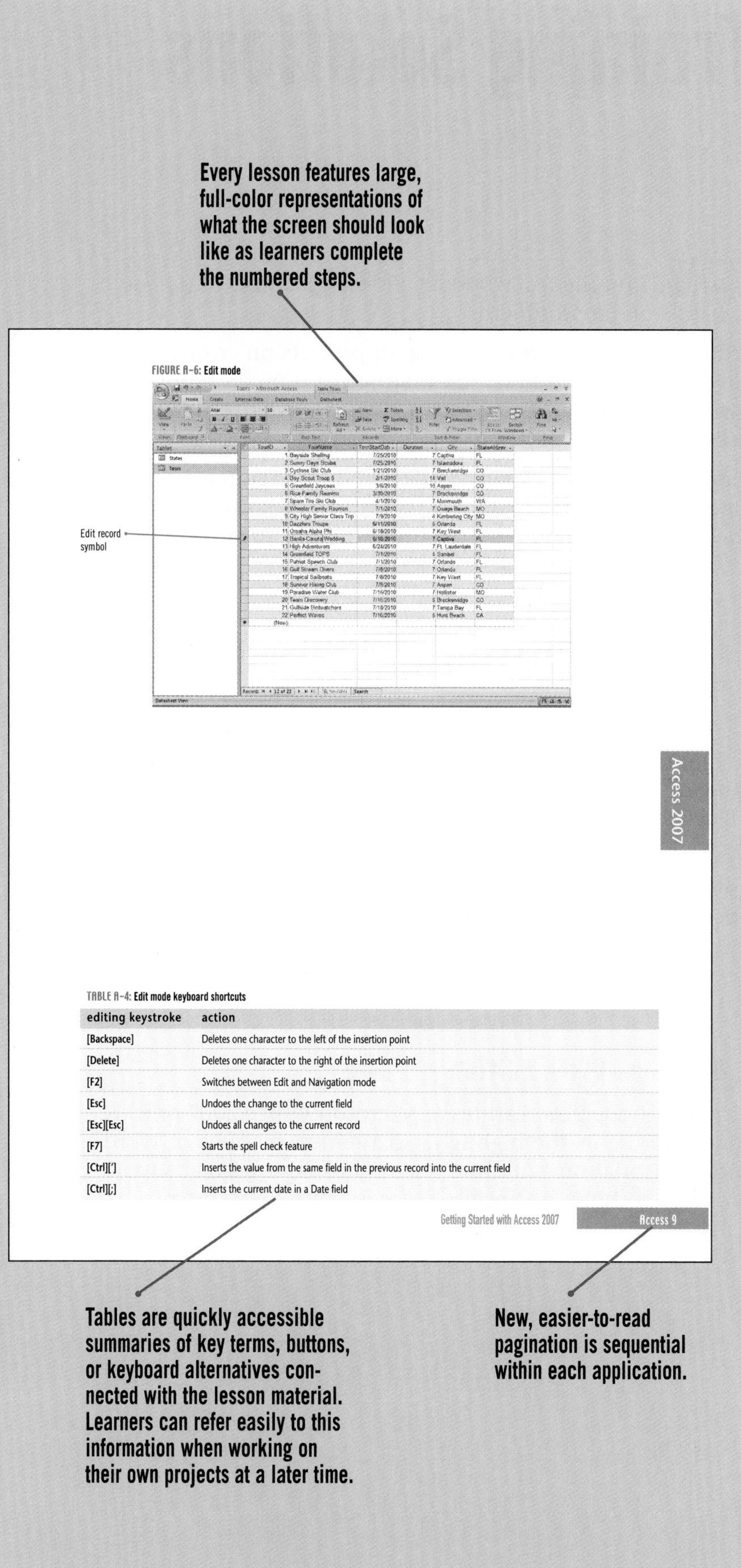

Every lesson features large, full-color representations of what the screen should look like as learners complete the numbered steps.
Edit record symbol
Access 2007
Tables are quickly accessible summaries of key terms, buttons, or keyboard alternatives connected with the lesson material. Learners can refer easily to this information when working on their own projects at a later time.
New, easier-to-read pagination is sequential within each application.

FIGURE A-6: Edit mode

TABLE A-4: Edit mode keyboard shortcuts

editing keystroke	action
[Backspace]	Deletes one character to the left of the insertion point
[Delete]	Deletes one character to the right of the insertion point
[F2]	Switches between Edit and Navigation mode
[Esc]	Undoes the change to the current field
[Esc][Esc]	Undoes all changes to the current record
[F7]	Starts the spell check feature
[Ctrl][']	Inserts the value from the same field in the previous record into the current field
[Ctrl][;]	Inserts the current date in a Date field

Getting Started with Access 2007 Access 9

- **New Case Study**—A new case study featuring Quest Specialty Travel provides a practical scenario that learners can relate to as they learn skills and promote skills retention. This fictional company offers a wide variety of tours around the world.
- **Content Improvements**—All of the content in every Illustrated Course Guide has been updated to cover Office 2007 and also to address customer feedback.

Assignments

The lessons use Quest Specialty Travel, a fictional adventure travel company, as the case study. The assignments on the light purple pages at the end of each unit increase in difficulty. Data Files and case studies provide a variety of interesting and relevant business applications to help reinforce learning and retain skills. Assignments include:

- **Concepts Reviews** consist of multiple choice, matching, and screen identification questions.
- **Skills Reviews** provide additional hands-on, step-by-step reinforcement.
- **Independent Challenges** are case projects requiring critical thinking and application of the unit skills. The Independent Challenges increase in difficulty, with the first one in each unit being the easiest. Independent Challenges 2 and 3 become increasingly open-ended, requiring more independent problem solving.
- **Real Life Independent Challenges** are practical exercises in which learners create projects to help them with their every day lives.
- **Advanced Challenge Exercises** set within the Independent Challenges provide optional steps for more advanced learners.
- **Visual Workshops** are practical, self-graded capstone projects that require independent problem solving.

Assessment & Training Solutions

SAM 2007

SAM 2007 helps bridge the gap between the classroom and the real world by allowing learners to train and test on important computer skills in an active, hands-on environment.

SAM 2007's easy-to-use system includes powerful interactive exams, training, or projects on critical applications such as Word, Excel, Access, PowerPoint, Outlook, Windows, the Internet, and much more. SAM simulates the application environment, allowing learners to demonstrate their knowledge and think through the skills by performing real-world tasks.

Designed to be used with the Illustrated Course Guides, SAM 2007 includes built-in page references so learners can print helpful study guides that match the Illustrated textbooks used in class. Powerful administrative options allow instructors to schedule exams and assignments, secure tests, and run reports with almost limitless flexibility.

Online Content

Blackboard is the leading distance learning solution provider and class-management platform today. Course Technology has partnered with Blackboard to bring you premium online content. Instructors: Content for use with this title is available in a Blackboard Course Cartridge and may include topic reviews, case projects, review questions, test banks, practice tests, custom syllabi, and more.

Course Technology also has solutions for several other learning management systems. Please visit *www.course.com* today to see what's available for this title.

A Guided Tour of Microsoft Office 2007, Windows Vista Edition

This CD of movie tutorials helps learners get exposed to the new features of Microsoft Office 2007 quickly. Dynamic and engaging author Corinne Hoisington presents the highlights of the new features of Word, Excel, Access, and PowerPoint plus a bonus movie tutorial on Windows Vista. This CD is a great supplement to this book, offering a fun overview of the software to inspire learners and show them what is possible.

Instructor Resources

The Instructor Resources CD is Course Technology's way of putting the resources and information needed to teach and learn effectively into your hands. With an integrated array of teaching and learning tools that offer you and your learners a broad range of technology-based instructional options, we believe this CD represents the highest quality and most cutting edge resources available to instructors today. Many of these resources are available at *www.course.com*. The resources available with this book are:

- **Instructor's Manual**—Available as an electronic file, the Instructor's Manual includes detailed lecture topics with teaching tips for each unit.
- **Sample Syllabus**—Prepare and customize your course easily using this sample course outline.
- **Course Outline**—Available online, the Course Outline includes suggested times for each unit (as well as time for breaks and lunch), to complete the Basic, Intermediate, or Advanced skills in one training day. You can customize it to suit your needs, or provide it as a hand out.
- **PowerPoint Presentations**—Each unit has a corresponding PowerPoint presentation that you can use in lecture, distribute to your learners, or customize to suit your course.
- **Figure Files**—The figures in the text are provided on the Instructor Resources CD to help you illustrate key topics or concepts. You can create traditional overhead transparencies by printing the figure files. Or you can create electronic slide shows by using the figures in a presentation program such as PowerPoint.
- **Solutions to Exercises**—Solutions to Exercises contains every file learners are asked to create or modify in the lessons and end-of-unit material. Also provided in this section, there is a document outlining the solutions for the end-of-unit Concepts Review, Skills Review, and Independent Challenges. An Annotated Solution File and Grading Rubric accompany each file and can be used together for quick and easy grading.
- **Data Files**—To complete most of the units in this book, learners will need Data Files. You can post the Data Files on a file server for learners to copy. The Data Files are available on the Instructor Resources CD, the Review Pack, and can also be downloaded from *www.course.com*. In this edition, we have included a lesson on downloading the Data Files for this book, see page xvi.

Instruct learners to use the Data Files List included on the Review Pack and the Instructor Resources CD. This list gives instructions on copying and organizing files.

- **ExamView**—ExamView is a powerful testing software package that allows you to create and administer printed, computer (LAN-based), and Internet exams. ExamView includes hundreds of questions that correspond to the topics covered in this text, enabling learners to generate detailed study guides that include page references for further review. The computer-based and Internet testing components allow learners to take exams at their computers, and also saves you time by grading each exam automatically.

CourseCasts—Learning on the Go. Always Available...Always Relevant.

Want to keep up with the latest technology trends relevant to you? Visit our site to find a library of podcasts, CourseCasts, featuring a "CourseCast of the Week," and download them to your mp3 player at *http://coursecasts.course.com.*

Our fast-paced world is driven by technology. You know because you're an active participant—always on the go, always keeping up with technological trends, and always learning new ways to embrace technology to power your life.

Ken Baldauf, a faculty member of the Florida State University Computer Science Department, is responsible for teaching technology classes to thousands of FSU learners each year. He knows what you know; he knows what you want to learn. He's also an expert in the latest technology and will sort through and aggregate the most pertinent news and information so you can spend your time enjoying technology, rather than trying to figure it out.

Visit us at *http://coursecasts.course.com* to learn on the go!

COURSECASTS

Brief Contents

Contents

Read This Before You Begin

Frequently Asked Questions

What are Data Files?

A Data File is a partially completed Access database, or another type of file that you use to complete the steps in the units and exercises to create the final document that you submit to your instructor. Each unit opener page lists the Data Files that you need for that unit.

Where are the Data Files?

Your instructor will provide the Data Files to you or direct you to a location on a network drive from which you can download them. Alternatively, you can follow the instructions on page xvi to download the Data Files from this book's Web page.

What software was used to write and test this book?

This book was written and tested using a typical installation of Microsoft Office 2007 installed on a computer with a typical installation of Microsoft Windows Vista. The browser used for any steps that require a browser is Internet Explorer 7.

If you are using this book on Windows XP, please see the "Important Notes for Windows XP Users" on the next page. If you are using this book on Windows Vista, please see the Appendix at the end of this book.

Do I need to be connected to the Internet to complete the steps and exercises in this book?

Some of the exercises in this book assume that your computer is connected to the Internet. If you are not connected to the Internet, see your instructor for information on how to complete the exercises.

What do I do if my screen is different from the figures shown in this book?

This book was written and tested on computers with monitors set at a resolution of 1024 × 768. If your screen shows more or less information than the figures in the book, your monitor is probably set at a higher or lower resolution. If you don't see something on your screen, you might have to scroll down or up to see the object identified in the figures.

The Ribbon (the blue area at the top of the screen) in Microsoft Office 2007 adapts to different resolutions. If your monitor is set at a lower resolution than 1024 × 768, you might not see all of the buttons shown in the figures. The groups of buttons will always appear, but the entire group might be condensed into a single button that you need to click to access the buttons described in the instructions. For example, the figures and steps in this book assume that the Editing group on the Home tab in Word looks like the following:

1024 × 768 Editing Group

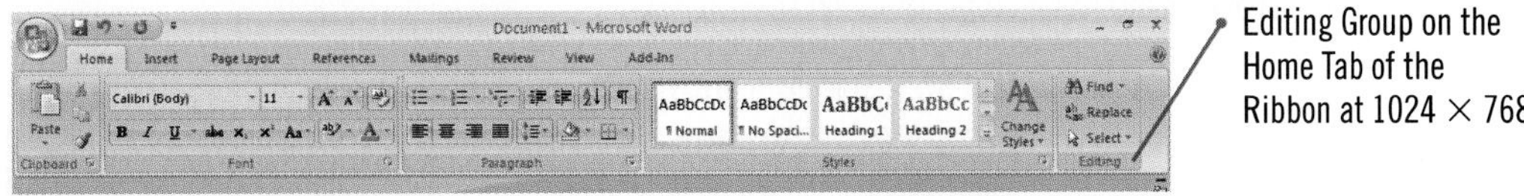

Editing Group on the Home Tab of the Ribbon at 1024 × 768

If your resolution is set to 800 × 600, the Ribbon in Word will look like the following figure, and you will need to click the Editing button to access the buttons that are visible in the Editing group.

800 × 600 Editing Group

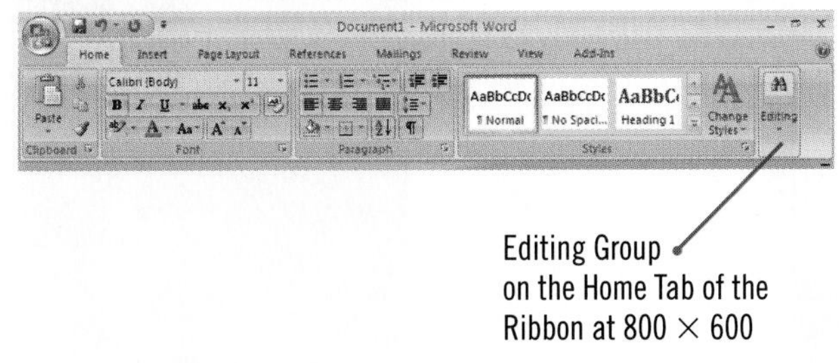

Editing Group on the Home Tab of the Ribbon at 800 × 600

800 × 600 Editing Group Clicked

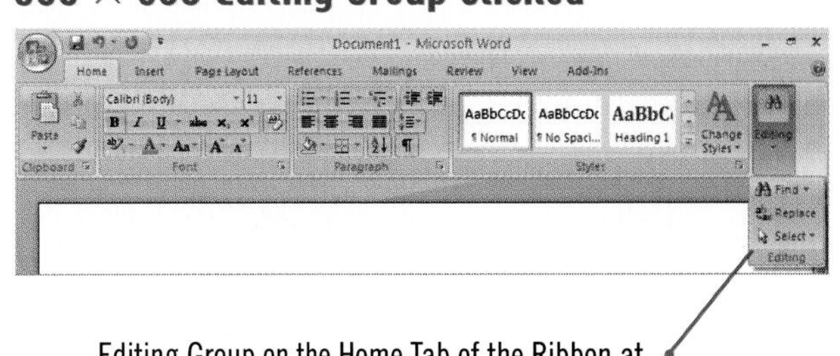

Editing Group on the Home Tab of the Ribbon at 800 × 600 is selected to show available buttons

Important Notes for Windows XP Users

The screen shots in this book show Microsoft Office 2007 running on Windows Vista. However, if you are using Microsoft Windows XP, you can still use this book because Office 2007 runs virtually the same on both platforms. There are a few differences that you will encounter if you are using Windows XP. Read this section to understand the differences.

Dialog boxes

If you are a Windows XP user, dialog boxes shown in this book will look slightly different than what you see on your screen. Dialog boxes for Windows XP have a blue title bar, instead of a gray title bar. However, beyond this difference in appearance, the options in the dialog boxes across platforms are the same. For instance, the screen shots below show the Font dialog box running on Windows XP and the Font dialog box running on Windows Vista.

FIGURE 1: Dialog box in Windows XP

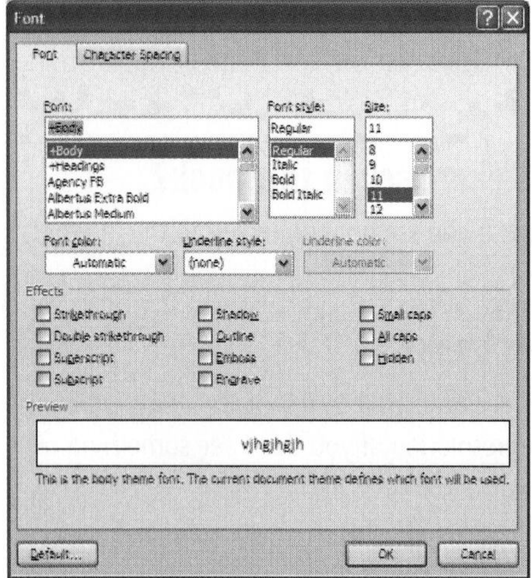

FIGURE 2: Dialog box in Windows Vista

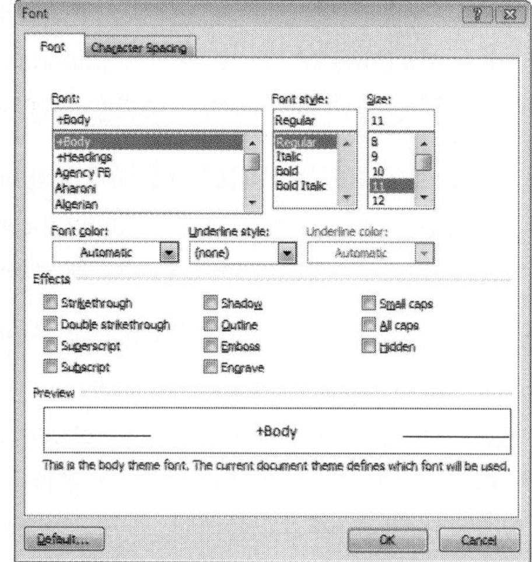

Alternate Steps for Windows XP Users

Nearly all of the steps in this book work exactly the same for Windows XP users. However, there are a few tasks that will require you to complete slightly different steps. This section provides alternate steps for a few specific skills.

Starting a program

1. Click the **Start button** on the taskbar
2. Point to **All Programs**, point to **Microsoft Office**, then click the application you want to use

FIGURE 3: Starting a program

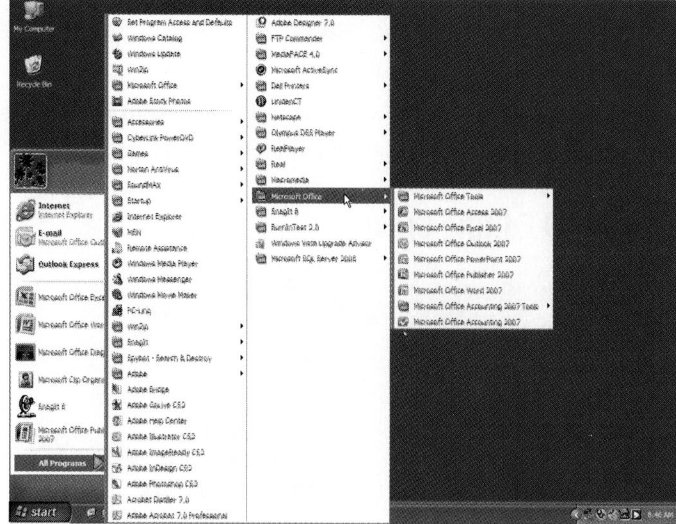

Saving a file for the first time

1. Click the **Office button**, then click **Save As**
2. Type a name for your file in the File name text box
3. Click the **Save in list arrow**, then navigate to the drive and folder where you store your Data Files
4. Click **Save**

FIGURE 4: Save As dialog box

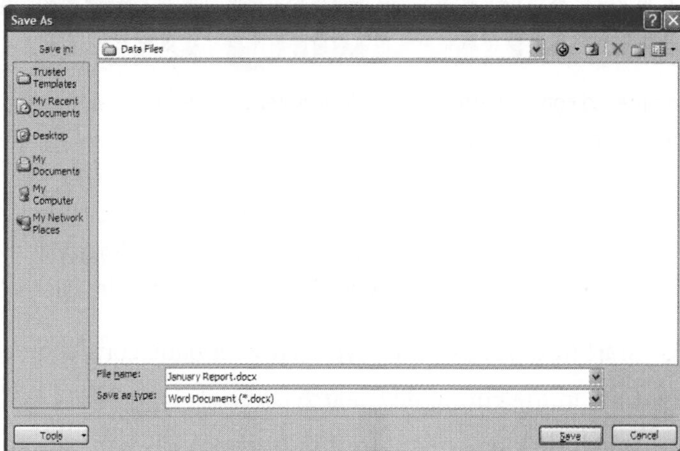

Opening a file

1. Click the **Office button**, then click **Open**
2. Click the **Look in list arrow**, then navigate to the drive and folder where you store your Data Files
3. Click the file you want to open
4. Click **Open**

FIGURE 5: Open dialog box

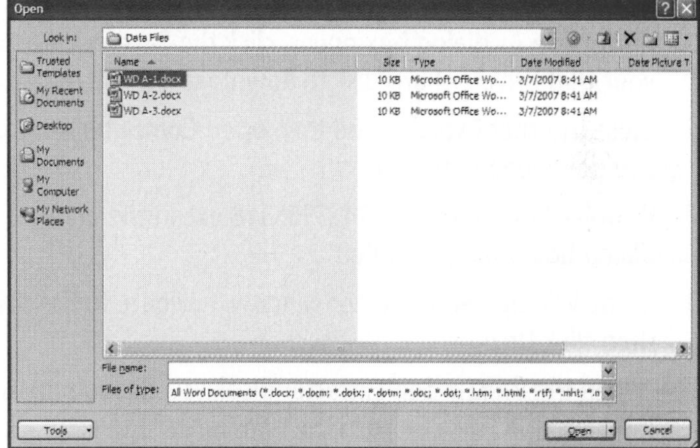

Downloading Data Files for This Book

In order to complete many of the lesson steps and exercises in this book, you are asked to open and save Data Files. A **Data File** is a partially completed file that you use as a starting point to complete the steps in the units and exercises. The benefit of using a Data File is that it saves you the time and effort needed to create a file; you can simply open a Data File, save it with a new name (so the original file remains intact), then make changes to it to complete lesson steps or an exercise. Your instructor will provide the Data Files to you or direct you to a location on a network drive from which you can download them. Alternatively, you can follow the instructions in this lesson to download the Data Files from this book's Web page.

1. **Start Internet Explorer, type** www.cengage.com/coursetechnology/ **in the address bar, then press** [Enter]
2. **Click in the Enter ISBN** Search text box, **type** 9781423905318, **then click** Search
3. **When the page opens for this textbook, click the** About this Product **link for the Student, point to** Student Downloads **to expand the menu, and then click the** Data Files for Students **link**
4. **If the File Download – Security Warning dialog box opens, click** Save. **(If no dialog box appears, skip this step and go to Step 6)**
5. **If the Save As dialog box opens, click the** Save in list arrow **at the top of the dialog box, select a folder on your USB drive or hard disk to download the file to, then click** Save
6. **Close Internet Explorer and then open Computer and display the contents of the drive and folder to which you downloaded the file**
7. **Double-click the file** 9781423905318.exe **in the drive or folder, then, if the Open File – Security Warning dialog box opens, click** Run
8. **In the WinZip Self-Extractor window, navigate to the drive and folder where you want to unzip the files to, then click** Unzip
9. **When the WinZip Self-Extractor displays a dialog box listing the number of files that have unzipped successfully, click** OK, **click** Close **in the WinZip Self-Extractor dialog box, then close Computer**

   The Data Files are now unzipped in the folder you specified in Step 8 and ready for you to open and use.

Getting Started with Microsoft Office 2007

Files You Will Need:
OFFICE A-1.xlsx

Microsoft Office 2007 is a group of software programs designed to help you create documents, collaborate with co-workers, and track and analyze information. Each program is designed so you can work quickly and efficiently to create professional-looking results. You use different Office programs to accomplish specific tasks, such as writing a letter or producing a sales presentation, yet all the programs have a similar look and feel. Once you become familiar with one program, you'll find it easy to transfer your knowledge to the others. This unit introduces you to the most frequently used programs in Office, as well as common features they all share.

OBJECTIVES

- Understand the Office 2007 Suite
- Start and exit an Office program
- View the Office 2007 user interface
- Create and save a file
- Open a file and save it with a new name
- View and print your work
- Get Help and close a file

Understanding the Office 2007 Suite

Microsoft Office 2007 features an intuitive, context-sensitive user interface, so you can get up to speed faster and use advanced features with greater ease. The programs in Office are bundled together in a group called a **suite** (although you can also purchase them separately). The Office suite is available in several configurations, but all include Word and Excel. Other configurations include PowerPoint, Access, Outlook, Publisher, and/or others. Each program in Office is best suited for completing specific types of tasks, though there is some overlap in terms of their capabilities.

DETAILS

The Office programs covered in this book include:

- **Microsoft Office Word 2007**
  When you need to create any kind of text-based document, such as memos, newsletters, or multi-page reports, Word is the program to use. You can easily make your documents look great by inserting eye-catching graphics and using formatting tools such as themes. **Themes** are predesigned combinations of color and formatting attributes you can apply, and are available in most Office programs. The Word document shown in Figure A-1 was formatted with the Solstice theme.
- **Microsoft Office Excel 2007**
  Excel is the perfect solution when you need to work with numeric values and make calculations. It puts the power of formulas, functions, charts, and other analytical tools into the hands of every user, so you can analyze sales projections, figure out loan payments, and present your findings in style. The Excel worksheet shown in Figure A-1 tracks personal expenses. Because Excel automatically recalculates results whenever a value changes, the information is always up-to-date. A chart illustrates how the monthly expenses are broken down.
- **Microsoft Office PowerPoint 2007**
  Using PowerPoint, it's easy to create powerful presentations complete with graphics, transitions, and even a soundtrack. Using professionally designed themes and clip art, you can quickly and easily create dynamic slideshows such as the one shown in Figure A-1.
- **Microsoft Office Access 2007**
  Access helps you keep track of large amounts of quantitative data, such as product inventories or employee records. The form shown in Figure A-1 was created for a grocery store inventory database. Employees use the form to enter data about each item. Using Access enables employees to quickly find specific information such as price and quantity, without hunting through store shelves and stockrooms.

Microsoft Office has benefits beyond the power of each program, including:

- **Common user interface: Improving business processes**
  Because the Office suite programs have a similar **interface**, or look and feel, your experience using one program's tools makes it easy to learn those in the other programs. Office documents are **compatible** with one another, meaning that you can easily incorporate, or **integrate**, an Excel chart into a PowerPoint slide, or an Access table into a Word document.
- **Collaboration: Simplifying how people work together**
  Office recognizes the way people do business today, and supports the emphasis on communication and knowledge-sharing within companies and across the globe. All Office programs include the capability to incorporate feedback—called **online collaboration**—across the Internet or a company network.

FIGURE A-1: Microsoft Office 2007 documents

Word document

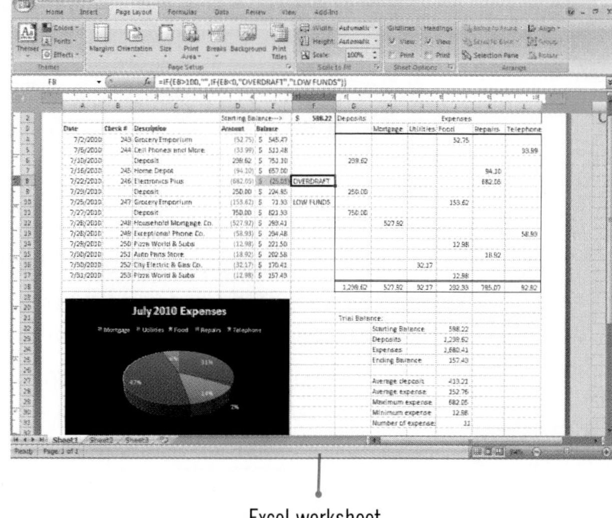

Excel worksheet

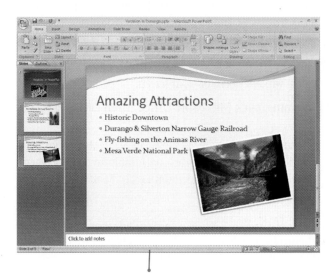

PowerPoint presentation

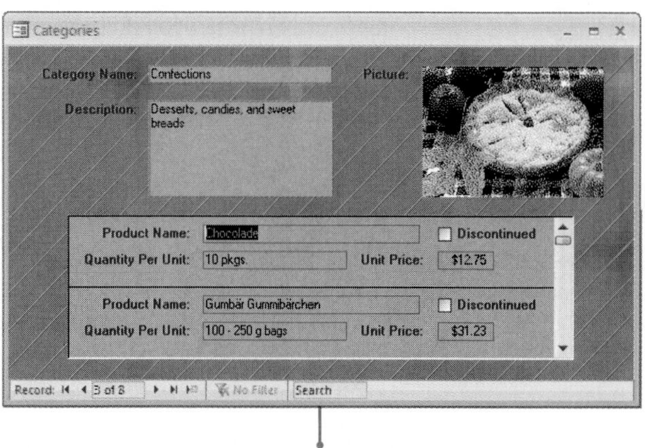

Access database form

Deciding which program to use

Every Office program includes tools that go far beyond what you might expect. For example, although Excel is primarily designed for making calculations, you can use it to create a database. So when you're planning a project, how do you decide which Office program to use? The general rule of thumb is to use the program best suited for your intended task, and make use of supporting tools in the program if you need them. Word is best for creating text-based documents, Excel is best for making mathematical calculations, PowerPoint is best for preparing presentations, and Access is best for managing quantitative data. Although the capabilities of Office are so vast that you *could* create an inventory in Excel or a budget in Word, you'll find greater flexibility and efficiency by using the program designed for the task. And remember, you can always create a file in one program, and then insert it in a document in another program when you need to, such as including sales projections (Excel) in a memo (Word).

Starting and Exiting an Office Program

The first step in using an Office program is of course to open, or **launch**, it on your computer. You have a few choices for how to launch a program, but the easiest way is to click the Start button on the Windows taskbar, or to double-click an icon on your desktop. You can have multiple programs open on your computer simultaneously, and you can move between open programs by clicking the desired program or document button on the taskbar or by using the [Alt][Tab] keyboard shortcut combination. When working, you'll often want to open multiple programs in Office, and switch among them throughout the day. Begin by launching a few Office programs now.

STEPS

QUICK TIP
You can also launch a program by double-clicking a desktop icon or clicking an entry on the Recent Items menu.

1. **Click the Start button on the taskbar**
   The Start menu opens, as shown in Figure A-2. If the taskbar is hidden, you can display it by pointing to the bottom of the screen. Depending on your taskbar property settings, the taskbar may be displayed at all times, or only when you point to that area of the screen. For more information, or to change your taskbar properties, consult your instructor or technical support person.

2. **Point to All Programs, click Microsoft Office, then click Microsoft Office Word 2007**
   Microsoft Office Word 2007 starts and the program window opens on your screen.

QUICK TIP
It is not necessary to close one program before opening another.

3. **Click on the taskbar, point to All Programs, click Microsoft Office, then click Microsoft Office Excel 2007**
   Microsoft Office Excel 2007 starts and the program window opens, as shown in Figure A-3. Word is no longer visible, but it remains open. The taskbar displays a button for each open program and document. Because this Excel document is **active**, or in front and available, the Microsoft Excel – Book1 button on the taskbar appears in a darker shade.

4. **Click Document1 – Microsoft Word on the taskbar**
   Clicking a button on the taskbar activates that program and document. The Word program window is now in front, and the Document1 – Microsoft Word taskbar button appears shaded.

QUICK TIP
If there isn't room on your taskbar to display the entire name of each button, you can point to any button to see the full name in a Screentip.

5. **Click on the taskbar, point to All Programs, click Microsoft Office, then click Microsoft Office PowerPoint 2007**
   Microsoft Office PowerPoint 2007 starts, and becomes the active program.

6. **Click Microsoft Excel – Book1 on the taskbar**
   Excel is now the active program.

QUICK TIP
As you work in Windows, your computer adapts to your activities. You may notice that after clicking the Start button, the name of the program you want to open appears in the Start menu; if so, you can click it to start the program.

7. **Click on the taskbar, point to All Programs, click Microsoft Office, then click Microsoft Office Access 2007**
   Microsoft Office Access 2007 starts, and becomes the active program.

8. **Point to the taskbar to display it, if necessary**
   Four Office programs are open simultaneously.

9. **Click the Office button, then click Exit Access, as shown in Figure A-4**
   Access closes, leaving Excel active and Word and PowerPoint open.

FIGURE A-2: Start menu

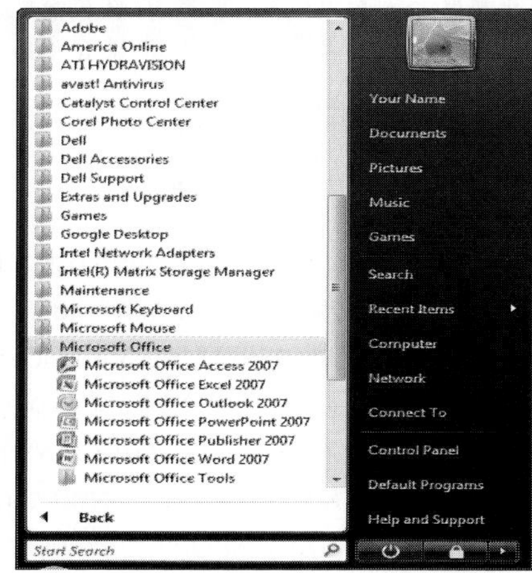

FIGURE A-3: Excel program window and Windows taskbar

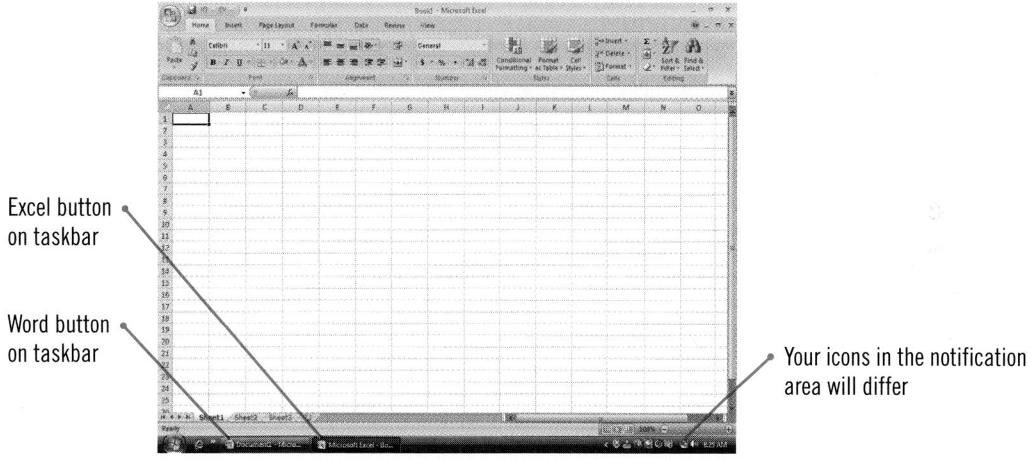

FIGURE A-4: Exiting Microsoft Office Access

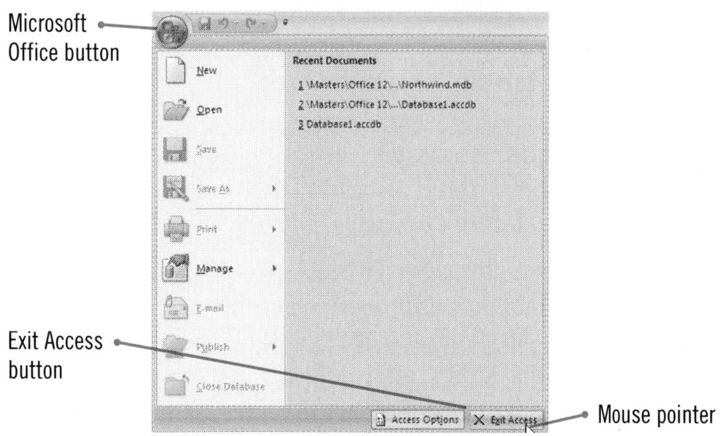

Using shortcut keys to move between Office programs

As an alternative to the Windows taskbar, you can use a keyboard shortcut to move among open Office programs. The [Alt][Tab] keyboard combination lets you either switch quickly to the next open program, or choose one from a palette. To switch immediately to the next open program, press [Alt][Tab]. To choose from all open programs, press and hold [Alt], then press and release [Tab] without releasing [Alt]. A palette opens on screen, displaying the icon and filename of each open program and file. Each time you press [Tab] while holding [Alt], the selection cycles to the next open file. Release [Alt] when the program/file you want to activate is selected.

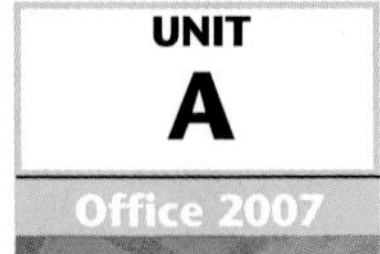

UNIT A Office 2007

Viewing the Office 2007 User Interface

One of the benefits of using Office is that the programs have much in common, making them easy to learn and making it simple to move from one to another. Individual Office programs have always shared many features, but the innovations in the Office 2007 user interface mean even greater similarity among them all. That means you can also use your knowledge of one program to get up to speed in another. A **user interface** is a collective term for all the ways you interact with a software program. The user interface in Office 2007 includes a more intuitive way of choosing commands, working with files, and navigating in the program window. Familiarize yourself with some of the common interface elements in Office by examining the PowerPoint program window.

STEPS

QUICK TIP
In addition to the standard tabs on the ribbon, **contextual tabs** open when needed to complete a specific task; they appear in an accent color, and close when no longer needed.

1. **Click Microsoft PowerPoint – [Presentation1] on the taskbar**

   PowerPoint becomes the active program. Refer to Figure A-5 to identify common elements of the Office user interface. The **document window** occupies most of the screen. In PowerPoint, a blank slide appears in the document window, so you can build your slide show. At the top of every Office program window is a **title bar**, which displays the document and program name. Below the title bar is the **Ribbon**, which displays commands you're likely to need for the current task. Commands are organized into **tabs**. The tab names appear at the top of the Ribbon, and the active tab appears in front with its name highlighted. The Ribbon in every Office program includes tabs specific to the program, but all include a Home tab on the far left, for the most popular tasks in that program.

2. **Click the Office button**

   The Office menu opens. This menu contains commands common to most Office programs, such as opening a file, saving a file, and closing the current program. Next to the Office button is the **Quick Access toolbar**, which includes buttons for common Office commands.

TROUBLE
If you accidentally click the wrong command and an unwanted dialog box opens, press [Esc].

3. **Click again to close it, then point to the Save button on the Quick Access toolbar, *but do not click it***

   You can point to any button in Office to see a description; this is a good way to learn the available choices.

4. **Click the Design tab on the Ribbon**

   To display a different tab, you click its name on the Ribbon. Each tab arranges related commands into **groups** to make features easy to find. The Themes group displays available themes in a **gallery**, or palette of choices you can browse. Many groups contain a **dialog box launcher**, an icon you can click to open a dialog box or task pane for the current group, which offers an alternative way to choose commands.

QUICK TIP
Live Preview is available in many galleries and palettes throughout Office.

5. **Move the mouse pointer over the Aspect theme in the Themes group as shown in Figure A-6, *but do not click the mouse button***

   Because you have not clicked the theme, you have not actually made any changes to the slide. With the **Live Preview** feature, you can point to a choice, see the results right in the document, and then decide whether you want to make the change.

QUICK TIP
If you accidentally click a theme, click the Undo button on the Quick Access toolbar.

6. **Move away from the Ribbon and towards the slide**

   If you clicked the Aspect theme, it would be applied to this slide. Instead, the slide remains unchanged.

7. **Point to the Zoom slider on the status bar, then drag to the right until the Zoom percentage reads 166%**

   The slide display is enlarged. Zoom tools are located on the status bar. You can drag the slider or click the plus and minus buttons to zoom in/out on an area of interest. The percentage tells you the zoom effect.

8. **Drag the Zoom slider on the status bar to the left until the Zoom percentage reads 73%**

FIGURE A-5: PowerPoint program window

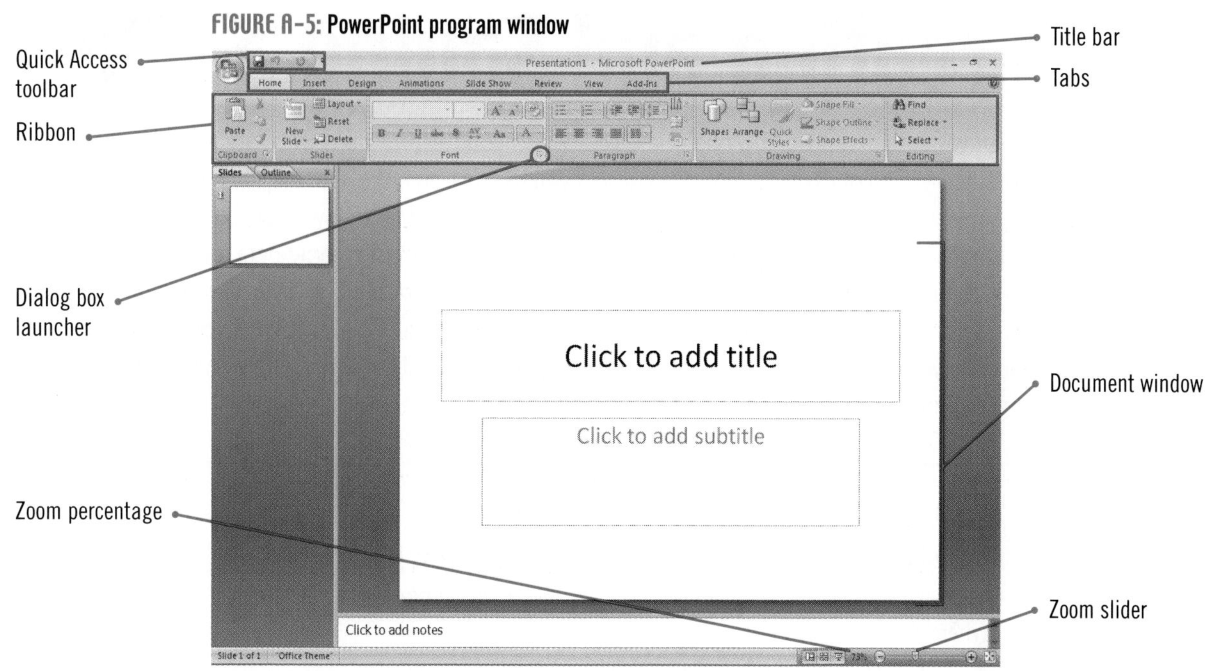

FIGURE A-6: Viewing a theme with Live Preview

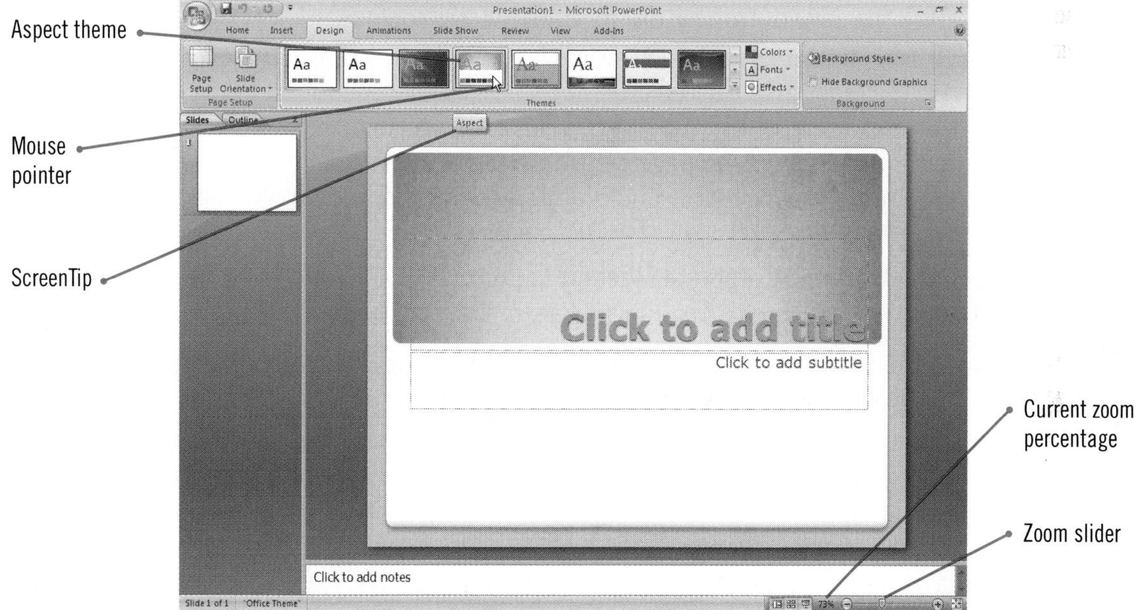

Customizing the Quick Access toolbar

You can customize the Quick Access toolbar to display your favorite commands. To do so, click the Customize Quick Access Toolbar button in the title bar, then click the command you want to add. If you don't see the command in the list, click More Commands to open the Customize tab of the Options dialog box. In the Options dialog box, use the Choose commands from list to choose a category, click the desired command in the list on the left, click Add to add it to the Quick Access toolbar, then click OK. To remove a button from the toolbar, click the name in the list on the right, then click Remove. To add a command to the Quick Access toolbar on the fly, simply right-click the button on the Ribbon, then click Add to Quick Access Toolbar on the shortcut menu. You can also use the Customize Quick Access Toolbar button to move the toolbar below the ribbon, by clicking Show Below the Ribbon, or to minimize the Ribbon so it takes up less space onscreen. If you click Minimize the Ribbon, the Ribbon is minimized to display only the tabs. When you click a tab, the Ribbon opens so you can choose a command; once you choose a command, the Ribbon closes again, and only the tabs are visible.

UNIT

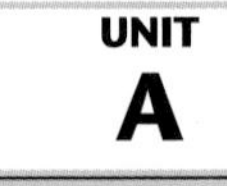

Office 2007

Creating and Saving a File

When working in a program, one of the first things you need to do is to create and save a file. A **file** is a stored collection of data. Saving a file enables you to work on a project now, then put it away and work on it again later. In some Office programs, including Word, Excel, and PowerPoint, a new file is automatically created when you start the program, so all you have to do is enter some data and save it. In Access, you must expressly create a file before you enter any data. You should give your files meaningful names and save them in an appropriate location, so they're easy to find. Use Microsoft Word to familiarize yourself with the process of creating and saving a document. First you'll type some notes about a possible location for a corporate meeting, then you'll save the information for later use.

STEPS

1. **Click Document1 – Microsoft Word on the taskbar**
2. **Type Locations for Corporate Meeting, then press [Enter] twice**

   The text appears in the document window, and a cursor blinks on a new blank line. The cursor indicates where the next typed text will appear.
3. **Type Las Vegas, NV, press [Enter], type Orlando, FL, press [Enter], type Chicago, IL, press [Enter] twice, then type your name**

   Compare your document to Figure A-7.

> **QUICK TIP**
> A filename can be up to 255 characters, including a file extension, and can include upper- or lowercase characters and spaces, but not ?, ", /, \, <, >, *, |, or :.

4. **Click the Save button on the Quick Access toolbar**

   Because this is the first time you are saving this document, the Save As dialog box opens, as shown in Figure A-8. The Save As dialog box includes options for assigning a filename and storage location. Once you save a file for the first time, clicking saves any changes to the file *without* opening the Save As dialog box, because no additional information is needed. In the Address bar, Office displays the default location for where to save the file, but you can change to any location. In the File name field, Office displays a suggested name for the document based on text in the file, but you can enter a different name.
5. **Type Potential Corporate Meeting Locations**

   The text you type replaces the highlighted text.

> **QUICK TIP**
> You can create a desktop icon that you can double-click to both launch a program and open a document, by saving it to the desktop.

6. **In the Save As dialog box, use the Address bar or Navigation pane to navigate to the drive and folder where you store your Data Files**

   Many students store files on a flash drive or Zip drive, but you can also store files on your computer, a network drive, or any storage device indicated by your instructor or technical support person.

> **QUICK TIP**
> To create a new blank file when a file is open, click the Office button, click New, then click Create.

7. **Click Save**

   The Save As dialog box closes, the new file is saved to the location you specified, then the name of the document appears in the title bar, as shown in Figure A-9. (You may or may not see a file extension.) See Table A-1 for a description of the different types of files you create in Office, and the file extensions associated with each. You can save a file in an earlier version of a program by choosing from the list of choices in the Save as type list arrow in the Save As dialog box.

TABLE A-1: Common filenames and default file extensions

File created in	is called a	and has the default extension
Excel	workbook	.xlsx
Word	document	.docx
Access	database	.accdb
PowerPoint	presentation	.pptx

FIGURE A-7: Creating a document in Word

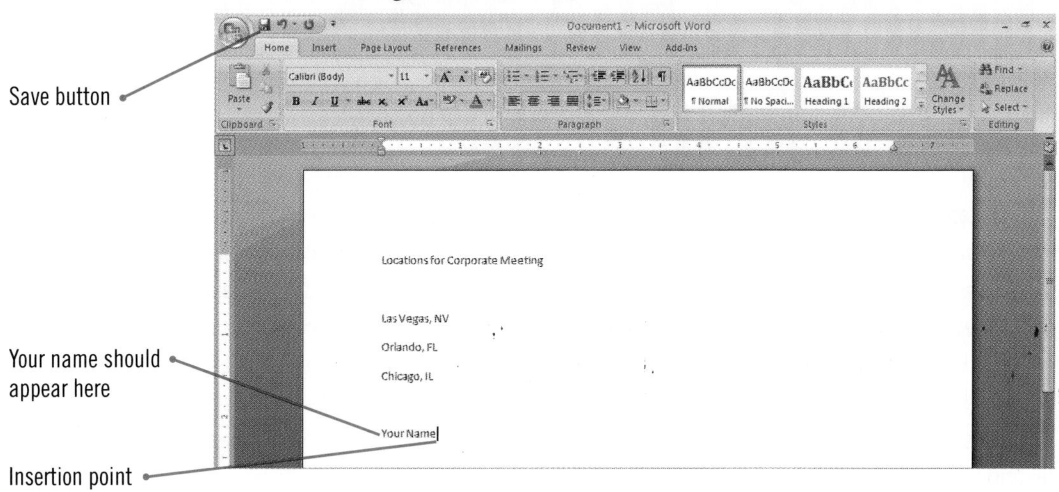

FIGURE A-8: Save As dialog box

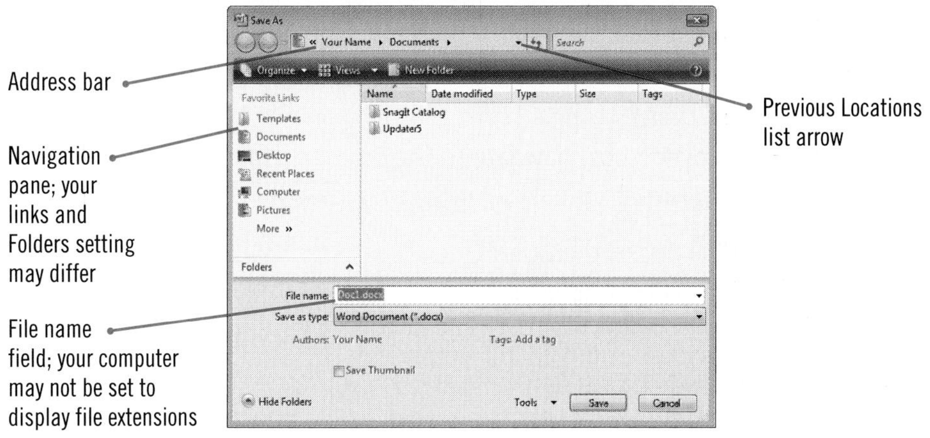

FIGURE A-9: Named Word document

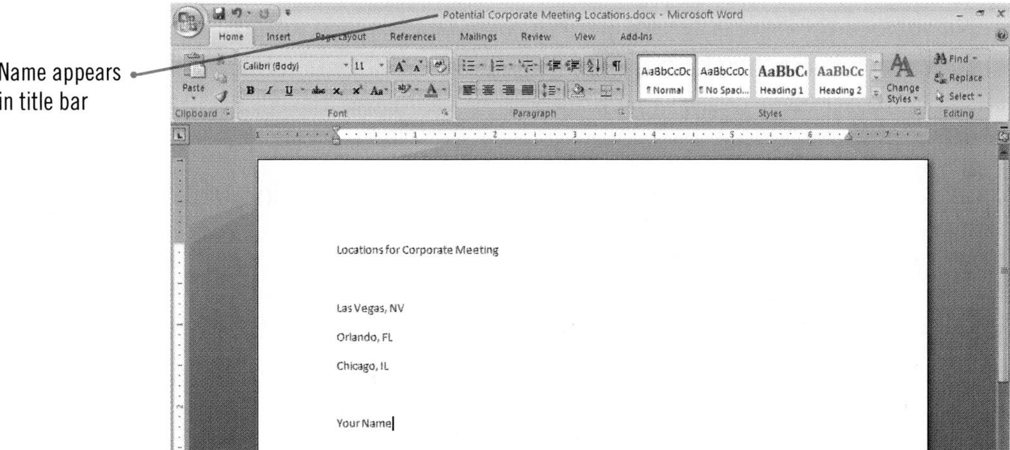

Using the Office Clipboard

You can use the Office Clipboard to cut and copy items from one Office program and paste them into others. The Clipboard can store a maximum of 24 items. To access it, open the Office Clipboard task pane by clicking the launcher in the Clipboard group in the Home tab. Each time you copy a selection, it is saved in the Office Clipboard. Each entry in the Office Clipboard includes an icon that tells you the program in which it was created. To paste an entry, click in the document where you want it to appear, then click the item in the Office Clipboard. To delete an item from the Office Clipboard, right-click the item, then click Delete.

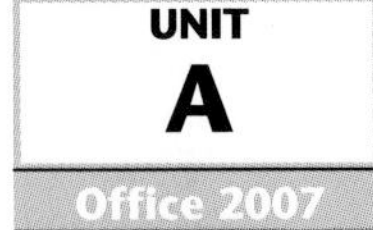

Opening a File and Saving it with a New Name

In many cases as you work in Office, you start with a blank document, but often you need to use an existing file. It might be a file you or a co-worker created earlier as a work-in-progress, or it could be a complete document that you want to use as the basis for another. For example, you might want to create a budget for this year using the budget you created last year; you could type in all the categories and information from scratch, or you could open last year's budget, save it with a new name, and just make changes to update it for the current year. By opening the existing file and saving it with the Save As command, you create a duplicate that you can modify to your heart's content, while the original file remains intact. Use Excel to open an existing workbook file, and save it with a new name so the original remains unchanged.

STEPS

QUICK TIP
If you point to a command on the Office menu that is followed by an arrow, a submenu opens displaying additional, related commands.

QUICK TIP
The Recent Items list on the Office menu displays recently opened documents; you can click any file to open it.

QUICK TIP
The Save As command works identically in all Office programs, except Access; in Access, this command lets you save a copy of the current database object, such as a table or form, with a new name, but not a copy of the entire database.

1. **Click Microsoft Excel – Book1 on the taskbar, click the Office button, then click Open**
   The Open dialog box opens, where you can navigate to any drive or folder location accessible to your computer to locate a file.
2. **In the Open dialog box, navigate to the drive and folder where you store your Data Files**
   The files available in the current folder are listed, as shown in Figure A-10. This folder contains one file.
3. **Click OFFICE A-1.xlsx, then click Open**
   The dialog box closes and the file opens in Excel. An Excel file is an electronic spreadsheet, so it looks different from a Word document or a PowerPoint slide.
4. **Click, then click Save As**
   The Save As dialog box opens, and the current filename is highlighted in the File name text box. Using the Save As command enables you to create a copy of the current, existing file with a new name. This action preserves the original file, and creates a new file that you can modify.
5. **Navigate to the drive and folder where your Data Files are stored if necessary, type Budget for Corporate Meeting in the File name text box, as shown in Figure A-11, then click Save**
   A copy of the existing document is created with the new name. The original file, Office A-1.xlsx, closes automatically.
6. **Click cell A19, type your name, then press [Enter], as shown in Figure A-12**
   In Excel, you enter data in cells, which are formed by the intersection of a row and a column. Cell A19 is at the intersection of column A and row 19. When you press [Enter], the cell pointer moves to cell A20.
7. **Click the Save button on the Quick Access toolbar**
   Your name appears in the worksheet, and your changes to the file are saved.

Exploring File Open options

You might have noticed that the Open button on the Open dialog box includes an arrow. In a dialog box, if a button includes an arrow you can click the button to invoke the command, or you can click the arrow to choose from a list of related commands. The Open button list arrow includes several related commands, including Open Read-Only and Open as Copy. Clicking Open Read-Only opens a file that you can only save by saving it with a new name; you cannot save changes to the original file. Clicking Open as Copy creates a copy of the file already saved and named with the word "Copy" in the title. Like the Save As command, these commands provide additional ways to use copies of existing files while ensuring that original files do not get inadvertently changed.

FIGURE A-10: Open dialog box

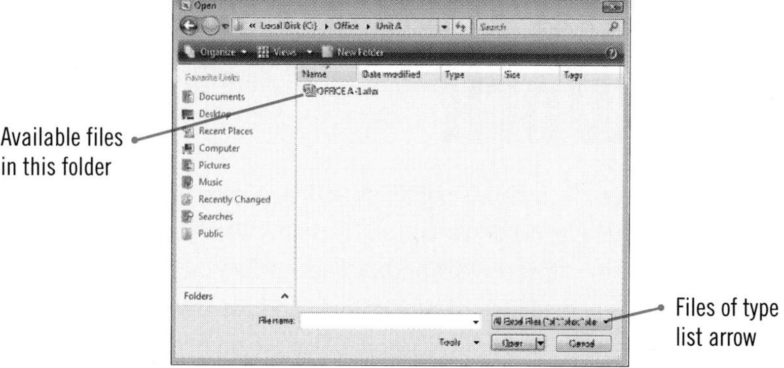

FIGURE A-11: Save As dialog box

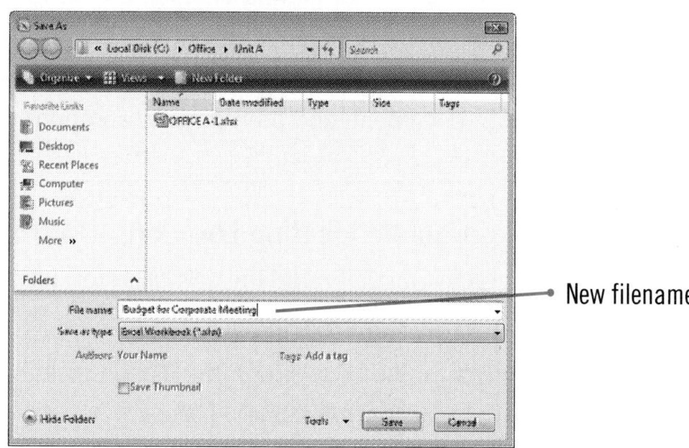

FIGURE A-12: Adding your name to the worksheet

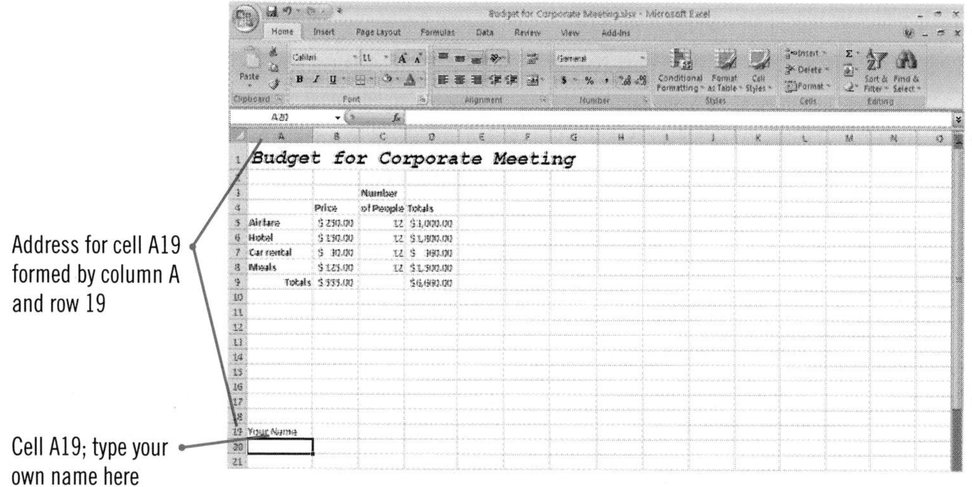

Working in Compatibility mode

Not everyone upgrades to the newest version of Office. As a general rule, new software versions are **backward-compatible**, meaning that documents saved by an older version can be read by newer software. The reverse is not always true, so Office 2007 includes a feature called Compatibility mode. When you open a file created in an earlier version of Office, "Compatibility Mode" appears in the title bar, letting you know the file was created in an earlier, but usable version of the program. If you are working with someone who may not be using the newest version of the software, you can avoid possible incompatibility problems by saving your file in another, earlier format. To do this, click the Office button, point to the Save As command, then click a choice on the Save As submenu. For example, if you're working in Excel, click Excel 97-2003 Workbook format. When the Save As dialog box opens, you'll notice that the Save as type box reads "Excel 97-2003 Workbook" instead of the default "Excel Workbook." To see more file format choices, such as Excel 97-2003 Template or Microsoft Excel 5.0/95 Workbook, click Other Formats on the Save As submenu. In the Save As dialog box, click the Save as type button, click the choice you think matches what your co-worker is using, then click Save.

Viewing and Printing Your Work

If your computer is connected to a printer or a print server, you can easily print any Office document. Printing can be as simple as clicking a button, or as involved as customizing the print job by printing only selected pages or making other choices, and/or **previewing** the document to see exactly what a document will look like when it is printed. (In order for printing and previewing to work, a printer must be installed.) In addition to using Print Preview, each Microsoft Office program lets you switch among various **views** of the document window, to show more or fewer details or a different combination of elements that make it easier to complete certain tasks, such as formatting or reading text. You can also increase or decrease your view of a document, so you can see more or less of it on the screen at once. Changing your view of a document does not affect the file in any way, it affects only the way it looks on screen. Experiment with changing your view of a Word document, and then preview and print your work.

STEPS

1. **Click Potential Corporate Meeting Locations – Microsoft Word on the taskbar**
   Word becomes the active program, and the document fills the screen.
2. **Click the View tab on the Ribbon**
   In most Office programs, the View tab on the Ribbon includes groups and commands for changing your view of the current document. You can also change views using the View buttons on the status bar.
3. **Click Web Layout button in the Document Views group on the View tab**
   The view changes to Web Layout view, as shown in Figure A-13. This view shows how the document will look if you save it as a Web page.
4. **Click the Zoom in button on the status bar eight times until the zoom percentage reads 180%**
   Zooming in, or choosing a higher percentage, makes a document appear bigger on screen, but less of it fits on the screen at once; **zooming out**, or choosing a lower percentage, lets you see more of the document but at a reduced size.

> **QUICK TIP**
> You can also use the Zoom button in the Zoom group of the View tab to enlarge or reduce a document's appearance.

5. **Drag the Zoom slider on the status bar to the center mark**
   The Zoom slider lets you zoom in and out without opening a dialog box or clicking buttons.
6. **Click the Print Layout button on the View tab**
   You return to Print Layout view, the default view in Microsoft Word.
7. **Click the Office button, point to Print, then click Print Preview**
   The Print Preview presents the most accurate view of how your document will look when printed, displaying the entire page on screen at once. Compare your screen to Figure A-14. The Ribbon in Print Preview contains a single tab, also known as a **program** tab, with commands specific to Print Preview. The commands on this tab facilitate viewing and changing overall settings such as margins and page size.
8. **Click the Print button on the Ribbon**
   The Print dialog box opens, as shown in Figure A-15. You can use this dialog box to change which pages to print, the number of printed copies, and even the number of pages you print on each page. If you have multiple printers from which to choose, you can change from one installed printer by clicking the Name list arrow, then clicking the name of the installed printer you want to use.

> **QUICK TIP**
> You can open the Print dialog box from any view by clicking the Office button, then clicking Print.

9. **Click OK, then click the Close Print Preview button on the Ribbon**
   A copy of the document prints, and Print Preview closes.

FIGURE A-13: Web Layout view

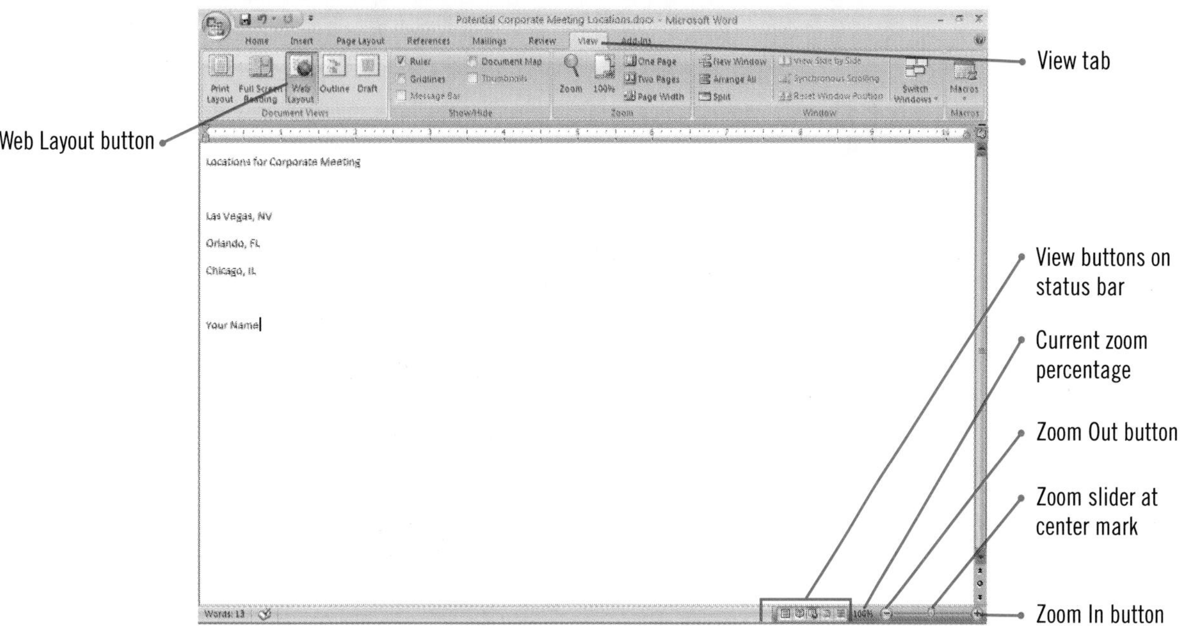

FIGURE A-14: Print Preview screen

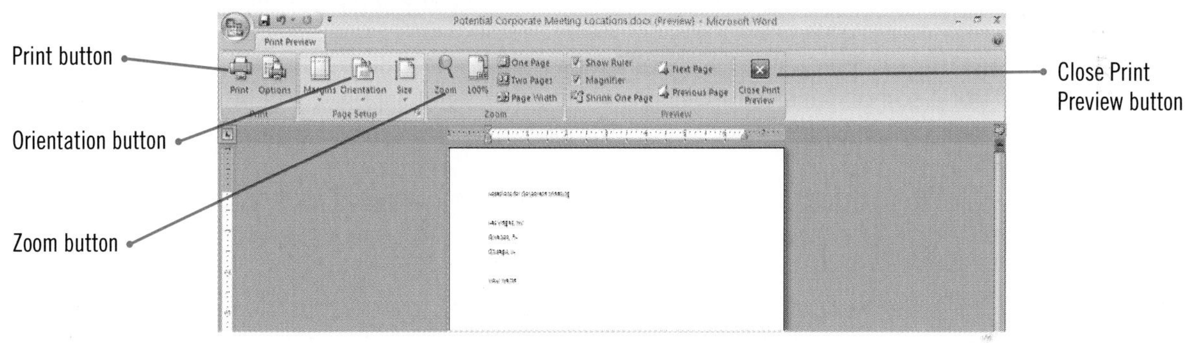

FIGURE A-15: Print dialog box

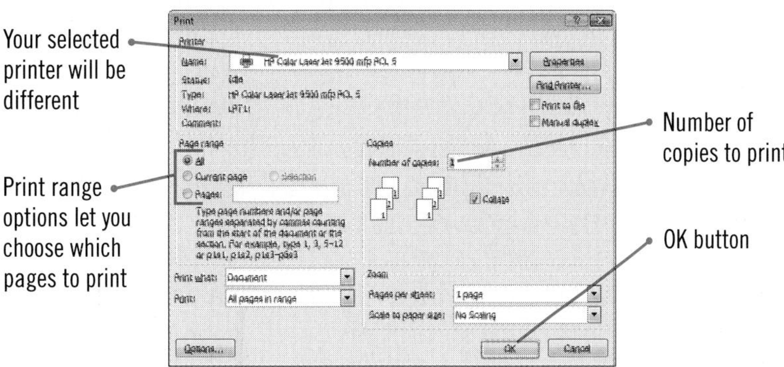

Using the Print Screen feature to create a screen capture

At some point you may want to create a screen capture. A **screen capture** is a snapshot of your screen, as if you took a picture of it with a camera. You might want to take a screen capture if an error message occurs and you want Technical Support to see exactly what's on the screen. Or perhaps your instructor wants to see what your screen looks like when you create a particular document. To create a screen capture, press [PrtScn]. (Keyboards differ, but you may find the [PrtScn] button on the Insert key in or near your keyboard's function keys. You may have to press the [F Lock] key to enable the Function keys.) Pressing this key places a digital image of your screen in the Windows temporary storage area known as the **Clipboard**. Open the document where you want the screen capture to appear, click the Home tab on the Ribbon (if necessary), then click Paste on the Home tab. The screen capture is pasted into the document.

Getting Help and Closing a File

You can get comprehensive help at any time by pressing [F1] in an Office program. You can also get help in the form of a ScreenTip by pointing to almost any icon in the program window. When you're finished working in an Office document, you have a few choices regarding ending your work session. You can close a file or exit a program by using the Office button or by clicking a button on the title bar. Closing a file leaves a program running, while exiting a program closes all the open files in that program as well as the program itself. In all cases, Office reminds you if you try to close a file or exit a program and your document contains unsaved changes. Explore the Help system in Microsoft Office, and then close your documents and exit any open programs.

STEPS

1. **Point to the Zoom button on the View tab of the Ribbon**

   A ScreenTip appears that describes how the Zoom button works.

2. **Press [F1]**

   The Word Help window opens, as shown in Figure A-16, displaying the home page for help in Word. Each entry is a hyperlink you can click to open a list of related topics. This window also includes a toolbar of useful Help commands and a Search field. The connection status at the bottom of the Help window indicates that the connection to Office Online is active. Office Online supplements the help content available on your computer with a wide variety of up-to-date topics, templates, and training.

> **QUICK TIP**
> If you are not connected to the Internet, the Help window displays only the help content available on your computer.

3. **Click the Getting help link in the Table of Contents pane**

   The icon next to Getting help changes and its list of subtopics expands.

> **QUICK TIP**
> You can also open the Help window by clicking the Microsoft Office Help button to the right of the tabs on the Ribbon.

4. **Click the Work with the Help window link in the topics list in the left pane**

   The topic opens in the right pane, as shown in Figure A-17.

5. **Click the Hide Table of Contents button on the Help toolbar**

   The left pane closes, as shown in Figure A-18.

> **QUICK TIP**
> You can print the current topic by clicking the Print button on the Help toolbar to open the Print dialog box.

6. **Click the Show Table of Contents button on the Help toolbar, scroll to the bottom of the left pane, click the Accessibility link in the Table of Contents pane, click the Use the keyboard to work with Ribbon programs link, read the information in the right pane, then click the Help window Close button**

7. **Click the Office button, then click Close; if a dialog box opens asking whether you want to save your changes, click Yes**

   The Potential Corporate Meeting Locations document closes, leaving the Word program open.

8. **Click, then click Exit Word**

   Microsoft Office Word closes, and the Excel program window is active.

9. **Click, click Exit Excel, click the PowerPoint button on the taskbar if necessary, click, then click Exit PowerPoint**

   Microsoft Office Excel and Microsoft Office PowerPoint both close.

FIGURE A-16: Word Help window

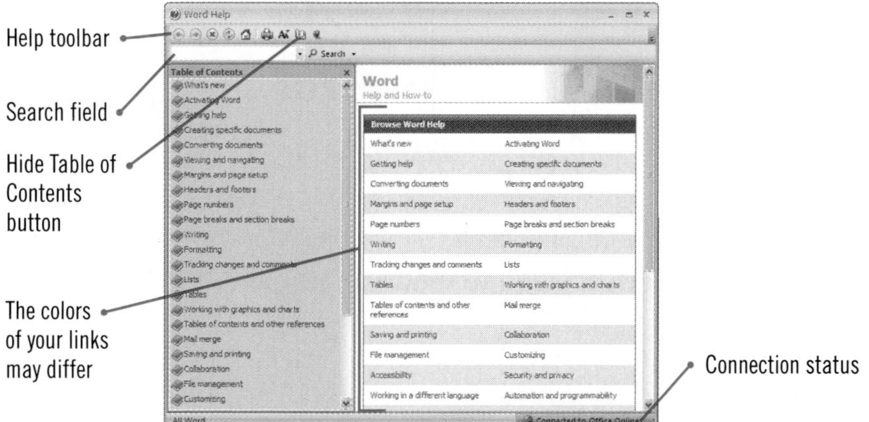

FIGURE A-17: Work with the Help window

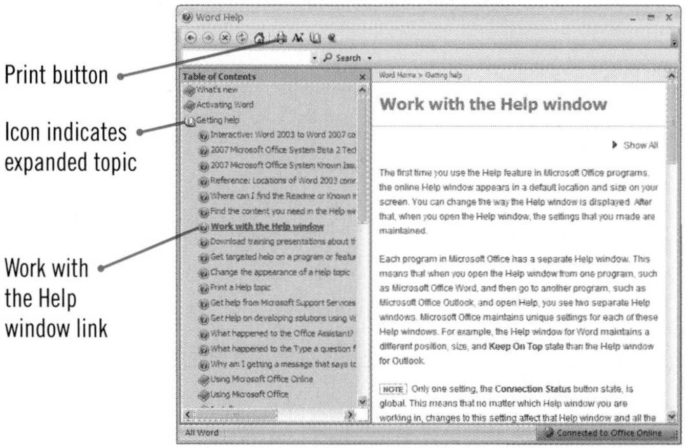

FIGURE A-18: Help window with Table of Contents closed

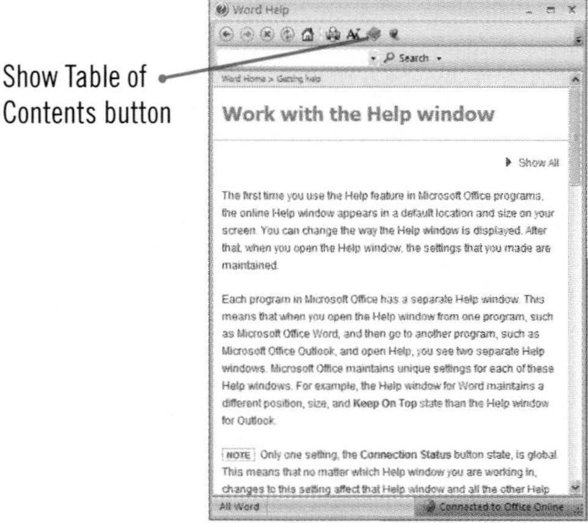

Recovering a document

Sometimes while you are using Office, you may experience a power failure or your computer may "freeze," making it impossible to continue working. If this type of interruption occurs, each Office program has a built-in recovery feature that allows you to open and save files that were open at the time of the interruption. When you restart the program(s) after an interruption, the Document Recovery task pane opens on the left side of your screen displaying both original and recovered versions of the files that were open. If you're not sure which file to open (original or recovered), it's usually better to open the recovered file because it will contain the latest information. You can, however, open and review all versions of the file that were recovered and save the best one. Each file listed in the Document Recovery task pane displays a list arrow with options that allow you to open the file, save it as is, delete it, or show repairs made to it during recovery.

Practice

If you have a SAM user profile, you may have access to hands-on instruction, practice, and assessment of the skills covered in this unit. Log in to your SAM account (http://sam2007.course.com/) to launch any assigned training activities or exams that relate to the skills covered in this unit.

▼ CONCEPTS REVIEW

Label the elements of the program window shown in Figure A-19.

FIGURE A-19

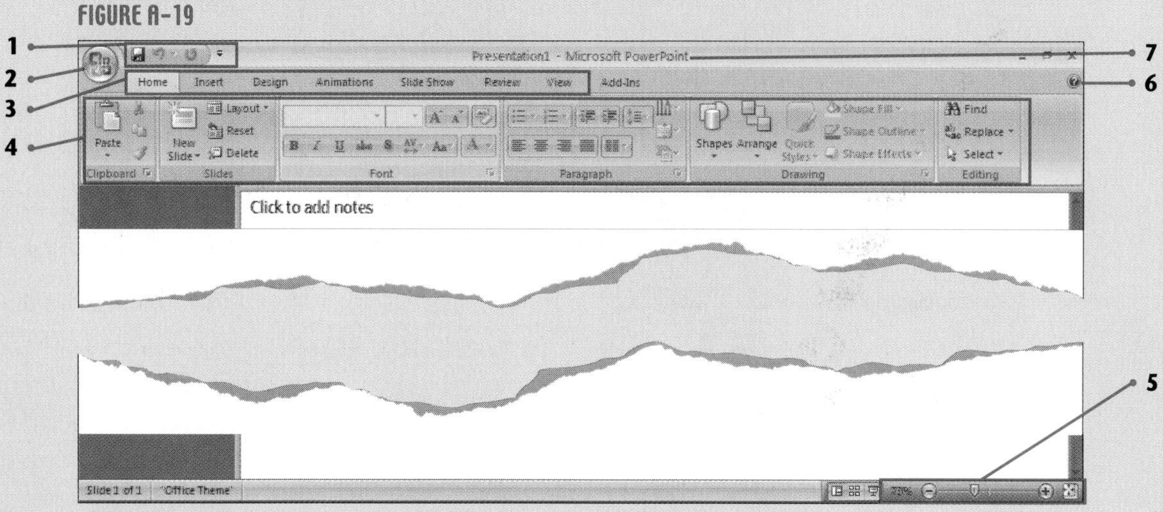

Match each project with the program for which it is best suited.

8. Microsoft Office PowerPoint

9. Microsoft Office Excel

10. Microsoft Office Word

11. Microsoft Office Access

a. Corporate expansion budget with expense projections

b. Business résumé for a job application

c. Auto parts store inventory

d. Presentation for Board of Directors meeting

▼ INDEPENDENT CHALLENGE 1

You just accepted an administrative position with a local car dealership that's recently invested in computers and is now considering purchasing Microsoft Office. You are asked to propose ways Office might help the dealership. You produce your proposal in Microsoft Word.

a. Start Word, then save the document as **Microsoft Office Proposal** in the drive and folder where you store your Data Files.

b. Type **Microsoft Office Word**, press [Enter] twice, type **Microsoft Office Excel**, press [Enter] twice, type **Microsoft Office PowerPoint**, press [Enter] twice, type **Microsoft Office Access**, press [Enter] twice, then type your name.

c. Click the line beneath each program name, type at least two tasks suited to that program, then press [Enter].

d. Save your work, then print one copy of this document.

Advanced Challenge Exercise

- Press the [PrtScn] button to create a screen capture, then press [Ctrl][V].
- Save and print the document.

e. Exit Word.

Getting Started with Access 2007

Files You Will Need:

Quest-A.accdb
RealEstate-A.accdb
Recycle-A.accdb
Media-A.accdb
Basketball-A.accdb

In this unit, you will learn the purpose, advantages, and terminology of Microsoft Office Access 2007, the relational database program in Microsoft Office 2007. You will create and modify tables, the basic building blocks of an Access relational database. You'll also navigate, enter, update, preview, and print data. Mark Rock is the tour developer for United States group travel at Quest Specialty Travel (QST), a tour company that specializes in cultural tourism and adventure travel. Mark uses Access to store, maintain, and analyze customer and tour information.

OBJECTIVES

- Understand relational databases
- Open a database
- Enter data
- Edit data
- Create a database
- Create a table
- Create primary keys
- Relate two tables
- Print a datasheet

Understanding Relational Databases

Microsoft Office Access 2007 is relational database software that runs on the Windows operating system. You use **relational database software** to manage data that is organized into lists, such as information about customers, products, vendors, employees, projects, or sales. Many small companies track customer, inventory, and sales information in a spreadsheet program such as Microsoft Office Excel. While Excel does offer some list management features, Access provides many more tools and advantages, mainly due to the "relational" nature of the lists that Access manages. Table A-1 compares the two programs. You and Mark Rock review the advantages of database software over spreadsheets for managing lists of information.

DETAILS

The advantages of using Access for database management include:

- **Duplicate data is minimized**

  Figures A-1 and A-2 compare how you might store sales data in a single Excel spreadsheet list versus three related Access tables. Note that with Access, you do not have to reenter information such as a customer's name and address or product description every time a sale is made, because lists can be linked, or "related," in relational database software.

- **Information is more accurate, reliable, and consistent because duplicate data is minimized**

  The relational nature of data stored in an Access database allows you to minimize duplicate data entry, which creates more accurate, reliable, and consistent information.

- **Data entry is faster and easier using Access forms**

  Data entry forms (screen layouts) make data entry faster and easier than entering data in a spreadsheet.

- **Information can be viewed and sorted in many ways using Access queries, forms, and reports**

  In Access, you can save queries (questions about the data), data entry forms, and reports, allowing you to use them over and over without performing extra work to re-create a particular view of the data.

- **Information is more secure using Access passwords and security features**

  Access databases can be password protected, and users can be given different privileges to view or update data.

- **Several users can share and edit information simultaneously**

  Unlike spreadsheets or word processing documents, Access databases are inherently multiuser. More than one person can be entering, updating, and analyzing data at the same time.

FIGURE A-1: Using a spreadsheet to organize sales data

	A	B	C	D	E	F	G	H	I	J	K	L	M	N	O	P
1	Cust No	First	Last	Street	City	State	Zip	Phone	Date	Invoice	Product No	Artist	Name	Format	Tracks	Cost
2	1	Kusong	Tse	222 Elm	Topeka	KS	66111	913-555-0000	8/1/2006	8111	11-222	Michael Smith	Always	CD	14	15
3	2	Paige	Denver	400 Oak	Lenexa	MO	60023	816-555-8877	8/1/2006	8112	11-222	Michael Smith	Always	CD	14	15
4	1	Kusong	Tse	222 Elm	Topeka	KS	66111	913-555-0000	8/2/2006	8113	22-333	Gold Flakes	Avalon	CD	13	14
5	3	Caitlyn	Baily	111 Ash	Ames	IA	50010	515-555-3333	8/3/2006	8114	22-333	Gold Flakes	Avalon	CD	13	14
6	2	Paige	Denver	400 Oak	Lenexa	MO	60023	816-555-8877	8/4/2006	8115	44-1111	Lungwort	Sounds	CD	15	13
7	3	Caitlyn	Baily	111 Ash	Ames	IA	50010	515-555-3333	8/4/2006	8116	44-1111	Lungwort	Sounds	CD	15	13
8	4	Max	Royal	500 Pine	Manilla	NE	55123	827-555-4422	8/5/2006	8117	44-1111	Lungwort	Sounds	CD	15	13
9																

Duplicate customer data is entered each time an existing customer makes an additional purchase

Duplicate product data is entered each time the same product is sold more than once

FIGURE A-2: Using a relational database to organize sales data

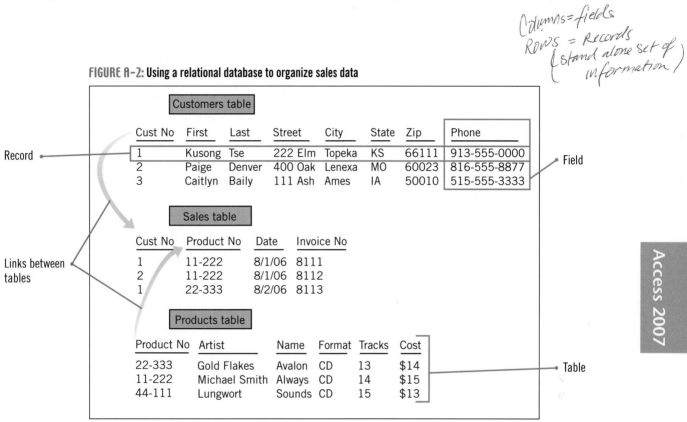

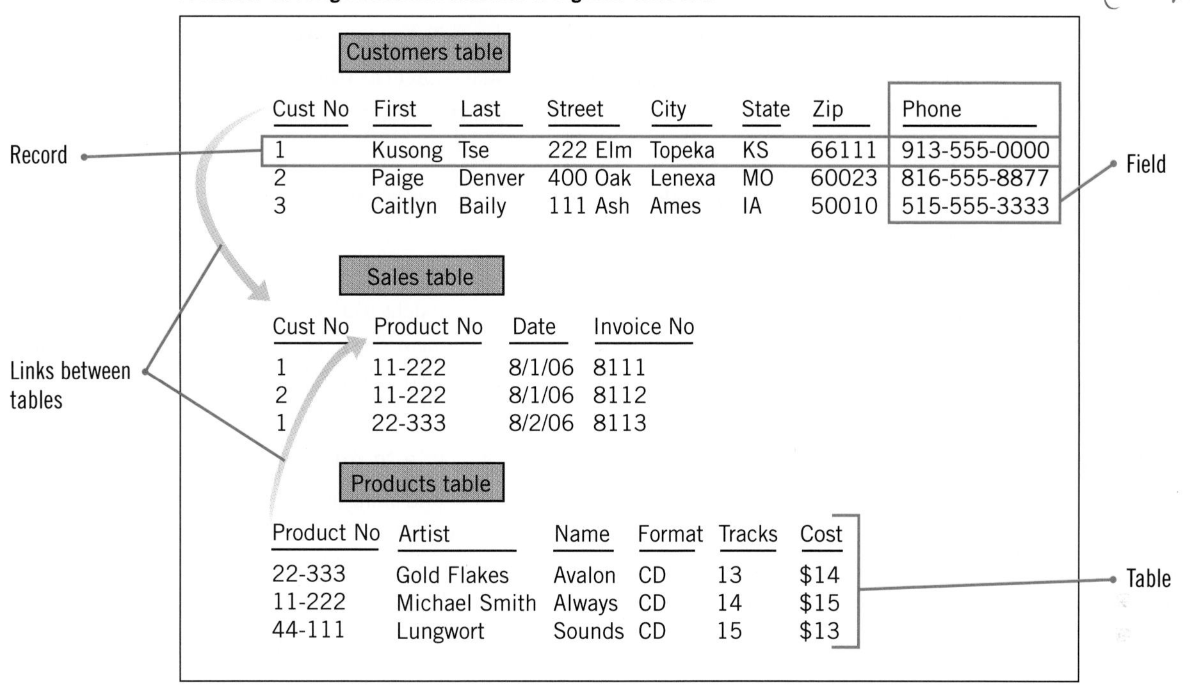

Customers table
Cust No First Last Street City State Zip Phone
1 Kusong Tse 222 Elm Topeka KS 66111 913-555-0000
2 Paige Denver 400 Oak Lenexa MO 60023 816-555-8877
3 Caitlyn Baily 111 Ash Ames IA 50010 515-555-3333
Record
Field
Sales table
Cust No Product No Date Invoice No
1 11-222 8/1/06 8111
2 11-222 8/1/06 8112
1 22-333 8/2/06 8113
Links between tables
Products table
Product No Artist Name Format Tracks Cost
22-333 Gold Flakes Avalon CD 13 $14
11-222 Michael Smith Always CD 14 $15
44-111 Lungwort Sounds CD 15 $13
Table

TABLE A-1: Comparing Excel to Access

feature	Excel	Access
Layout	Provides a natural tabular layout for easy data entry	Provides a natural tabular layout as well as the ability to create customized data entry screens
Storage	Limited to approximately 65,000 records per sheet	Stores any number of records up to 2 GB
Linked tables	Manages single lists of information	Allows links between lists of information to reduce data redundancy
Reporting	Limited to the current spreadsheet arrangement of data	Creates and saves multiple presentations of data
Security	Limited to file security options such as marking the file "read-only" or protecting a range of cells	Allows users to access only the records and fields they need
Multiuser capabilities	Does not easily allow multiple users to simultaneously enter and update data	Allows multiple users to simultaneously enter and update data
Data entry	Provides limited data entry screens	Provides the ability to create extensive data entry screens called forms

UNIT
A
Access 2007

Opening a Database

You can start Access from the Start menu, which opens when you click the Start button on the Windows taskbar, or from an Access shortcut icon on the desktop. Access opens to the Getting Started with Microsoft Office Access page, which shows different ways to work with Access. To open a specific database in Access, you can click a database in the Open Recent Database list or click the More link to navigate to a different database. You can also start Access and open a database at the same time by opening the database directly from a My Computer or Windows Explorer window. Mark Rock has entered some tour information in a database called Quest-A. He asks you to start Access and review this database.

STEPS

TROUBLE
If a Security Warning bar appears below the Ribbon, click the Options button, click Enable this content, then click OK.

TROUBLE
If the Navigation Pane is not open, click the Shutter Bar Open/Close button » to open it and view database table names.

QUICK TIP
For more information on using features of the Access window that are new to Microsoft Office 2007, see the unit "Getting Started with Office 2007."

1. **Start Access**

   Access starts and opens the Getting Started with Microsoft Office Access page, shown in Figure A-3, which helps you create a new database from a template, create a new blank database, or open an existing database.

2. **Click the More link in the Open Recent Database list, navigate to the drive and folder where you store your Data Files, click the Quest-A.accdb database file, click Open, then click the Maximize button if the Access window is not already maximized**

   The Quest-A database contains two tables of data named States and Tours.

3. **In the Navigation Pane, double-click the Tours table to open it, then click on the Tours table**

   The Tours table opens in Datasheet View, as shown in Figure A-4. **Tables** are the fundamental building blocks of a relational database because they store all of the data. **Datasheet View** displays the data in a table in a spreadsheet-like view of fields and records called the **datasheet**. The Tours datasheet contains six fields and 21 records. **Field names** are listed at the top of each column. Important database terminology is summarized in Table A-2.

4. **In the Navigation Pane, double-click the States table to open it**

   The States table contains only two fields, StateAbbreviation and StateName, and four records. By using a separate States table, you only need to enter full state names such as Colorado and Florida once, rather than every time you enter a record for a particular state in the Tours table. The Tours and States tables are linked together via the common StateAbbreviation field. Later in this unit, you learn more about how multiple lists of information, defined as tables in Access, are linked to create relational databases.

FIGURE A-3: Getting Started with Microsoft Office Access page

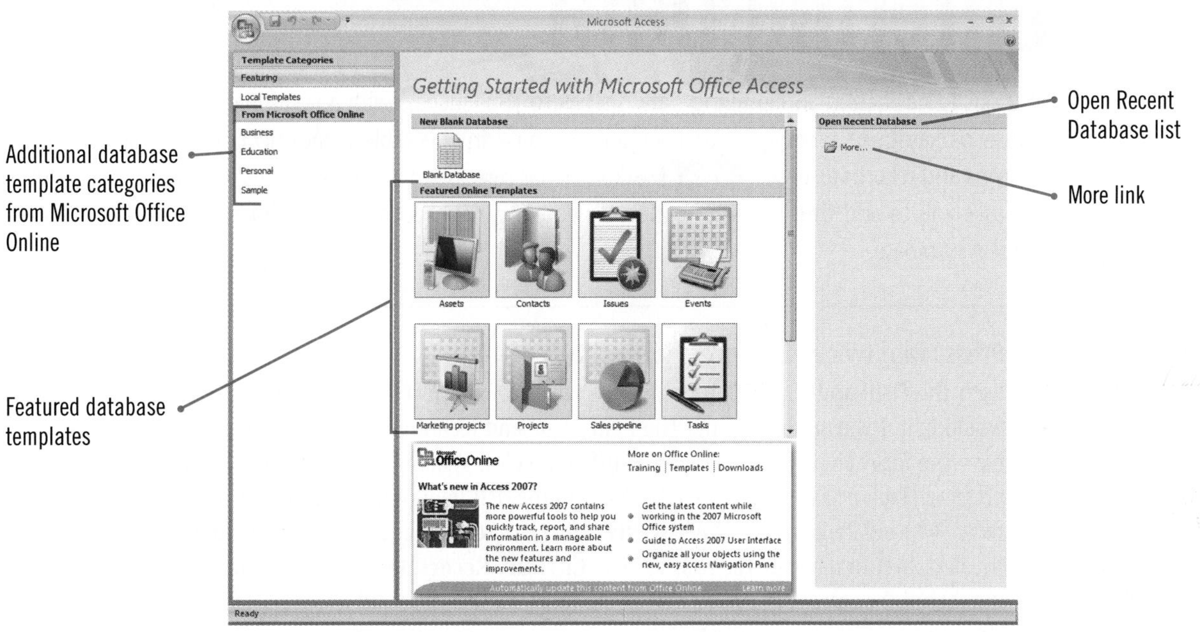

FIGURE A-4: Tours table

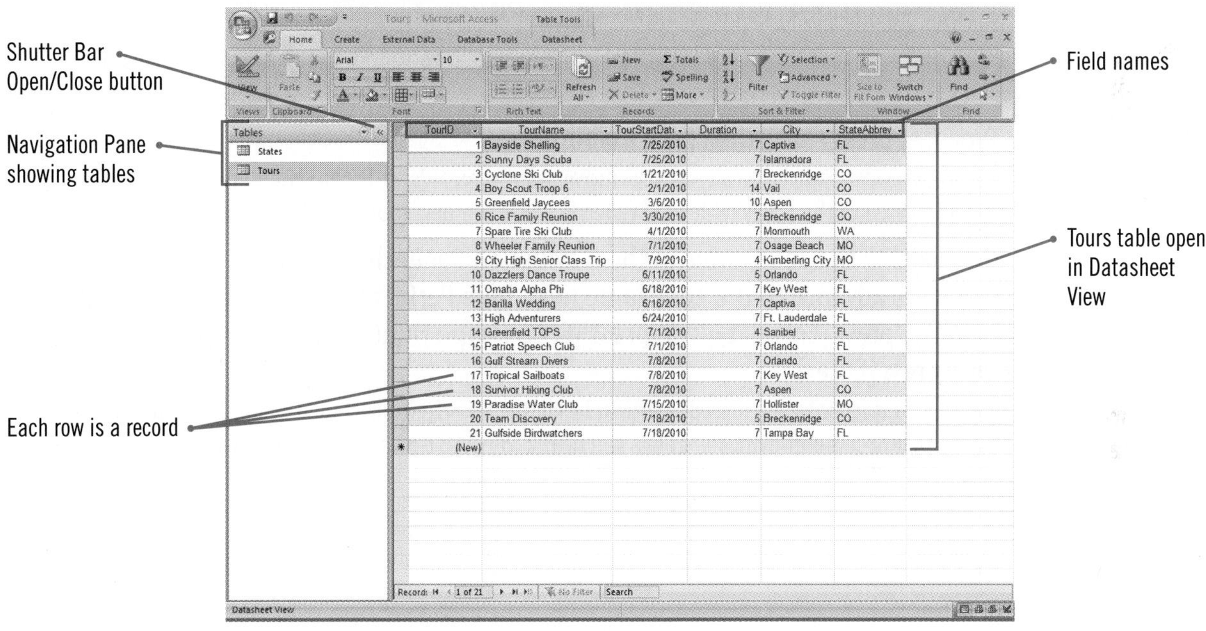

Access 2007

TABLE A-2: Important database terminology

term	description
Field	The smallest unit of data organization; consists of a specific category of data such as a customer's name, city, state, or phone number
Record	A group of related fields that describe a person, place, or thing
Key field	A field that contains unique information for each record, such as a customer number for a customer
Table	A collection of records for a single subject
Database	A collection of tables associated with a general topic
Relational database	An Access database with multiple tables that are linked together by a common field
Objects	The parts of an Access database that help you view, edit, manage, and analyze the data, such as **tables**, **queries**, **forms**, **reports**, **macros**, and **modules**

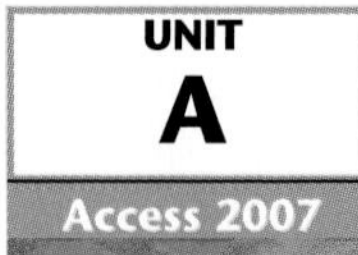

Entering Data

Your skill in navigating and entering data is a key to your success with a relational database. You use either mouse or keystroke techniques to navigate the data in the table's datasheet, which displays fields as columns and records as rows. Mark Rock has developed some new tours for Quest Specialty Travel, and asks you to add this tour information by entering new records in the States and Tours tables of the Quest-A database.

STEPS

1. **Press [Tab] twice, then press [Enter] twice**

   Both the [Tab] and [Enter] keys move the focus to the next field. The **focus** refers to which data you would edit if you started typing. The field name and record selector button for the field and record that have the focus are highlighted with a different color. When you navigate to the last field of the record, pressing [Tab] or [Enter] advances the focus to the first field of the next record. You can also use the Next record and Previous record **navigation buttons** on the navigation bar in the lower-left corner of the datasheet to navigate the records. The **Current Record** text box on the navigation bar tells you the number of the current record as well as the total number of records in the datasheet.

2. **Click the StateAbbrev field below WA to position the insertion point to enter a new record**

   You can also use the New (blank) record button on the navigation bar to move to a new record. You enter new records at the end of the datasheet. You learn how to sort and reorder them later. A complete list of navigation keystrokes is shown in Table A-3.

3. **Type CA, press [Tab], then type California**

   Access saves data automatically as you move among records or within the database. With the California record entered in the States table, you're ready to enter a new tour record in the Tours table.

4. **Double-click the Tours table in the Navigation Pane, click (New) in the last row, press [Enter] to advance to the TourName field, type Perfect Waves, press [Enter], type 7/16/10, press [Enter], type 5, press [Enter], type Hunt Beach, press [Enter], type CA, then press [Enter]**

   The new tour record you entered is shown in Figure A-5. The TourID field is an **AutoNumber** field, which means that Access automatically enters the next consecutive number into the field as it creates the record.

Changing from Navigation mode to Edit mode

If you navigate to another area of the datasheet by clicking with the mouse pointer instead of pressing [Tab] or [Enter], you change from **Navigation mode** to Edit mode. In **Edit mode**, Access assumes that you are trying to make changes to the current field value, so keystrokes such as [Ctrl][End], [Ctrl][Home], [←], and [→] move the insertion point *within* the field. To return to Navigation mode, press [Tab] or [Enter] (thus moving the focus to the next field), or press [↑] or [↓] (thus moving the focus to a different record).

FIGURE A-5: New record in the Tours table

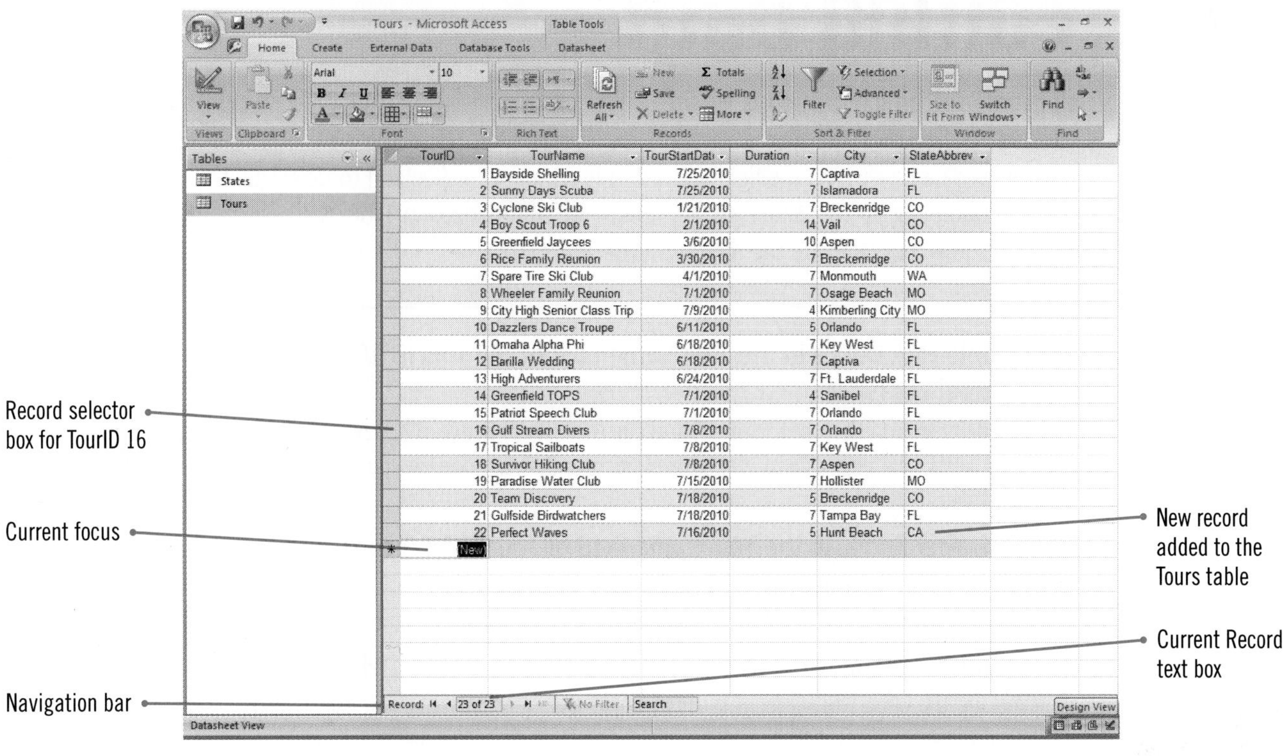

TABLE A-3: Navigation mode keyboard shortcuts

shortcut key	moves to the
[Tab], [Enter], or [→]	Next field of the current record
[Shift][Tab] or [←]	Previous field of the current record
[Home]	First field of the current record
[End]	Last field of the current record
[Ctrl][Home] or [F5]	First field of the first record
[Ctrl][End]	Last field of the last record
[↑]	Current field of the previous record
[↓]	Current field of the next record

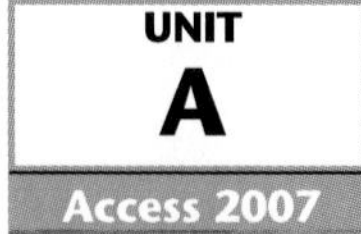

Editing Data

Updating existing information is another critical data management task. To change the contents of an existing record, click the field you want to change, then type the new information. You can delete unwanted data by clicking the field and using [Backspace] or [Delete] to delete text to the left or right of the insertion point. Other data-entry keystrokes are summarized in Table A-4. Mark Rock asks you to make some corrections to the records in the Tours table.

STEPS

1. **Double-click Dance in the TourName field of the TourID 10 record, and press the [Delete] key twice**
   You deleted both the word "Dance" and the extra space between "Dazzlers" and "Troupe." Access automatically saves new records and changes to existing data as soon as you move to another record or close the datasheet.
2. **Click after Barilla in the TourName field of TourID 12 record, and type -Cavuto**
   When you are editing a record, the **edit record symbol**, which looks like a small pencil, appears in the record selector box to the left of the current record, as shown in Figure A-6, to indicate you are in Edit mode.
3. **Double-click Speech in the TourID 15 record, and type Debate**
   You use the same editing techniques in an Access datasheet that you use in an Excel spreadsheet or Word document.
4. **Click the TourStartDate field in the TourID 22 record, click the Calendar icon, then navigate to and click August 27, 2010**
   The **calendar picker**, a pop-up calendar from which you can choose dates for a date field, is a new feature for Access 2007. You can also type the date directly into the field as 8/27/2010.
5. **Press [Esc]**
   Pressing [Esc] once removes the current field's editing changes, so the TourStartDate changes back to 7/16/2010. Pressing [Esc] twice removes all changes to the current record. Once you move to another record, the edits are saved, you return to Navigation mode, and you can no longer use [Esc] to remove editing changes to the current record. You can, however, click the Undo button on the Quick Access toolbar to undo the last change you made.
6. **Click the record selector for the TourID 16 record, click the Delete button in the Records group on the Home tab, then click Yes**
   A message warns that you cannot undo a record deletion operation. Notice that the Undo button is dimmed, indicating that it cannot be used now.
7. **Click the Close button on the title bar to close both the Quest-A.accdb database and Access 2007**
   Because Access saves data as you work in a database, you are not prompted to save data when you close the database or the Access itself.

QUICK TIP

The ScreenTip for the Undo button displays the action you can undo.

Resizing and moving datasheet columns

You can resize the width of a field in a datasheet by dragging the **column separator**, the thin line that separates the field names to the left or right. The pointer changes to ↔ as you make the field wider or narrower. Release the mouse button when you have resized the field. To adjust the column width to accommodate the widest entry in the field, double-click the column separator. To move a column, click the field name to select the entire column, then drag the field name left or right.

FIGURE A-6: **Edit mode**

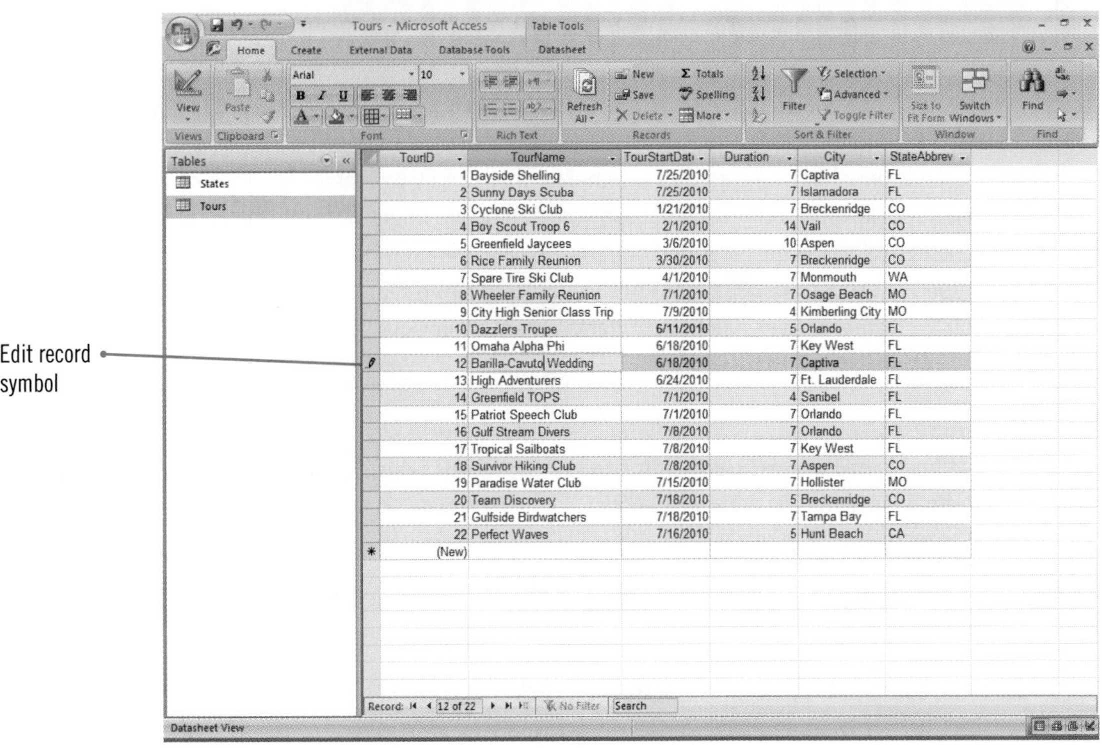

TourID	TourName	TourStartDate	Duration	City	StateAbbrev
1	Bayside Shelling	7/25/2010	7	Captiva	FL
2	Sunny Days Scuba	7/25/2010	7	Islamadora	FL
3	Cyclone Ski Club	1/21/2010	7	Breckenridge	CO
4	Boy Scout Troop 6	2/1/2010	14	Vail	CO
5	Greenfield Jaycees	3/6/2010	10	Aspen	CO
6	Rice Family Reunion	3/30/2010	7	Breckenridge	CO
7	Spare Tire Ski Club	4/1/2010	7	Monmouth	WA
8	Wheeler Family Reunion	7/1/2010	7	Osage Beach	MO
9	City High Senior Class Trip	7/9/2010	4	Kimberling City	MO
10	Dazzlers Troupe	6/11/2010	5	Orlando	FL
11	Omaha Alpha Phi	6/18/2010	7	Key West	FL
12	Barilla-Cavuto Wedding	6/18/2010	7	Captiva	FL
13	High Adventurers	6/24/2010	7	Ft. Lauderdale	FL
14	Greenfield TOPS	7/1/2010	4	Sanibel	FL
15	Patriot Speech Club	7/1/2010	7	Orlando	FL
16	Gulf Stream Divers	7/8/2010	7	Orlando	FL
17	Tropical Sailboats	7/8/2010	7	Key West	FL
18	Survivor Hiking Club	7/8/2010	7	Aspen	CO
19	Paradise Water Club	7/15/2010	7	Hollister	MO
20	Team Discovery	7/18/2010	5	Breckenridge	CO
21	Gulfside Birdwatchers	7/18/2010	7	Tampa Bay	FL
22	Perfect Waves	7/16/2010	5	Hunt Beach	CA
(New)					

Access 2007

TABLE A-4: **Edit mode keyboard shortcuts**

editing keystroke	action
[Backspace]	Deletes one character to the left of the insertion point
[Delete]	Deletes one character to the right of the insertion point
[F2]	Switches between Edit and Navigation mode
[Esc]	Undoes the change to the current field
[Esc][Esc]	Undoes all changes to the current record
[F7]	Starts the spell check feature
[Ctrl][']	Inserts the value from the same field in the previous record into the current field
[Ctrl][;]	Inserts the current date in a Date field

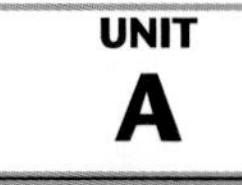

UNIT A

Access 2007

Creating a Database

You can create a new database using an Access **template**, a sample database provided within the Microsoft Access program, or you can start with a blank database to create a database from scratch. Your decision depends on whether Access has a template that closely resembles the type of data you plan to manage. If it does, building your own database from a template might be faster than creating the database from scratch. Regardless of which method you use, you can always modify the database later, tailoring it to meet your specific needs. Mark Rock wants to organize Quest's clients, prospects, and vendors, and asks you to create an Access database to track contacts. You'll use the Contacts template to get started.

STEPS

QUICK TIP

To create a new blank database, use the Blank Database icon.

TROUBLE

If an Access Help window or Security Warning bar opens, close it. If a Microsoft Office Genuine Advantage dialog box opens, click Continue.

1. **Start Access**

   The "Getting Started with Microsoft Office Access" page opens, which you can use to create a database from a template. Some templates are stored on your computer when you install Access, and others are available from Microsoft Office Online.

2. **In the Featured Online Templates pane click Contacts, then click Download in the lower-right corner**

3. **Click the Watch This link on the left, then click the Watch this >> link to watch a short video on the Contact Management Database template**

   A short video plays explaining some of the features of the Microsoft Contact Management Database template. Note how to use the Options button to enable content.

4. **Close the Microsoft Office Online window, the Access Help window, and the Getting Started window**

   The Contact List form opens, as shown in Figure A-7.

5. **Click the Options button, click the Enable this content option button, click OK, close the Getting Started window if it opens again, enter your own name and e-mail address for the first record, use school information for the Business Phone and Company field, use Student for the Job Title field, then press [↓]**

   Although you are entering this record in an **Access form** (an easy-to-use data entry screen) instead of directly in a table, the data is stored in the underlying table. Forms and tables are database objects, and are displayed in the Navigation Pane. The **Navigation Pane** provides a way to move between objects (tables, queries, forms, and reports) in the database. Tables are the most important objects because they physically store all of the data. Table A-5 defines the four primary Access objects—tables, queries, forms, and reports—and the icon that identifies each in the Navigation Pane. When you created this database, the Contacts template not only created the Contact List form you used to enter your name, but also the Contact Details form and two reports, Directory and Phone Book.

TROUBLE

If the Phone Book report still shows your last name instead of "Johnson," close the report by right-clicking its tab and clicking Close, then double-click the report in the Navigation Pane to reopen it.

6. **Double-click the Contacts table in the Navigation Pane, double-click your last name in the Last Name field, type Johnson, then press [↓] to save the data**

   The Contacts table appears with the record you entered using the Contact List form. All data is physically stored in Access table objects when you move from record to record, even if the data is entered through a query or form.

7. **Double-click the Phone Book report in the Navigation Pane**

   All reports that depend on this data are automatically updated, as shown in Figure A-8.

8. **Click the Close button on the title bar to close both the Contacts database and Access 2007**

FIGURE A-7: Contact List form provided by the Contacts template

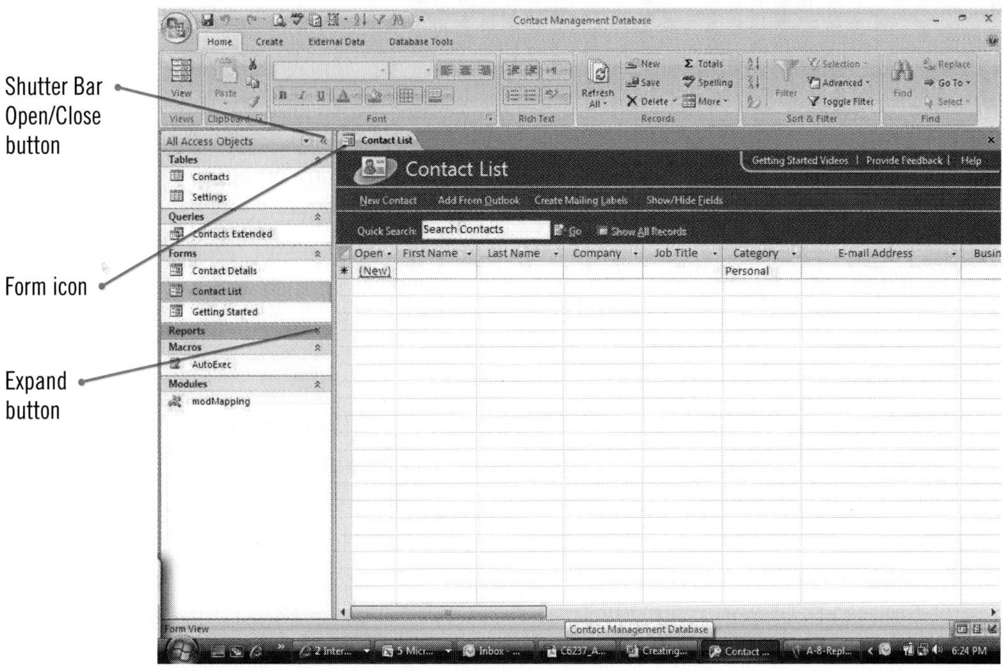

FIGURE A-8: Phone Book report provided by the Contacts template

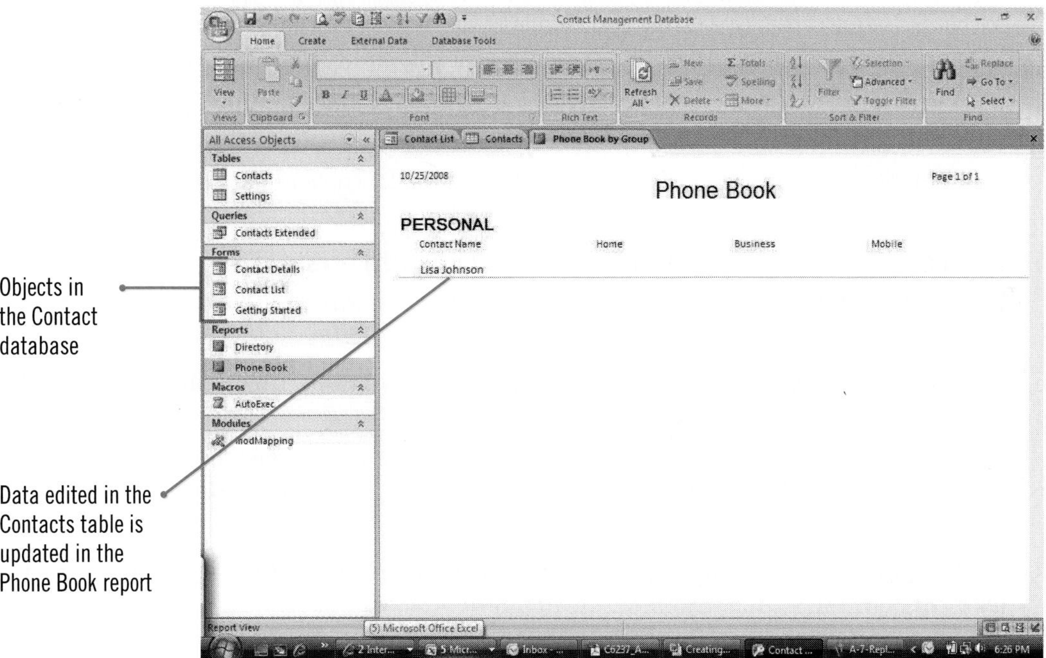

Access 2007

TABLE A-5: Access objects and their purpose

object	Navigation Pane icon	purpose
Table		Contains all of the raw data within the database in a spreadsheet-like view; tables are linked with a common field to create a relational database, which minimizes redundant data
Query		Allows the user to select a subset of fields or records from one or more tables; queries are created when a user has a question about the data
Form		Provides an easy-to-use data entry screen
Report		Provides a professional printout of data that can contain enhancements such as headers, footers, graphics, and calculations on groups of records

UNIT A
Access 2007

Creating a Table

After establishing your database, you often need to create a new table. You can use one of the table templates Access provides or you can create your own table from scratch. Creating a table consists of three essential tasks: meaningfully naming each field in the table, selecting an appropriate data type for each field, and naming the table itself. The **data type** determines what kind of data can be entered into a field, such as numbers, text, or dates. Data types are described in Table A-6. Mark Rock asks you to create a small table that lists the different types of tours Quest offers, such as Educational, Adventure, and Cultural. Because Access does not have a template for such a table, you'll create the table yourself.

STEPS

1. **Reopen the Quest-A.accdb database, enable content if prompted, click the Create tab on the Ribbon, click the Table button, then click the Maximize button**

   A new, blank table datasheet appears, as shown in Figure A-9, with one sample field named ID that has an AutoNumber data type. You don't need this sample field in the table, so you can rename the first field and use it to identify tour categories.

2. **Click the ID field name, then click the Rename button on the Datasheet tab**

   ID in the column header is highlighted, allowing you to enter a new field name.

3. **Type Category, then press [↓]**

   The new field, renamed Category, is now the first field. With the field named appropriately, the next step is to choose the correct data type for the field. Currently, the field has an AutoNumber data type, but because this field will store the name of each tour category, you need to change its data type to Text.

4. **Click the Data Type list arrow (which currently displays AutoNumber) on the Datasheet tab, then click Text**

   For this table, you want to create one more field called TourDescription that also has a Text data type because it will store text descriptions of each tour.

5. **Double-click Add New Field, type TourDescription, then press [↓]**

   Because Text is the default data type for new fields, the TourDescription field has already been assigned with the correct data type.

6. **Click the blank cell below the Category field, type Adventure, then enter the remaining records as shown in Figure A-10**

   After naming the fields, assigning the data types, and entering the data, you save the table with an appropriate name. Table1 is the default name, but it is not very descriptive. You cannot rename a table that is open, so you'll close it and give it a descriptive name when prompted.

7. **Click the Close Window button for the new table, click Yes, type TourCategories, then click OK**

QUICK TIP

Widen the TourDescription field by dragging the resize pointer ✛ to resize the column.

TROUBLE

The Close Window button for the table is on the Ribbon (not on the title bar). You can also click the Office button, then click Close to close the table.

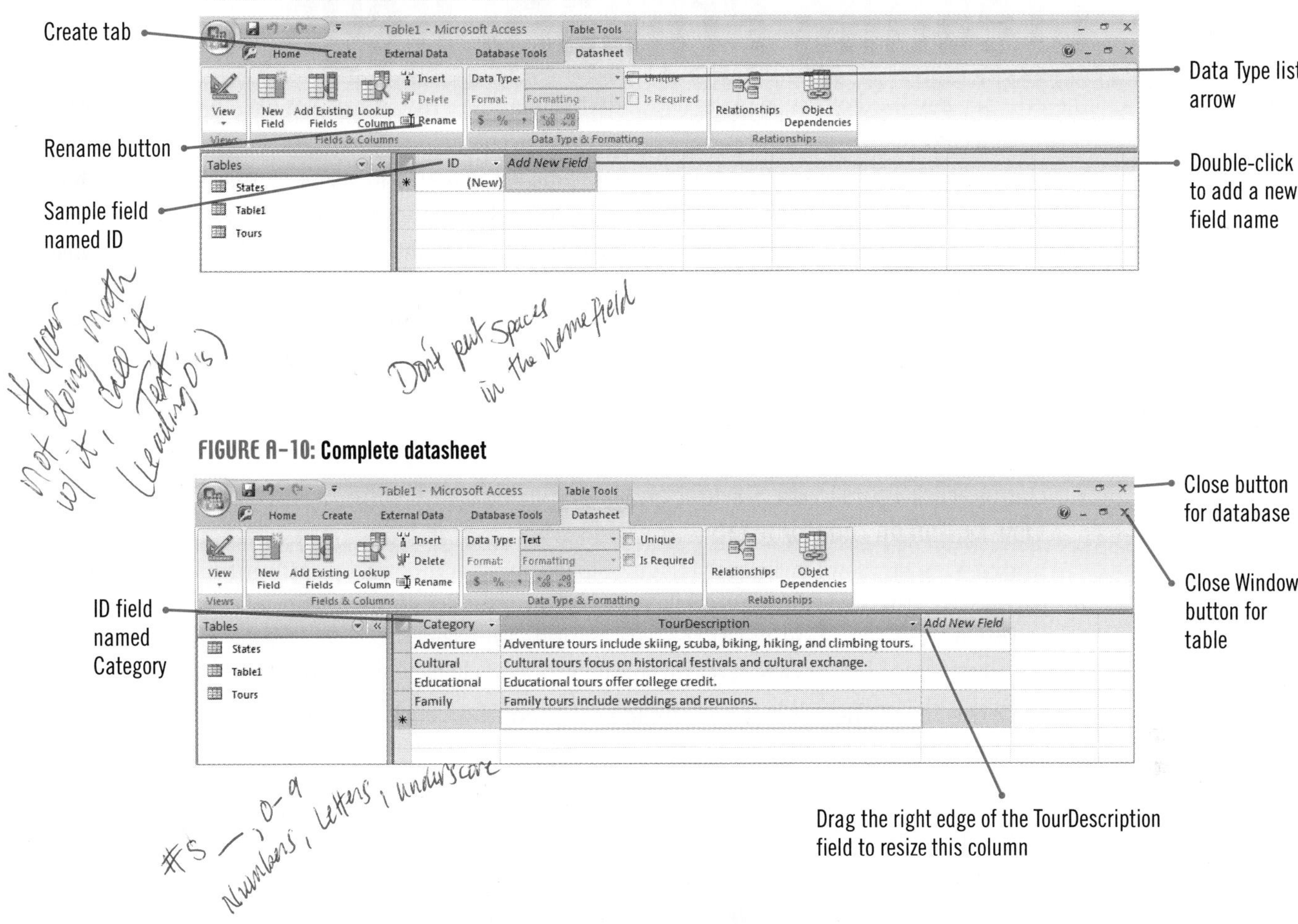

FIGURE A-9: New blank table in Datasheet View

FIGURE A-10: Complete datasheet

TABLE A-6: Data types

data type	description of data	size
Text	Text information or combinations of text and numbers, such as a street address, name, or phone number	Up to 255 characters
Memo	Lengthy text, such as comments or notes	Up to 65,535 characters
Number	Numeric information, such as quantities	Several sizes available to store numbers with varying degrees of precision
Date/Time	Dates and times	Size controlled by Access to accommodate dates and times across thousands of years (for example, 1/1/1850 and 1/1/2150 are valid dates)
Currency	Monetary values	Size controlled by Access; accommodates up to 15 digits to the left of the decimal point and four digits to the right
AutoNumber	Integers assigned by Access to sequentially order each record added to a table	Size controlled by Access
Yes/No	Only one of two values stored (Yes/No, On/Off, True/False)	Size controlled by Access
OLE Object	Office and Windows files that can be linked or embedded (OLE) such as pictures, sound clips, documents, or spreadsheets	Up to 2 GB
Attachment	Any supported file type including .jpg images, spreadsheets, and documents (new for Office 2007)	Up to 1 GB
Hyperlink	Web and e-mail addresses	Size controlled by Access

Creating Primary Keys

The **primary key field** of a table serves two important purposes. First, it contains data that uniquely identifies each record. No two records can have the exact same entry in the field designated as the primary key field. Secondly, the primary key field helps relate one table to another in a **one-to-many relationship**, where one record from one table is related to many records in the second table. For example, one state record in the States table might be related to many tours in the Tours table. In the States table, StateAbbreviation is the primary key field. This field is duplicated in the Tours table, providing the link between one state and many tours. The primary key field is always on the "one" side of a one-to-many relationship between two tables. Mark Rock asks you to check that a primary key field has been appropriately identified for each table.

STEPS

1. **Double-click Tours in the Navigation Pane, maximize the window, then click the Design View button on the Home tab**

   Design View, as shown in Figure A-11, is used to modify and define field properties that are not available in Datasheet View. You see many of a field's **properties** (characteristics that define a field) in the lower half of Design View. Some field properties, such as Field Name and Data Type, can be specified in either Datasheet View or Design View. Specifying the primary key field requires that you work in Design View.

2. **Click the TourID field if it is not already selected, then click the Primary Key button on the Design tab**

   A field designated as the primary key field for a table appears with the key icon, as shown in Figure A-12.

3. **Close and save the Tours table**

   Next, you'll use Design View to set the primary key fields for the other two tables.

4. **Double-click States in the Navigation Pane, click the Design View button, click StateAbbreviation if it is not already selected, click the Primary Key button, then close and save the States table**

   You'll use the Category field as the primary key field in the TourCategories table.

5. **Double-click TourCategories in the Navigation Pane, click the Design View button, make sure the Category field is the primary key, then close the TourCategories table**

   Now that each table has been modified to contain an appropriate primary key field, you no longer have to worry that two tour records in the Tours table could be assigned the same TourID, two states in the States table could be given the same StateAbbreviation, or two tour categories could be assigned to the same Category. In other words, assigning an appropriate primary key field to each table helps prevent you from entering incorrect and duplicate records. The second purpose of the primary key field is to help tie tables together in one-to-many relationships, which you learn about in the next lesson.

FIGURE A-11: Design View of the Tours table

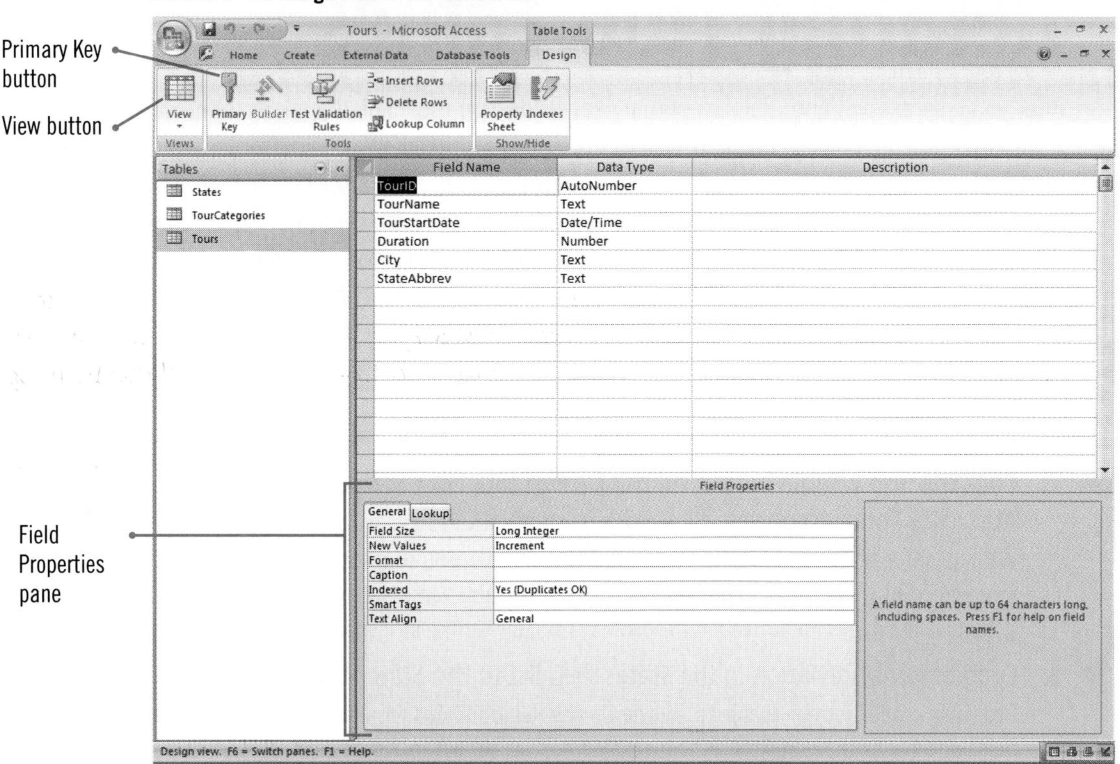

FIGURE A-12: TourID is set as the primary key field

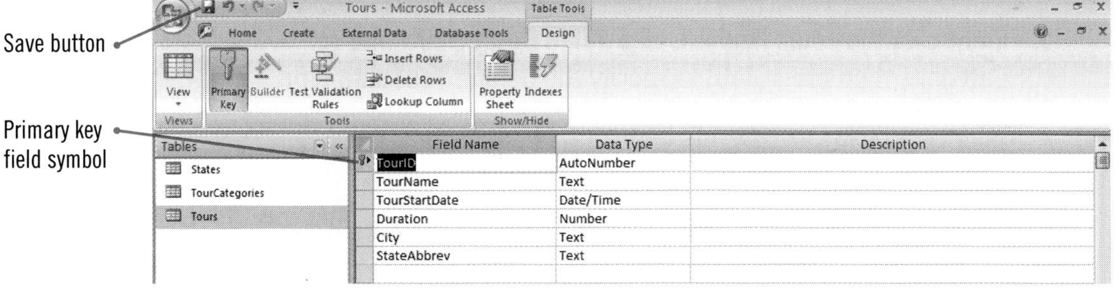

Access 2007

Learning about field properties

Properties are the characteristics that define the field. Two properties are required for every field: Field Name and Data Type. Many other properties, such as Field Size, Format, Caption, and Default Value, are defined in the Field Properties pane in the lower half of a table's Design View. As you add more property entries, you are generally restricting the amount or type of data that can be entered in the field, which increases data entry accuracy. For example, you might change the Field Size property for a State field to 2 in order to eliminate an incorrect entry such as FLL. Field properties change depending on the data type of the selected field. For example, there is no Field Size property for date fields, because Access controls the size of fields with a Date/Time data type.

UNIT A
Access 2007

Relating Two Tables

After you create tables and establish primary key fields, you must link the tables together in one-to-many relationships before you can build queries, forms, or reports that display fields from more than one table. A one-to-many relationship between two tables means that one record from the first table is related to many records in the second table. You use a common linking field, which is always the primary key field in the table on the "one" side of the relationship, to establish this connection. Mark Rock mentions that he plans to create reports that include tour, category, and state information. To help in creating the reports, you define the one-to-many relationships between the tables of the Quest-A database.

STEPS

1. **Click the Database Tools tab on the Ribbon, then click the Relationships button**

QUICK TIP
Drag the table's title bar to move the field list.

2. **Click the Show Table button on the Design tab, click States, click Add, click Tours, click Add, click TourCategories, click Add, then click Close**
With all three tables visible in the Relationships window, you're ready to link them together. Each table is represented by a small **field list** window that displays the names of the fields in the table. The primary key field in each table is identified with the key symbol, as shown in Figure A-13.

QUICK TIP
Drag the bottom border of the field list to display all of the fields.

3. **Drag StateAbbreviation in the States field list to the StateAbbrev field in the Tours field list**
Dragging a field from one table to another in the Relationships window links the two tables by the selected fields and opens the Edit Relationships dialog box, as shown in Figure A-14. **Referential integrity**, a set of Access rules that govern data entry, helps ensure data accuracy.

QUICK TIP
Right-click a relationship line, then click Delete if you need to delete a relationship and start over.

4. **Click the Enforce Referential Integrity check box in the Edit Relationships dialog box, then click Create**
The **one-to-many line** shows the link between the StateAbbreviation field of the States table (the "one" side) and the StateAbbrev field of the Tours table (the "many" side, indicated by the **infinity symbol**). Similarly, you need to create a one-to-many relationship between the TourCategories table and the Tours table, so that one category can be associated with many tours. However, because these tables do not have a common field, you must establish one before you can join the tables.

5. **Right-click the Tours field list, click Table Design, click the cell below StateAbbrev, type Category, then press [Tab] to specify the default Text data type**
A field added to the "many" table to help establish a one-to-many relationship is called the **foreign key field**. Now that you created the foreign key field for the link between the Tours and TourCategories, you can join the tables in a one-to-many relationship.

6. **Close and save the Tours table, drag the Category field from the TourCategories table to the Category field of the Tours table, then click Create in the Edit Relationships dialog box**
The final Relationships window should look like Figure A-15. The relationship line between the Tours and TourCategories tables is also a one-to-many relationship, but the "one" and "many" symbols do not appear because you did not establish referential integrity on this relationship. The primary key field for the Tours table is TourID, but because it participates on the "many" side of two different one-to-many relationships, it contains two foreign key fields, StateAbbrev and Category.

7. **Close and save the Relationships window**

FIGURE A-13: Relationships window

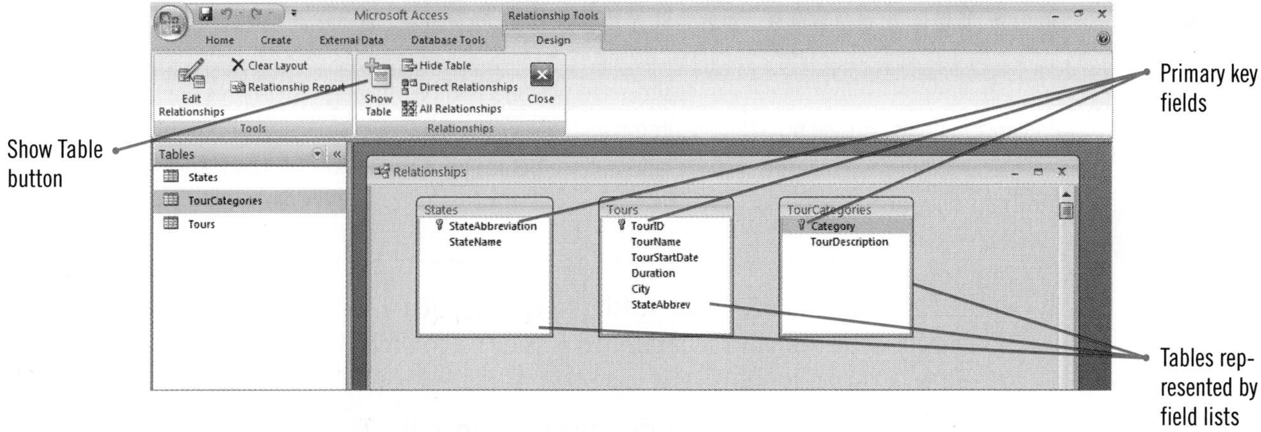

FIGURE A-14: Edit Relationships dialog box

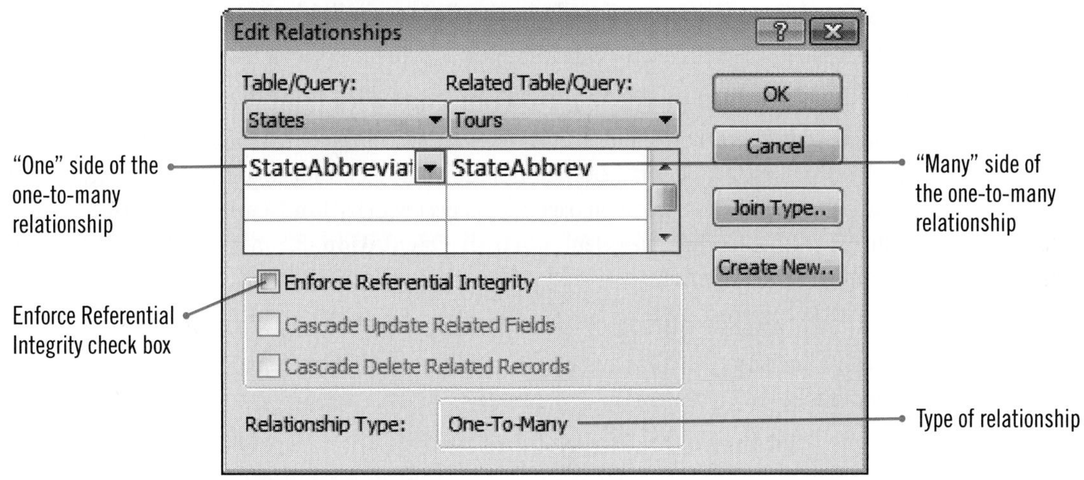

FIGURE A-15: Final Relationships window

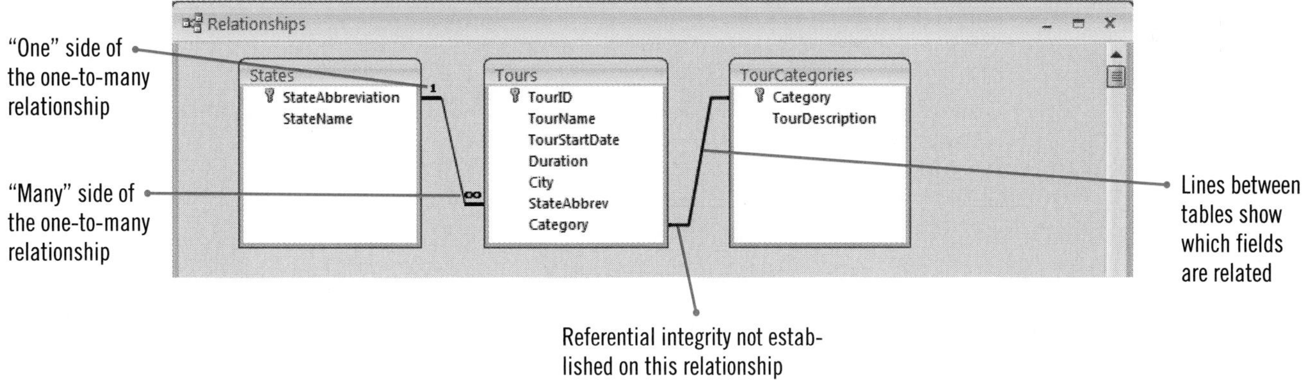

Access 2007

Enforcing referential integrity

Referential integrity is a set of rules that helps reduce invalid entries and orphan records. An **orphan record** is a record in the "many" table that doesn't have a matching entry in the linking field of the "one" table. With referential integrity enforced on a one-to-many relationship, you cannot enter a value in a foreign key field of the "many" table that does not have a match in the linking field of the "one" table. Referential integrity also prevents you from deleting a record in the "one" table if a matching entry exists in the foreign key field of the "many" table. You should enforce referential integrity on all one-to-many relationships if possible. If you are working with a database that already contains orphan records, you cannot enforce referential integrity on that relationship.

Printing a Datasheet

Printing and previewing Access data is similar to printing and previewing other types of Office documents. Previewing helps you see how the document will look when printed so you can make printing adjustments, such as changing the margins or page orientation, before printing it. Mark Rock asks you to print the Tours datasheet.

STEPS

1. **In the Navigation Pane, double-click the Tours table to open it in Datasheet View, then double-click each column separator to resize the columns to their best fit**
   One more new tour needs to be added to the list before you print it—a family reunion.
2. **Add a new record with your last name's Reunion in the TourName field, today's date in the TourStartDate field, 4 in the Duration field, your hometown in the City field, FL in the StateAbbrev field, and Family in the Category field**
   You decide to preview the datasheet before printing it to make sure it fits on one sheet of paper.
3. **Click the Office button, point to Print, then click Print Preview**
   The Tours table appears on a miniature page, as shown in Figure A-16, formatted as it will look when you print it. By previewing the datasheet, you realize that it is too wide to print on one page. (The Category and StateAbbrev fields do not appear on page 1.) You decide to try **landscape orientation** (11 inches wide by 8.5 inches tall) rather than the default **portrait orientation** (8.5 inches wide by 11 inches tall) to see if the printout fits on one page.
4. **Click the Landscape button on the Print Preview tab**
   The navigation buttons on the navigation bar in the lower-left corner in Figure A-17 are dim, indicating that the printout fits on one page.
5. **Click the Print button on the Print Preview tab, then click OK**
   If you need to change printing options, you can use the Page Setup dialog box.
6. **Click the Close button on the title bar to close both the Quest-A.accdb database and Access 2007**

QUICK TIP

Click the Close Print Preview button on the Print Preview tab to close the preview window and return to Datasheet View.

FIGURE A-16: Datasheet in print preview—portrait orientation

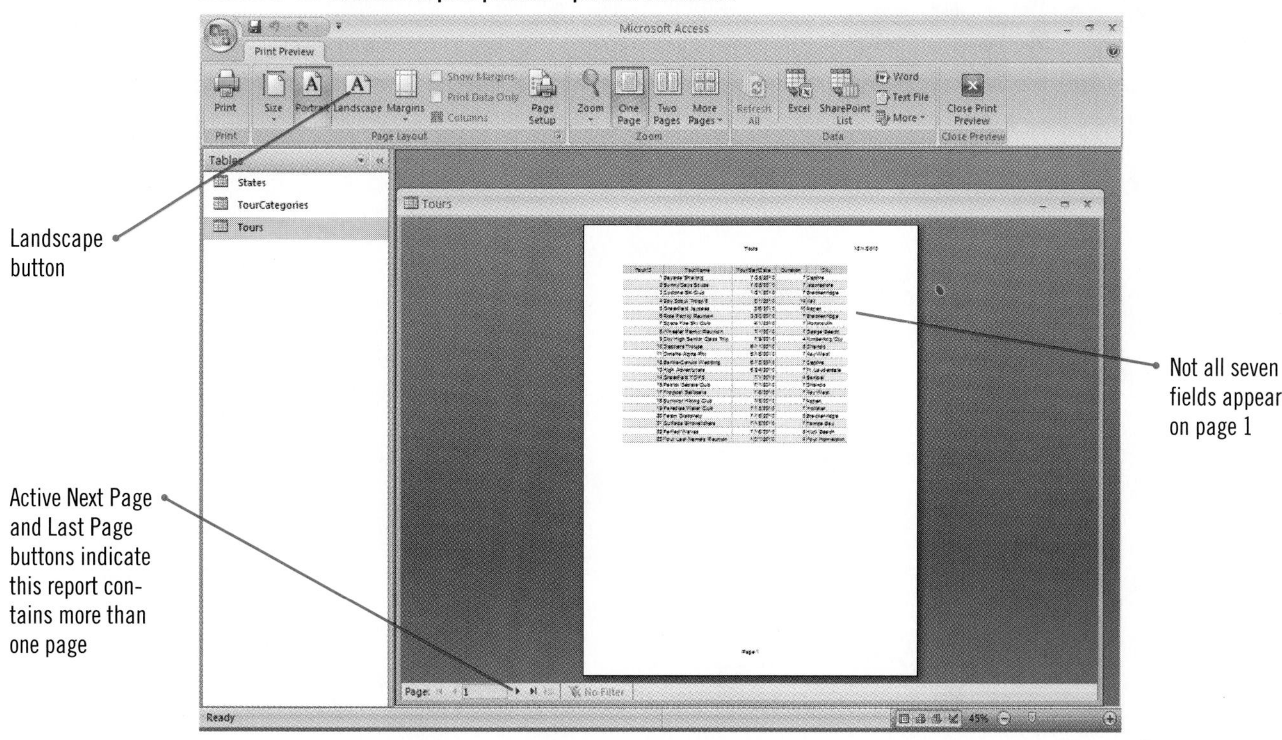
Landscape button
Not all seven fields appear on page 1
Active Next Page and Last Page buttons indicate this report contains more than one page

FIGURE A-17: Datasheet in print preview—landscape orientation

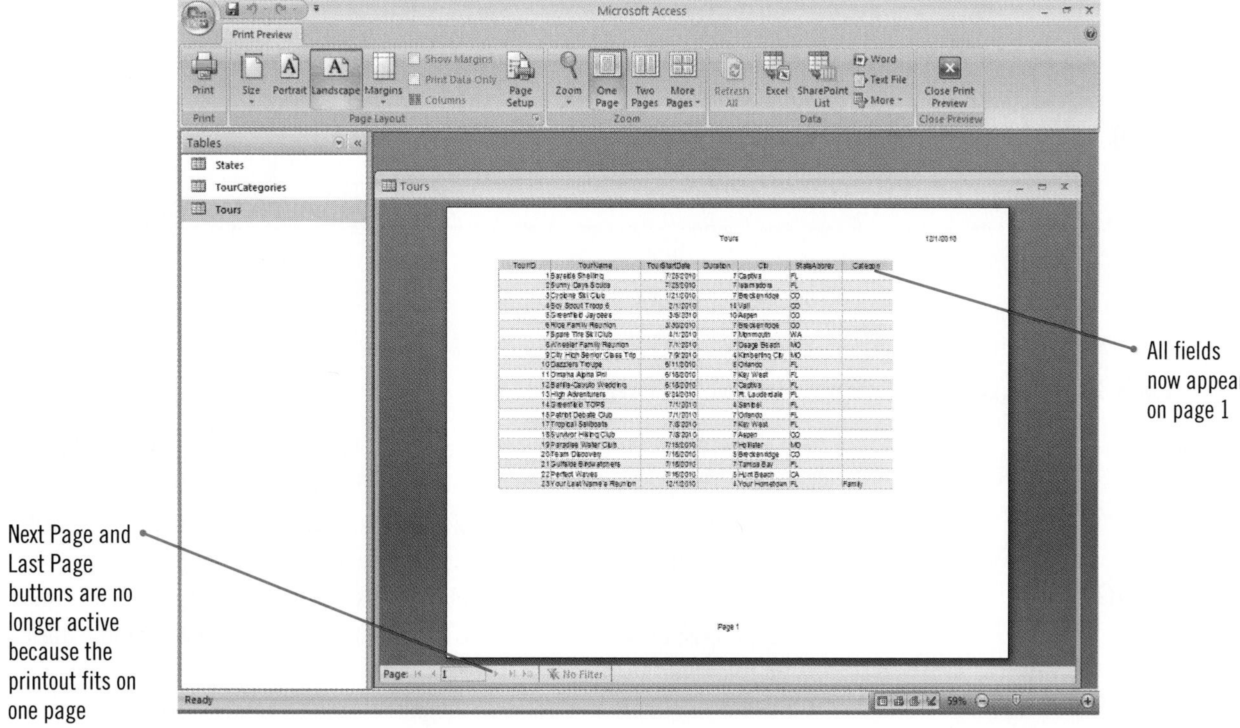
All fields now appear on page 1
Next Page and Last Page buttons are no longer active because the printout fits on one page

Access 2007

Practice

If you have a SAM user profile, you may have access to hands-on instruction, practice, and assessment of the skills covered in this unit. Log in to your SAM account (http://sam2007.course.com/) to launch any assigned training activities or exams that relate to the skills covered in this unit.

▼ CONCEPTS REVIEW

Label each element of the Access window shown in Figure A-18.

FIGURE A-18

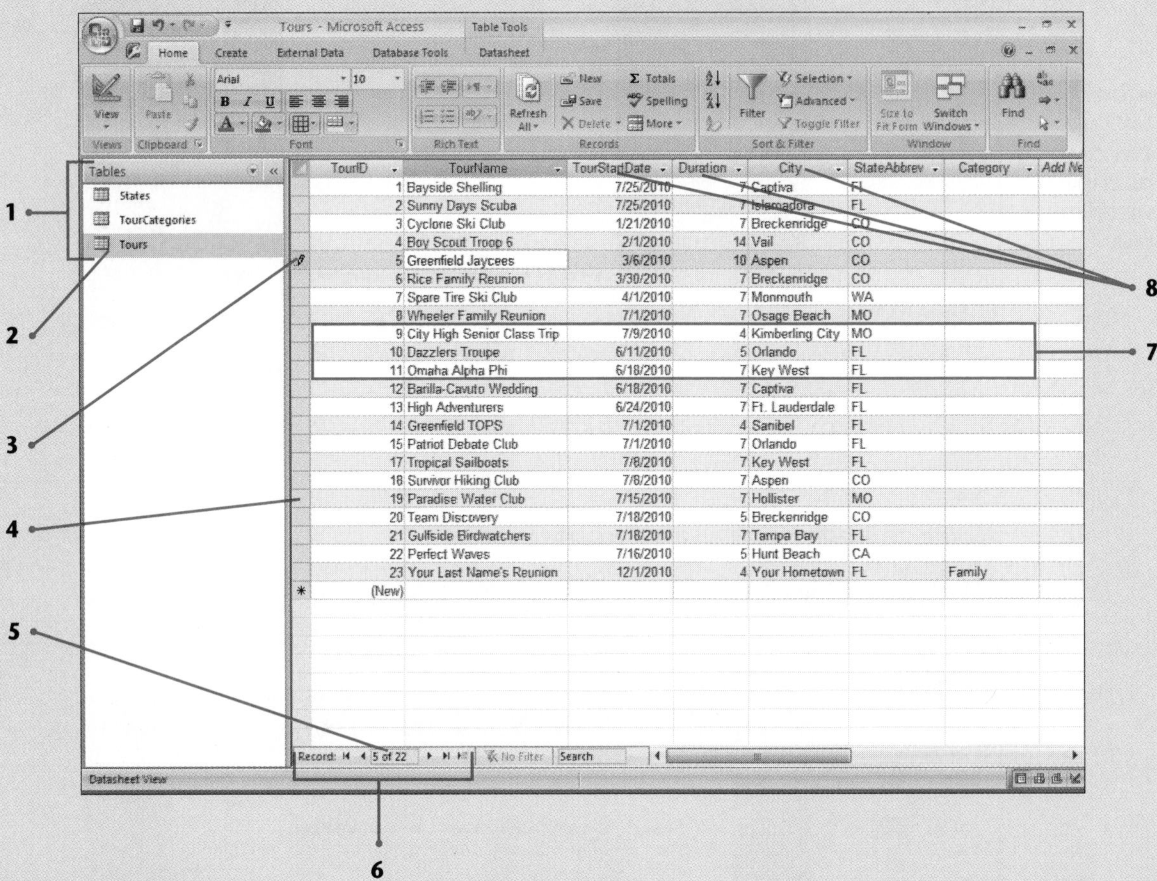

Match each term with the statement that best describes it.

9. Objects	**a.** Seven types of these are contained in an Access database and are used to enter, enhance, and use the data within the database
10. Table	**b.** A collection of records for a single subject, such as all the customer records
11. Record	**c.** A small pencil icon that appears in the record selector box
12. Field	**d.** A spreadsheet-like grid that displays fields as columns and records as rows
13. Datasheet	**e.** A group of related fields for one item, such as all of the demographic information for one customer
14. Form	**f.** A category of information in a table, such as a customer's name, city, or state
15. Edit record symbol	**g.** An Access object that provides an easy-to-use data entry screen

Select the best answer from the list of choices.

16. Which of the following is *not* a typical benefit of relational databases?

- **a.** More accurate data
- **b.** Automatic correction of data as it is entered
- **c.** Faster information retrieval
- **d.** Minimized duplicate data entry

17. Which of the following is *not* an advantage of managing data with relational database software such as Access versus spreadsheet software such as Excel?

- **a.** Uses a single table to store all data
- **b.** Reduces duplicate data entry
- **c.** Provides greater security
- **d.** Allows multiple users to enter data simultaneously

18. The object that creates a professional printout of data that includes headers, footers, and graphics is the:

- **a.** Query.
- **b.** Table.
- **c.** Report.
- **d.** Form.

19. The object that contains all of the database data is the:

- **a.** Report.
- **b.** Form.
- **c.** Page.
- **d.** Table.

20. What can you use to quickly create a new database?

- **a.** Template
- **b.** Object
- **c.** Module
- **d.** Form

▼ SKILLS REVIEW

1. Understand relational databases.

- **a.** Identify five advantages of managing database information in Access versus using a spreadsheet.
- **b.** Explain how a relational database organizes data to minimize redundant information. Use an example involving a database with two related tables, Customers and States, in your explanation.

2. Open a database.

- **a.** Explain the relationship between a field, a record, a table, and a database.
- **b.** Start Access.
- **c.** Open the **RealEstate-A.accdb** database from the drive and folder where you store your Data Files. Enable content if a Security Warning message appears.
- **d.** Open each of the three tables. On a sheet of paper, complete the following table:

table name	number of records	number of fields

3. Enter data.

- **a.** Enter the following records into the Agents table, then print it. Tab through the AgentNo field as it is defined with an AutoNumber data type and it automatically increments as you enter the rest of the data in the record.

AgentNo	AgentFirst	AgentLast	AgentPhone	AgencyNo
(10)	(Your first name)	(Your last name)	555-888-9999	1
(11)	(Your instructor's first name)	(Your instructor's last name)	555-888-5555	3

Access 2007

▼ SKILLS REVIEW (CONTINUED)

b. Enter the following record into the Agencies table, then print it. Tab through the AgencyNo field because it is an AutoNumber field.

AgencyNo	AgencyName	Street	City	State	Zip	AgencyPhone
(4)	(Your last name) Realty	(Your school's street address)	(Your school's city)	(Your school's state)	(Your school's zip code)	555-888-4444

4. Edit data.

a. Open the Listings table datasheet.

b. Change the Area field for ListingNo 7 from Shell Knob to **Ozark Mountain**.

c. Change the SqFt field for ListingNo 14 from 3500 to **5500**.

d. Delete the record for ListingNo 6. Resize the columns to their best fit. Your Listings table datasheet should look similar to the one in Figure A-19.

FIGURE A-19

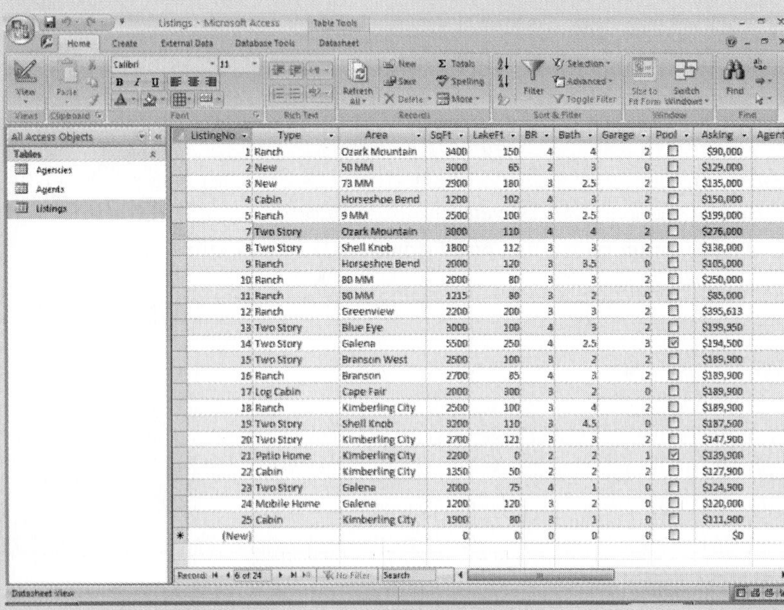

ListingNo	Type	Area	SqFt	LakeFt	BR	Bath	Garage	Pool	Asking
1	Ranch	Ozark Mountain	3400	150	4	4	2	☐	$90,000
2	New	50 MM	3000	65	2	3	0	☐	$129,000
3	New	73 MM	2900	180	3	2.5	2	☐	$135,000
4	Cabin	Horseshoe Bend	1200	102	4	3	2	☐	$150,000
5	Ranch	9 MM	2500	100	3	2.5	0	☐	$199,000
7	Two Story	Ozark Mountain	3000	110	4	4	2	☐	$276,000
8	Two Story	Shell Knob	1800	112	3	3	2	☐	$138,000
9	Ranch	Horseshoe Bend	2000	120	3	3.5	0	☐	$105,000
10	Ranch	80 MM	2000	80	3	3	2	☐	$250,000
11	Ranch	80 MM	1215	80	3	2	0	☐	$85,000
12	Ranch	Greenview	2200	200	3	3	2	☐	$395,613
13	Two Story	Blue Eye	3000	100	4	3	2	☐	$199,950
14	Two Story	Galena	5500	250	4	2.5	3	☑	$194,500
15	Two Story	Branson West	2500	100	3	2	2	☐	$189,900
16	Ranch	Branson	2700	85	4	3	2	☐	$189,900
17	Log Cabin	Cape Fair	2000	300	3	2	0	☐	$189,900
18	Ranch	Kimberling City	2500	100	3	4	2	☐	$189,900
19	Two Story	Shell Knob	3200	110	3	4.5	0	☐	$187,500
20	Two Story	Kimberling City	2700	121	3	3	2	☐	$147,900
21	Patio Home	Kimberling City	2200	0	2	2	1	☑	$139,900
22	Cabin	Kimberling City	1350	50	2	2	2	☐	$127,900
23	Two Story	Galena	2000	75	4	1	0	☐	$124,900
24	Mobile Home	Galena	1200	120	3	2	0	☐	$120,000
25	Cabin	Kimberling City	1900	80	3	1	0	☐	$111,900
(New)			0	0	0	0	0	☐	$0

e. Enter one new record, using your own last name in the Area field, then print the first page only of the datasheet in landscape orientation. (*Hint*: Click the Pages option button in the Print dialog box, then enter 1 in both the From and To boxes.)

f. Close the RealEstate-A.accdb database and Access 2007.

5. Create a database.

a. Open Access 2007, then use the Student database template in the Education category to create a new database. This requires you to be connected to the Internet. Close any windows that open before the database does.

b. In the Student List form that opens, enter your first and last names. Use any valid entries for the E-mail Address, Business Phone, Company, and Job Title fields.

c. Print the record.

d. Expand the Navigation Pane, then use it to complete the following table on a sheet of paper to identify the number and names of the objects that were automatically created by the Students database template. The first row is completed for you.

object type	number created	names of the objects
Tables	2	Students, Guardians
Queries		
Forms		
Reports		

▼ SKILLS REVIEW (CONTINUED)

6. **Create a table.**
   - **a.** Create a new table called States with the following fields and data types:
     StateName Text
     StateAbbreviation Text
   - **b.** Enter your own state in the first record.
   - **c.** Close the States table, close the Students.accdb database, then exit Access 2007.
7. **Create primary keys.**
   - **a.** Open the **RealEstate-A.accdb** database used in earlier steps. Enable content if prompted.
   - **b.** Open the Agencies table in Design View, then set AgencyNo as the primary key field.
   - **c.** Open the Agents table in Design View, then set AgentNo as the primary key field.
   - **d.** Open the Listings table in Design View, then set ListingNo as the primary key field.
   - **e.** Save all your changes.
   - **f.** On another sheet of paper, answer the following questions:
     Why is a field with an AutoNumber data type a good candidate for the primary key field for that table?
     Why is a field with an AutoNumber data type *not* a good candidate for the foreign key field for a one-to-many relationship?
8. **Relate two tables.**
   - **a.** In the Relationships window, set a one-to-many relationship between the Agencies and Agents table, using the common AgencyNo field. Apply referential integrity to this relationship.
   - **b.** In the Relationships window, set a one-to-many relationship between the Agents and Listings table, using the common AgentNo field. Apply referential integrity to this relationship.
   - **c.** Click the Relationship Report button on the Design tab, then print the report that is created.
   - **d.** Close the Relationships report without saving changes, then close the Relationships window.
9. **Print a datasheet.**
   - **a.** Preview and print the Agencies table datasheet in landscape orientation.
   - **b.** Preview and print the Agents table datasheet in landscape orientation.
   - **c.** Close the RealEstate-A.accdb database, and exit Access 2007.

▼ INDEPENDENT CHALLENGE 1

Review the following twelve examples of database tables:

- Telephone directory
- College course offerings
- Restaurant menu
- Cookbook
- Movie listing
- Islands of the Caribbean
- Encyclopedia
- Shopping catalog
- International product inventory
- Party guest list
- Members of the U.S. House of Representatives
- Ancient wonders of the world

For each example, write a brief answer for the following.

- **a.** What field names would you expect to find in each table?
- **b.** Provide an example of two possible records for each table.

▼ INDEPENDENT CHALLENGE 2

You are working with several civic groups to coordinate a community-wide cleanup effort. You have started a database called Recycle-A that tracks the clubs, their trash deposits, and the trash collection centers that are participating.

a. Start Access, then open the **Recycle-A.accdb** database from the drive and folder where you store your Data Files.
b. Open each table's datasheet, and write the number of records and fields in each of the tables.
c. In the Centers table datasheet, modify the ContactFirst and ContactLast names for the Trash Can record to your name.
d. Preview the Centers table datasheet in landscape orientation, print the datasheet if your instructor requests it, then close the table.
e. Open the Relationships window and complete the following table on a sheet of paper:

type of relationship	table on the "one" side of the relationship	table on the "many" side of the relationship	linking field name in the "one" table	linking field name in the "many" table
One-to-many				
One-to-many				

Advanced Challenge Exercise

- Open the datasheet for the Clubs table. Click the expand button to the left of each record (which looks like a small plus sign) to view related records from the Deposits table.
- Close the datasheet for the Clubs table. Open the datasheet for the Centers table. Click the expand button to the left of each record to view related records from the Deposits table.

f. Close the Centers table, close the Recycle-A.accdb database, then exit Access.

▼ INDEPENDENT CHALLENGE 3

You are working for an advertising agency that provides advertising media for small and large businesses in the Midwestern United States. You have started a database called Media-A which tracks your company's customers.

a. Start Access and open the **Media-A.accdb** database from the drive and folder where you store your Data Files. Enable content as needed.
b. Add a new record to the Customers table, using your own first and last names, **$7,788.99** in the YTDSales field, and any reasonable entry for the rest of the fields.
c. Edit the Rocket Laboratory record. The Company name should be **Johnson County Labs**, and the Street value should be **2145 College St**.
d. Preview the Customers datasheet in landscape orientation, print the datasheet if your instructor requests it, then close the table.
e. Create a States table with two fields, **StateName** and **StateAbbreviation**, both with a Text data type.
f. Enter at least three records into the States table, making sure that all of the states used in the Customers datasheet are entered in the States table. This includes Kansas KS, Missouri MO, and any other state you entered in previous steps.
g. In Design View, set the StateAbbreviation field as the primary key field, then save and close the States table.

▼ INDEPENDENT CHALLENGE 3 (CONTINUED)

Advanced Challenge Exercise

- Open the Relationships window, add both table field lists to the window, then expand the size of the Customers field list so that all fields are visible.
- Drag the StateAbbreviation field from the States table to the State field of the Customers table, to create a one-to-many relationship between the two tables. Enforce referential integrity on the relationship. If you are unable to enforce referential integrity, it means that there is a value in the State field of the Customers table that doesn't have a match in the StateAbbreviation field of the States table. Open both datasheets, making sure every state in the Customers table is also represented in the States table, close all datasheets, and reestablish the one-to-many relationship between the two tables with referential integrity.
- Click the Relationship Report button on the Design tab, then print the report that is created.
- Close the Relationships report without saving changes, then close the Relationships window.

h. Close the Media-A.accdb database, then exit Access 2007.

▼ REAL LIFE INDEPENDENT CHALLENGE

This Independent Challenge requires an Internet connection.

Now that you've learned about Microsoft Access and relational databases, brainstorm how you might use an Access database in your daily life or career. Start by visiting the Microsoft Web site, and explore what's new about Access 2007.

a. Connect to the Internet, and use your browser to go to your favorite search engine. Use the keywords "benefits of a relational database" or "benefits of Microsoft Access" to find articles that discuss the benefits of organizing data in a relational database.

b. Read several articles about the benefits of organizing data in a relational database such as Access, identifying three distinct benefits. As you read the articles, list all of the terminology unfamiliar to you as well, identifying at least five items.

c. Using a search engine or a Web site that provides a computer glossary such as *www.whatis.com* or *www.webopedia.com*, look up the definition of the five or more new terms you have identified.

d. Using the research you have conducted on the Web, create a one-page document that lists the three benefits of using a relational database you identified in Step b as well as the five or more technical terms that you researched in Step c. In order to document the original sources of your information, be sure to list the Internet Web page addresses (URLs such as *www.microsoft.com*) for each source you reference for benefits and definitions.

e. Apply this research to a job you have had or would like to secure in the future. In one paragraph, describe the job and give at least one example of how Access might be used to manage data important to that job. In a second paragraph, discuss how the benefits of using a relational database might apply to this example.

▼ VISUAL WORKSHOP

Open the **Basketball-A.accdb** database from the drive and folder where you store your Data Files, then open the Players table datasheet. Modify the first three records in the existing Players table to reflect the changes shown in the First, Last, and Height fields of Figure A-20. Note that your name should be entered in the First and Last fields of the first record. Resize all columns to show all data, print the first page of the datasheet in landscape orientation, close the Players table, close the Basketball-A.accdb database, then exit Access.

FIGURE A-20

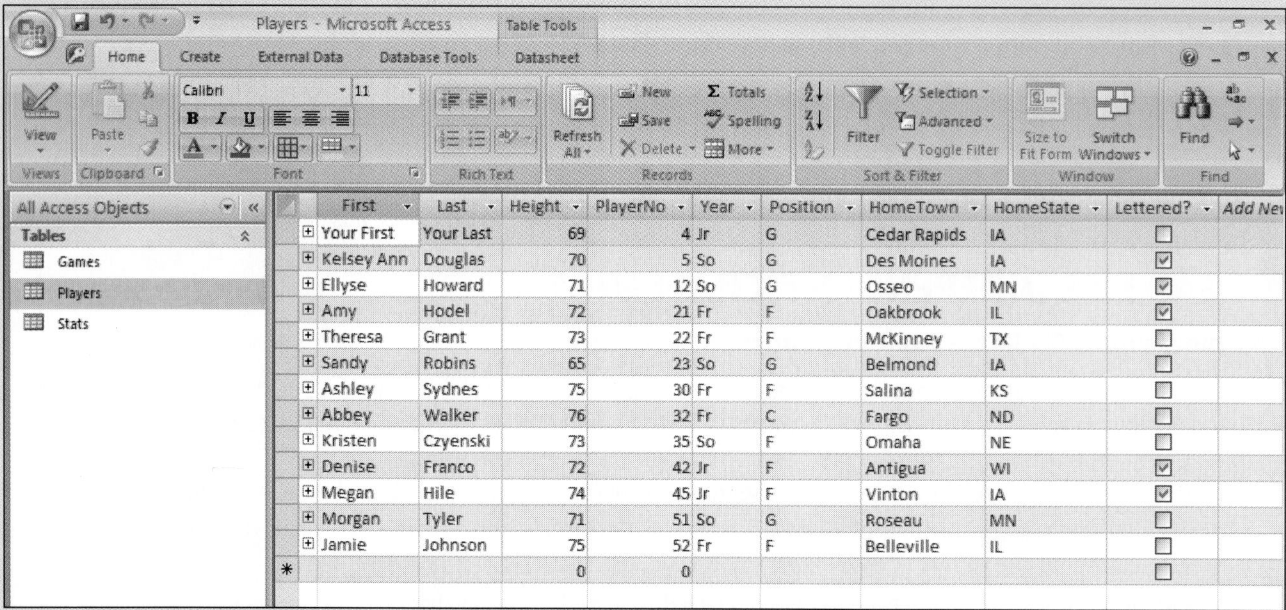

First	Last	Height	PlayerNo	Year	Position	HomeTown	HomeState	Lettered?	Add New
Your First	Your Last	69	4	Jr	G	Cedar Rapids	IA	☐	
Kelsey Ann	Douglas	70	5	So	G	Des Moines	IA	☑	
Ellyse	Howard	71	12	So	G	Osseo	MN	☑	
Amy	Hodel	72	21	Fr	F	Oakbrook	IL	☑	
Theresa	Grant	73	22	Fr	F	McKinney	TX	☐	
Sandy	Robins	65	23	So	G	Belmond	IA	☐	
Ashley	Sydnes	75	30	Fr	F	Salina	KS	☐	
Abbey	Walker	76	32	Fr	C	Fargo	ND	☐	
Kristen	Czyenski	73	35	So	F	Omaha	NE	☐	
Denise	Franco	72	42	Jr	F	Antigua	WI	☑	
Megan	Hile	74	45	Jr	F	Vinton	IA	☑	
Morgan	Tyler	71	51	So	G	Roseau	MN	☐	
Jamie	Johnson	75	52	Fr	F	Belleville	IL	☐	
*		0	0					☐	

UNIT
B
Access 2007

Building and Using Queries

Files You Will Need:

Quest-B.accdb
RealEstate-B.accdb
Vet-B.accdb
Membership-B.accdb
Recycle-B.accdb
Capitals-B.accdb
Basketball-B.accdb

You build queries in an Access database to ask "questions" about data, such as which adventure tours are scheduled for June or what types of tours take place in California. Queries present the answer in a datasheet, which you can sort, filter, and format. Because queries are stored in the database, they can be used multiple times. Each time a query is opened, it presents a current view of the latest updates to the database. Mark Rock, tour developer for U.S. group travel at Quest Travel Services, has several questions about the customer and tour information in the Quest database. You'll develop queries to provide Mark with up-to-date answers.

OBJECTIVES

- Create a query
- Use Query Design View
- Modify queries
- Sort and find data
- Filter data
- Apply AND criteria
- Apply OR criteria
- Format a datasheet

UNIT
B
Access 2007

Creating a Query

A **query** allows you to select a subset of fields and records from one or more tables and then present the selected data as a single datasheet. A major benefit of working with data through a query is that you can focus on the information you need to answer your questions, rather than navigating the fields and records from many large tables. You can enter, edit, and navigate data in a query datasheet just like a table datasheet. However, keep in mind that Access data is physically stored only in tables, even though you can view and edit it through other Access objects such as queries and forms. Because a query doesn't physically store the data, a query datasheet is sometimes called a **logical view** of the data. Technically, a query is a set of **SQL** (Structured Query Language) instructions, but because Access provides several easy-to-use query tools, knowledge of SQL is not required to build or use Access queries. You use the Simple Query Wizard to build a query to display a few fields from the States and Tours tables in one datasheet.

STEPS

1. **Start Access, open the Quest-B.accdb database, then enable content, if prompted**
   Access provides several tools to create a new query. One way is to use the **Simple Query Wizard**, which prompts you for information needed to create a new query.
2. **Click the Create tab on the Ribbon, click the Query Wizard button, then click OK to start the Simple Query Wizard**
   The first Simple Query Wizard dialog box opens, prompting you to select the fields you want to view in the new query.
3. **Click the Tables/Queries list arrow, click Table: Tours, double-click TourName, double-click City, then double-click Category**
   So far, you've selected three fields from the Tours table for this query. You also want to add the full state name, a field stored only in the States table.
4. **Click the Tables/Queries list arrow, click Table: States, then double-click StateName**
   You've selected three fields from the Tours table and one from the States table for your new query, as shown in Figure B-1. Because the Tours and States tables are linked together in this database by a common field (StateAbbrev), you can create queries by selecting individual fields from each of the linked tables to present a datasheet with a subset of desired fields.
5. **Click Next, select Tours Query, type ToursByState in the text box, click Finish, then maximize the datasheet**
   The ToursByState datasheet opens, displaying three fields from the Tours table and the StateName field from the States table, as shown in Figure B-2.

TROUBLE

Click the Remove Single Field button < if you need to remove a field from the Selected Fields list.

FIGURE B-1: Selecting fields in the Simple Query Wizard

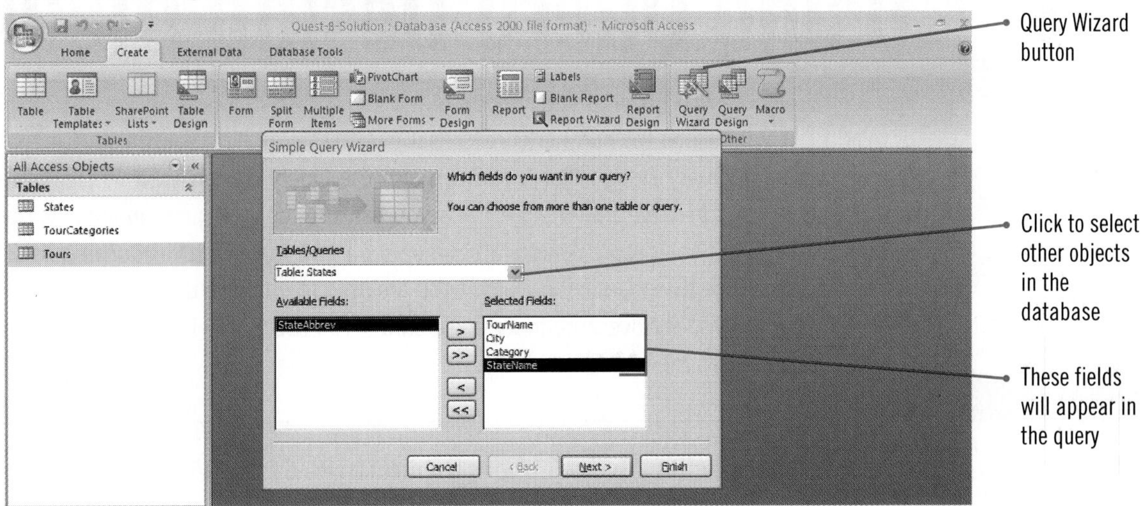

FIGURE B-2: ToursByState query datasheet

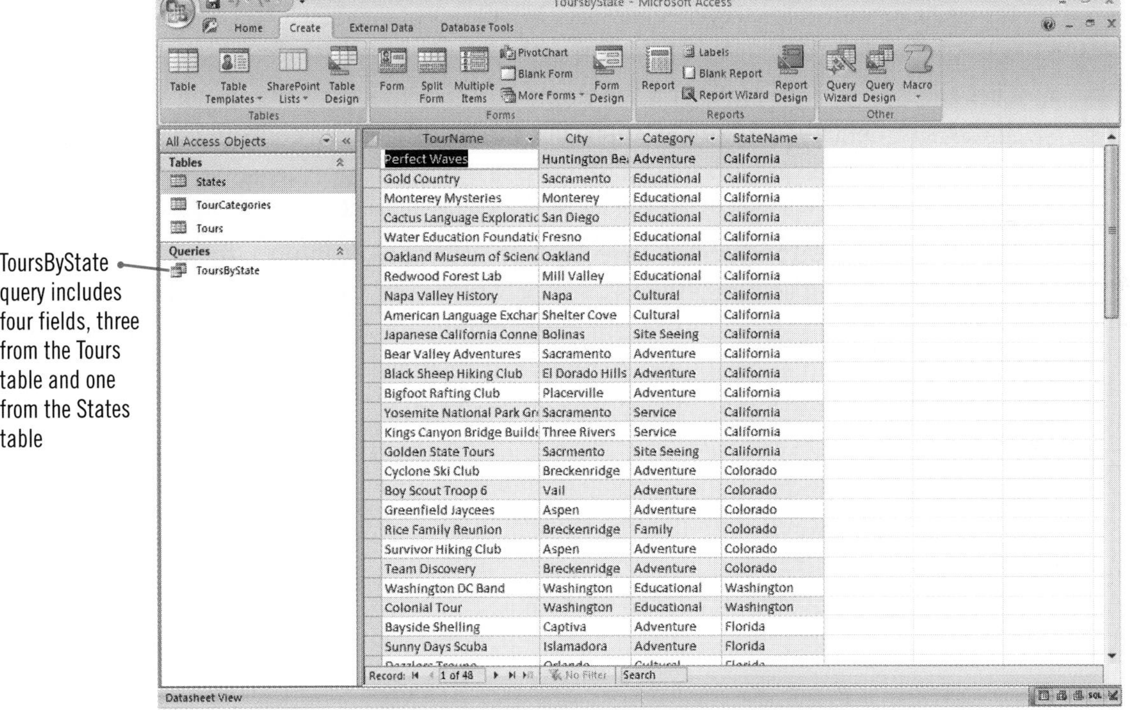

UNIT B

Access 2007

Using Query Design View

You use **Query Design View** to add, delete, or move the fields in an existing query, to specify sort orders, or to add **criteria** to limit the number of records shown in the resulting datasheet. (Criteria are limiting conditions you set in Query Design View.) You can also use Query Design View to create a new query from scratch. Query Design View presents the fields you can use for that query in small windows called **field lists**. If the fields of two or more related tables are used in the query, the relationship between two tables is displayed with a **join line** identifying which fields are used to establish the relationship. Mark Rock asks you to print a list of Adventure tours in Colorado. You use Query Design View to modify the existing ToursByState query to meet his request.

STEPS

1. **Click the Home tab on the Ribbon, then click the Design View button to switch to Query Design View for the ToursByState query**

   The Query Design View opens as shown in Figure B-3, showing the field lists for the States and Tours tables in the upper pane of the window, as well as the one-to-many relationship established between the two tables via the common StateAbbrev field. The four fields you previously requested for this query are displayed in the **query design grid** in the lower pane of the window.

2. **Click the first Criteria cell for the Category field, then type adventure**

   By adding the word "adventure" to the first Criteria cell for the Category field, only those records with this value in the Category field will be displayed in the datasheet.

3. **Click the Datasheet View button on the Design tab to switch to Datasheet View**

   The resulting datasheet lists the Adventure tours. To further narrow this list to tours in Colorado, you return to Query Design View and enter more criteria.

4. **Click the Design View button on the Home tab, click the first Criteria cell for the StateName field, type Colorado, then click the Datasheet View button on the Design tab**

   Now only five records are displayed, as only five of the Adventure tours are in the state of Colorado, as shown in Figure B-4. You want to save this query with a different name.

5. **Click the Office button, click Save As, type ColoradoAdventures, then click OK**

   Now two queries are included in the Queries list on the Navigation Pane: ToursByState and ColoradoAdventures.

QUICK TIP

Query criteria are not case sensitive.

TROUBLE

If you see more than five records, return to Query Design View and make sure your criteria are on the same row.

FIGURE B-3: **Query Design View of the TourByState query**

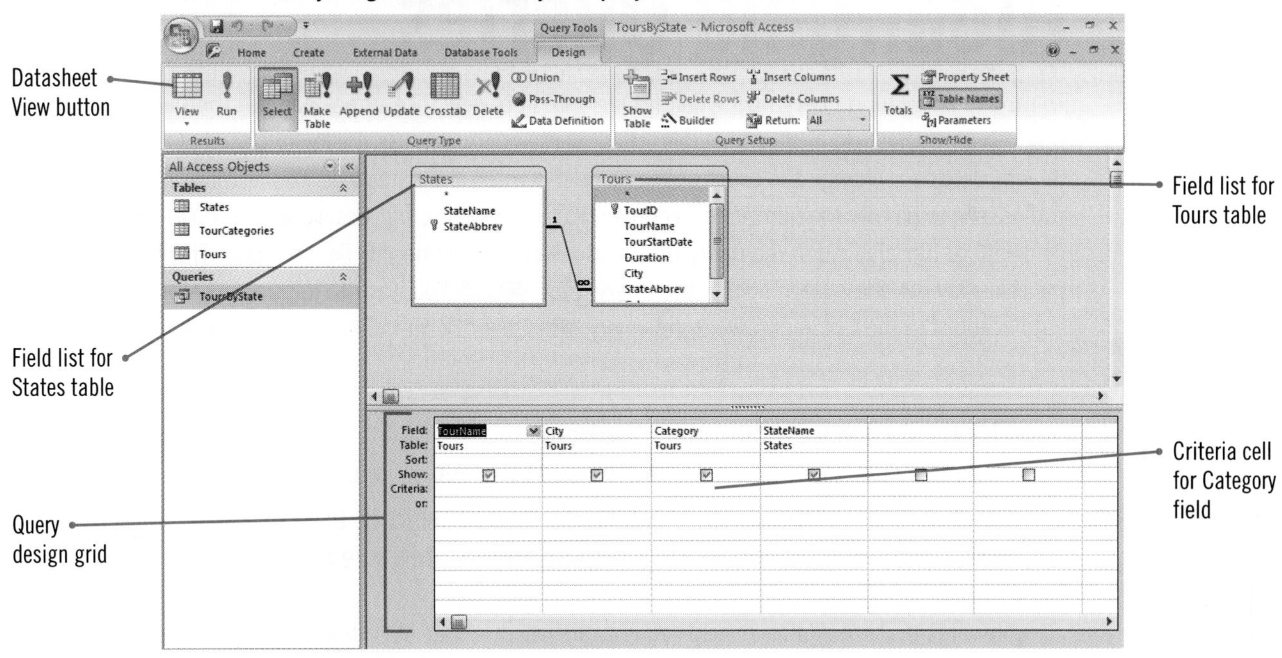

FIGURE B-4: **ColoradoAdventures datasheet**

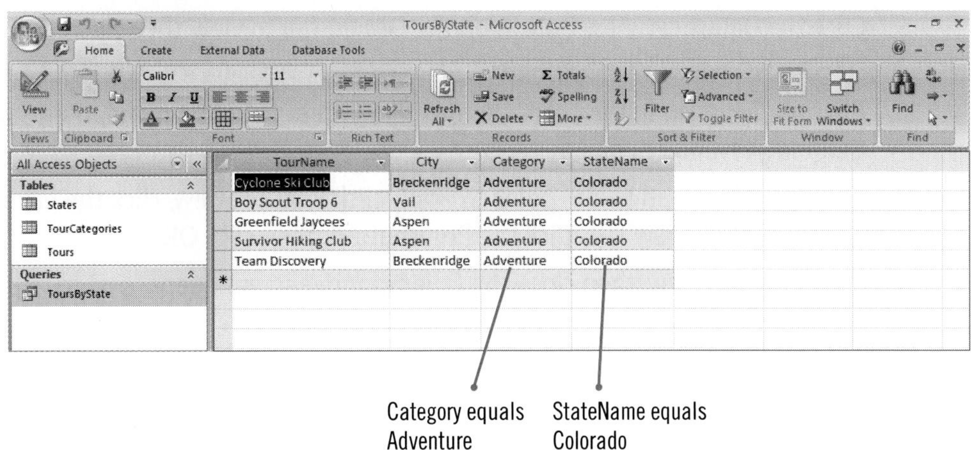

Access 2007

UNIT B

Access 2007

Modifying Queries

To modify an existing query, you work in Query Design View. The upper pane of the Query Design View window shows the field lists for the tables used by the query. You use the lower pane of Query Design View to add, delete, or change the order of the fields shown on the datasheet. You also use the lower pane to add criteria to narrow the number of records selected, to define sort orders, and to build calculated fields. To delete or move a field in the query grid, you select it by clicking its field selector. The **field selector** is the thin gray bar above each field in the query grid. You want to add more fields and make other modifications to the ColoradoAdventures query. Use Query Design View to make the changes.

STEPS

1. **Click the Design View button on the Home tab**

   You want to move the StateName field to the third field position, immediately after the City field.

2. **Click the field selector for the StateName field to select it, then drag the StateName field selector one column to the left to position StateName between the City and Category fields**

   A black vertical line appears to help you visualize where you are repositioning the field. You also want to sort the records in ascending order based on the TourName field.

3. **Click the Sort cell for the TourName field, click the list arrow, then click Ascending**

   Defining the sort order in Query Design View allows you to permanently save the sort order with the query object so that every time you open the query, the specified sort is applied. Selecting an ascending sort order for the TourName field lists the query results in alphabetic order (A-Z) by TourName. You also want to add the TourStartDate and Duration fields to this query so they appear immediately after the TourName field.

4. **Drag the TourStartDate field from the Tours field list to the second column, then drag the Duration field from the Tours field list to the third column**

   The existing fields in the query grid move to the right to accommodate the addition of new fields to the grid, as shown in Figure B-5.

5. **Click the Datasheet View button on the Design tab to view the selected data**

   The datasheet is shown in Figure B-6. Note the order of the fields and sort order of the records.

6. **Change Discovery in the Team Discovery record to your last name, then save the ColoradoAdventures query**

7. **Click the Office button, point to Print, click Print Preview, click the Landscape button on the Print Preview tab, click the Print button, then click OK**

8. **Close Print Preview, then close the ColoradoAdventures query**

QUICK TIP

Drag the lower edge of a field list down to expand the number of fields displayed, and drag the split bar down to resize the two panes of Query Design View.

QUICK TIP

To delete a field from a query, click its field selector button, then press [Delete]. Deleting a field from a query does not delete it from the underlying table; the field is only deleted from the query's logical view of the data.

FIGURE B-5: Modified query in Design View

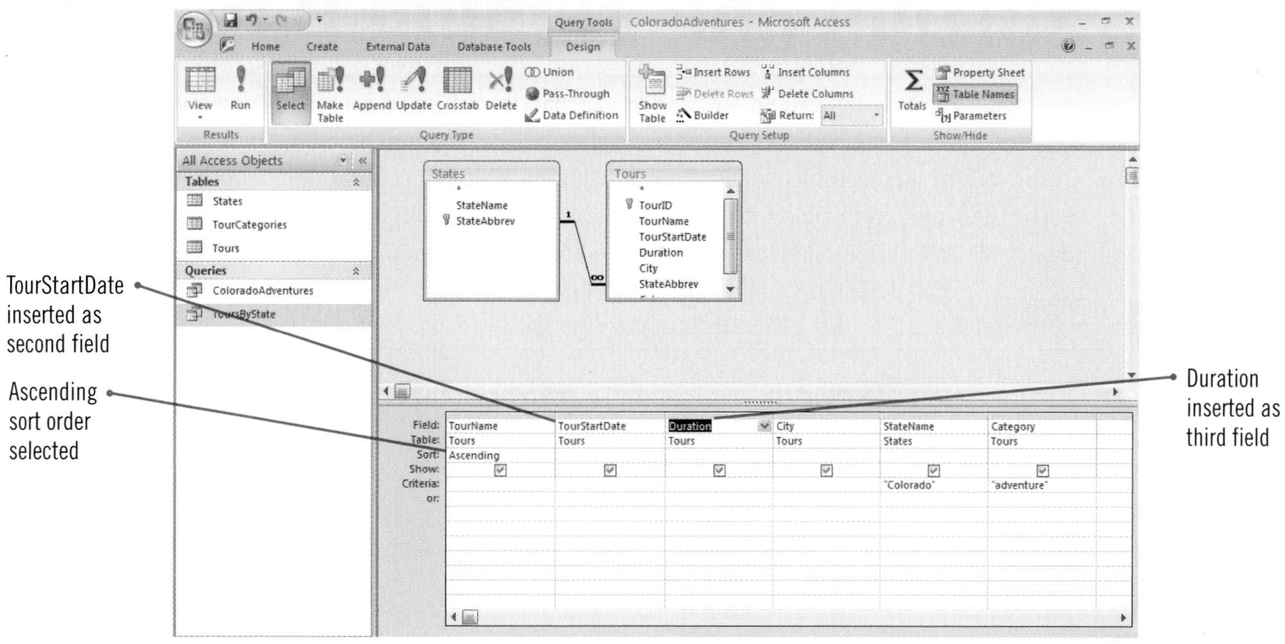

FIGURE B-6: Modified datasheet

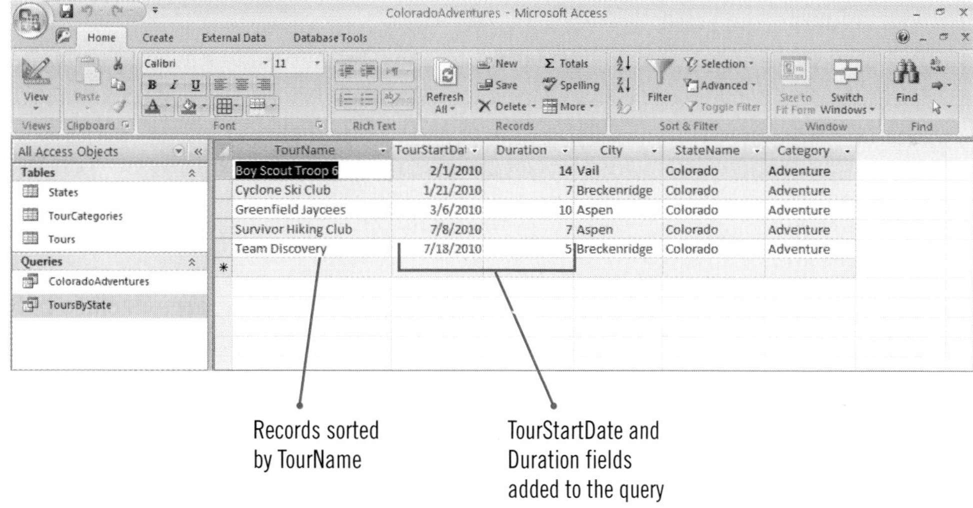

Adding or deleting a table to a query

You might want to add a table's field list to the upper pane of Query Design View in order to select fields from that table for the query. To add a new table to Query Design View, click the Design tab on the Ribbon, click the Show Table button, then add the desired table(s). To delete an unneeded table from Query Design View, click its title bar, then press [Delete].

UNIT
B
Access 2007

Sorting and Finding Data

The Access sort and find features are handy tools that help you quickly organize and find data. Table B-1 describes the Sort and Find buttons on the Home tab. Besides using these buttons, you can also click the list arrow on a datasheet's column heading, and then click a sorting option. Sorting and finding data works exactly the same way in table and query datasheets. Mark Rock asks you to provide a list of tours sorted by TourStartDate, and then by Duration. He also asks you to correct two tours by changing the entry of "Site Seeing" to "Cultural" in the Category field.

STEPS

QUICK TIP
Click the Navigation Pane list arrow, then make sure All Access Objects is checked to show all tables, queries, and other objects.

1. **Double-click Tours in the Navigation Pane to open the Tours datasheet, then maximize the window**
   By default, records in a table datasheet are sorted on the primary key field. For the Tours table, the primary key field is the TourID field.

QUICK TIP
A sort arrow appears next to the field name by which the datasheet is sorted.

2. **Click any value in the TourStartDate field, then click the Ascending button on the Home tab**
   The records are re-sorted based on the TourStartDate field. Notice that some tours start on the same date. You can specify a second sort order to further sort the records that have the same date in the TourStartDate field.

TROUBLE
To clear the current sort order, click the Clear All Sorts button.

3. **Drag across the TourStartDate and Duration field selector buttons to select both columns, then click**
   The records are now listed in ascending order, first by TourStartDate, then by the values in the Duration field, as shown in Figure B-7. Sort orders always work left to right, so you might need to rearrange the fields before applying a sort order that uses more than one field. Your next task is to replace all occurrences of "Site Seeing" with "Cultural" in the Category field.

TROUBLE
If your find and replace did not work correctly, click the Undo button and repeat step 4.

4. **Click the Category column heading to select that field, click the Replace button on the Home tab, type Site Seeing in the Find What box, press [Tab], type Cultural in the Replace With box, click Find Next to find the first occurrence of Site Seeing, click Replace, click Replace again to replace the next occurrence of "Site Seeing," then click Cancel**
   Access replaced two occurrences of "Site Seeing" with "Cultural" in the Category field, as shown in Figure B-8.

5. **Replace Rice in the TourID 26 record with your last name, then print the first page of the Tours datasheet**

6. **Save the Tours table**
   If you close a datasheet without saving the changes, the records return to the original sort order based on the values in the primary key field. If you close a datasheet and save layout changes, the last sort order is saved.

FIGURE B-7: Tours datasheet sorted by TourStartDate and Duration fields

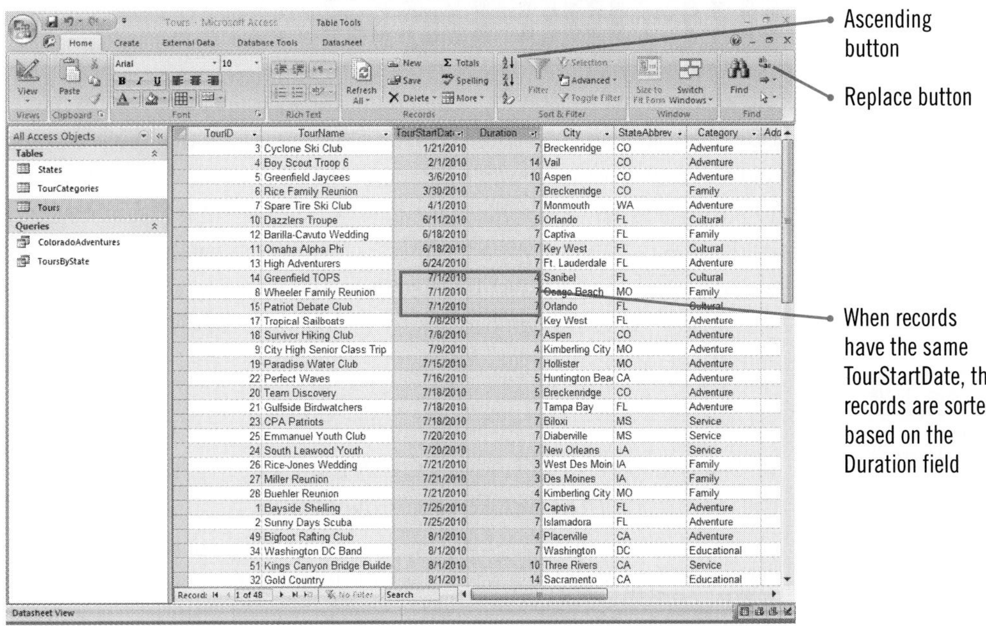
Ascending button
Replace button
When records have the same TourStartDate, the records are sorted based on the Duration field

FIGURE B-8: "Site Seeing" replaced with "Cultural" in the Category field

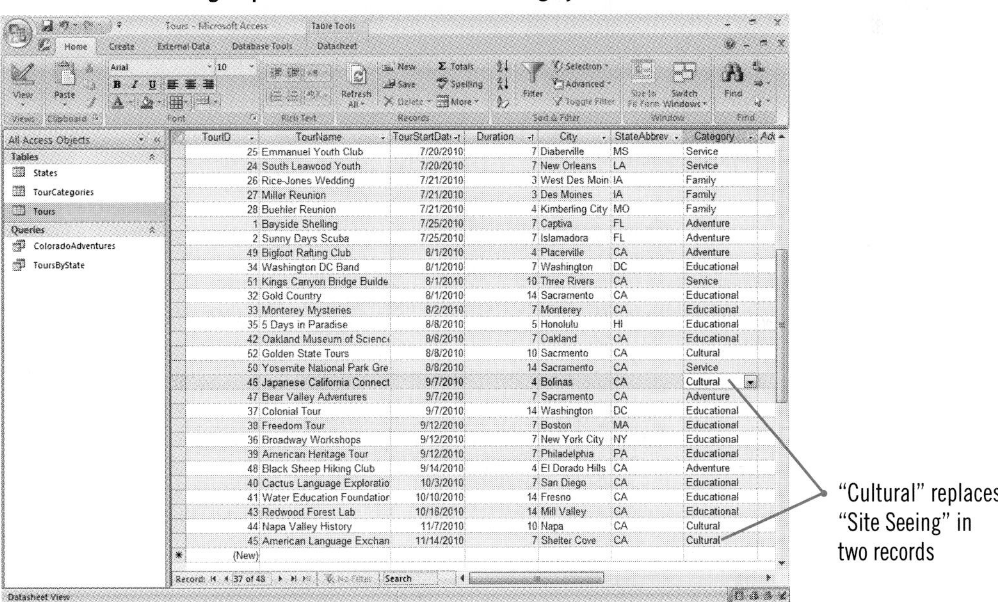
"Cultural" replaces "Site Seeing" in two records

TABLE B-1: Sort and Find buttons

name	button	purpose
Ascending	A↓Z	Sorts records based on the selected field in ascending order (0 to 9, A to Z)
Descending	Z↓A	Sorts records based on the selected field in descending order (Z to A, 9 to 0)
Clear All Sorts		Removes the current sort order
Find		Opens the Find and Replace dialog box, which allows you to find data in a single field or in the entire datasheet
Replace	ab→ac	Opens the Find and Replace dialog box, which allows you to find and replace data
Go To	➡	Helps you navigate to the first, previous, last, or new record
Select		Helps you select a single record or all records in a datasheet

UNIT
B
Access 2007

Filtering Data

Filtering a table or query datasheet temporarily displays only those records that match given criteria. Recall that criteria are limiting conditions you set. For example, you might want to show only those tours in the state of Florida, or those tours with a duration of less than seven days. While filters provide a quick and easy way to display a subset of records in the current datasheet, they are not nearly as powerful or flexible as queries. For example, a query is a saved object within the database, whereas filters are temporary. Filters are removed when the datasheet is closed, but if you want to apply a filter over and over again, you can save it as a query. Table B-2 compares filters and queries. Mark Rock asks you to find all Adventure tours offered in the month of July. You can filter the Tours datasheet to provide this information.

STEPS

QUICK TIP
You can also click the list arrow on a column heading, click the Select All check box to clear all the check boxes, then click the value to use as the filter.

1. **Click any occurrence of Adventure in the Category field, click the Selection button on the Home tab, then click Equals "Adventure"**

   Seventeen records are selected, as shown in Figure B-9. Filtering by a given field value, called **Filter By Selection**, is a fast and easy way to filter the records for an exact match. To filter for comparative data (for example, where TourStartDate is *equal to or greater than* 7/1/2010), you must use the **Filter By Form** feature. Filter buttons are summarized in Table B-3.

QUICK TIP
To save a filter permanently as a query object, click the Advanced button, then click Save As Query.

2. **Click the Advanced button on the Home tab, then click Filter By Form**

   The Filter by Form window opens. The previous Filter By Selection criterion, "Adventure" in the Category field, is still in the grid. Access distinguishes between text and numeric entries by placing quotation marks around text criteria.

QUICK TIP
If you need to clear previous criteria, click the Advanced button, then click Clear Grid.

3. **Click the TourStartDate cell, then type 7/*/2010 as shown in Figure B-10**

   Filter by Form also allows you to apply two or more criteria at the same time. An asterisk (*) in the day position of the date criterion works as a wildcard, selecting any date in the month of July (the seventh month) in the year 2010.

4. **Click the Toggle Filter button on the Home tab**

   The datasheet redisplays all nine records that match both filter criteria, as shown in Figure B-11. Note that filter icons appear next to the TourStartDate and Category field names as both fields are involved in the filter.

QUICK TIP
Be sure to remove existing filters before applying a completely new filter, or you filter the current subset of records instead of applying the filter to the entire datasheet.

5. **Change Bayside in TourID 1 to your last name, then print the filtered datasheet**

   To remove the current filter, you click the Toggle Filter button.

6. **Click to remove the filter, then save and close the Tours datasheet**

Using wildcard characters

To search for a pattern, you can use a **wildcard** character to represent any character in the criteria entry. Use a ? (question mark) to search for any single character and an * (asterisk) to search for any number of characters. Wildcard characters are often used with the Like operator. For example, the criterion Like "12/*/10" would find all dates in December of 2010, and the criterion Like "F*" would find all entries that start with the letter F.

FIGURE B-9: Filtering for Adventure records

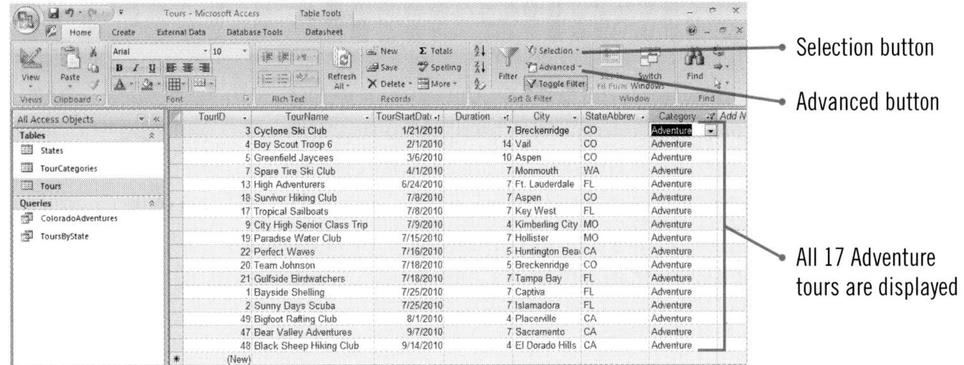

FIGURE B-10: Filter by Form window

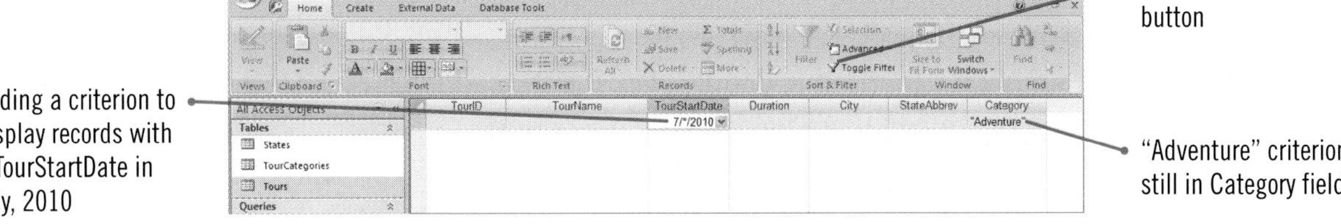

FIGURE B-11: Filtering for Adventure records in July, 2010

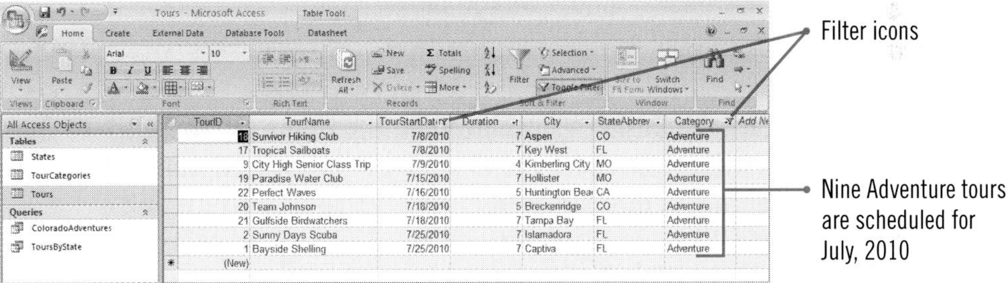

Access 2007

TABLE B-2: Filters versus queries

characteristics	filters	queries
Are saved as an object in the database	No	Yes
Can be used to select a subset of records in a datasheet	Yes	Yes
Can be used to select a subset of fields in a datasheet	No	Yes
Resulting datasheet used to enter and edit data	Yes	Yes
Resulting datasheet used to sort, filter, and find records	Yes	Yes
Commonly used as the source of data for a form or report	No	Yes
Can calculate sums, averages, counts, and other types of summary statistics across records	No	Yes
Can be used to create calculated fields	No	Yes

TABLE B-3: Filter buttons

name	button	purpose
Filter		Provides a list of values in the selected field by which to customize a filter
Selection		Filters records that equal, do not equal, or are otherwise compared to the current value
Advanced		Provides advanced filter features such as Filter By Form, Save As Query, and Clear Grid
Toggle Filter		Applies or removes the current filter

UNIT
B
Access 2007

Applying AND Criteria

As you have seen, you can limit the number of records that appear on a query datasheet by entering criteria into Query Design View. Criteria are tests, or limiting conditions, for which the record must be true to be selected for a datasheet. To create **AND criteria**, which means that *all* criteria must be true in order for the record to be selected, enter two or more criteria on the *same* Criteria row of the query design grid. Mark Rock asks you to provide a list of all educational tours in the state of California with a duration of greater than seven days. Use Query Design View to create the query with AND criteria to meet his request.

STEPS

QUICK TIP

Drag the bottom border of the Tours field list down to display all of the fields. The scroll bar disappears when all fields are displayed.

1. **Click the Create tab on the Ribbon, click the Query Design button, double-click Tours, click Close in the Show Table dialog box, then maximize the query window**
   You want to add four fields to this query.
2. **Double-click TourName, double-click Duration, double-click StateAbbrev, and double-click Category to add these fields to the query grid**
   Start by adding criteria to select only those records in California. Because you are using the StateAbbrev field, you need to use the two-letter state abbreviation for California, CA, as the Criteria entry.
3. **Click the first Criteria cell for the StateAbbrev field, type CA, then click the Datasheet View button on the Design tab**
   Querying for only those tours in the state of California selects 16 records. Next, you add criteria to select only those records in the Educational category.
4. **Click the Design View button on the Home tab to switch to Query Design View, click the first Criteria cell for the Category field, type Educational, then click the Datasheet View button on the Design tab**
   Criteria added to the same line of the query design grid are AND criteria. When entered on the same line, each criterion must be true for the record to appear in the resulting datasheet. Querying for both California and Educational tours selects six records. Every time you add AND criteria, you *narrow* the number of records that are selected because the record must be true for *all* criteria.
5. **Click the Design View button on the Home tab, click the first Criteria cell for the Duration field, then type >7, as shown in Figure B-12**
   Access assists you with **criteria syntax**, rules by which criteria need to be entered. Access automatically adds quotation marks around text criteria in Text fields and pound signs (#) around date criteria in Date/Time fields. The criteria in Number, Currency, and Yes/No fields are not surrounded by any characters. See Table B-4 for more information about comparison operators such as > (greater than).

TROUBLE

If your datasheet doesn't match Figure B-13, return to Query Design View and compare your criteria to that of Figure B-12.

6. **Click the Datasheet View button on the Design tab**
   The third AND criterion further narrows the number of records selected to three, as shown in Figure B-13.
7. **Click the Save button on the Quick Access toolbar, type CaliforniaEducational as the query name, then click OK**
   The query is saved with the new name, CaliforniaEducational, as a new object in the Quest-B database.

Searching for blank fields

Is Null and **Is Not Null** are two other types of common criteria. The Is Null criterion finds all records where no entry has been made in the field. Is Not Null finds all records where there is any entry in the field, even if the entry is 0. Primary key fields cannot have a null entry.

FIGURE B-12: Query Design View with criteria on one row (AND criteria)

Datasheet View button

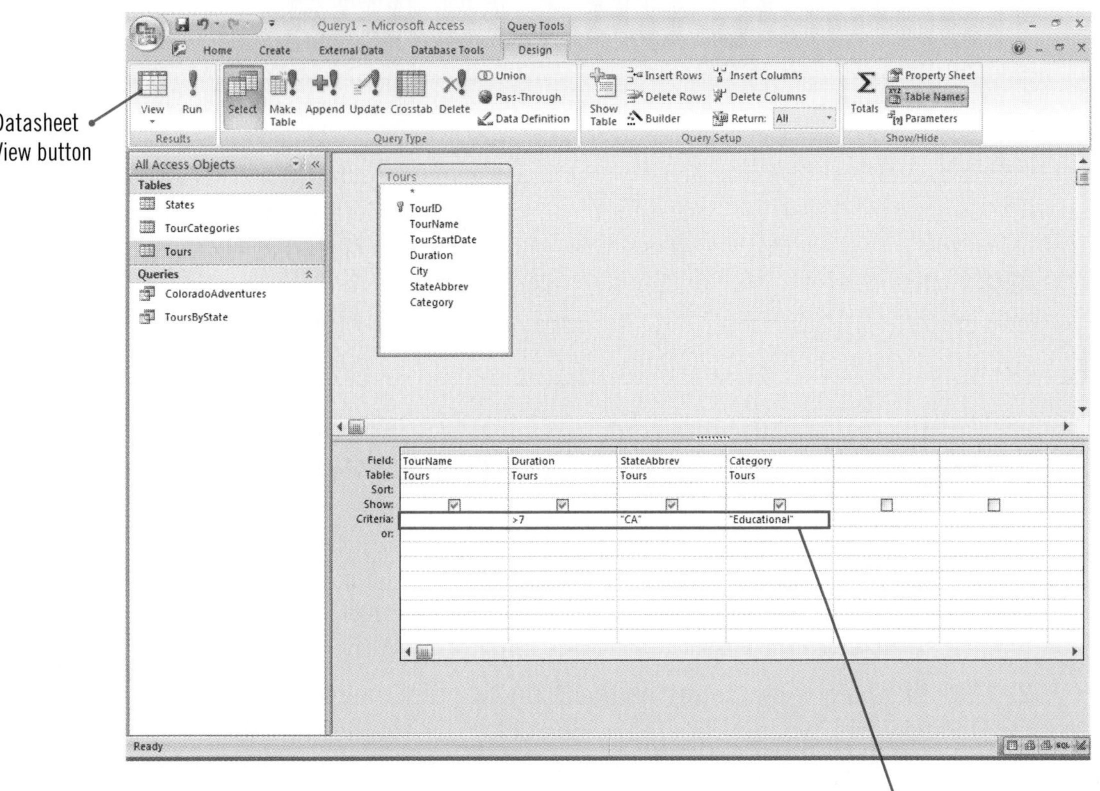

Criteria for displaying Educational tours in California that are longer than one week

FIGURE B-13: Datasheet of CaliforniaEducational query

Design View button

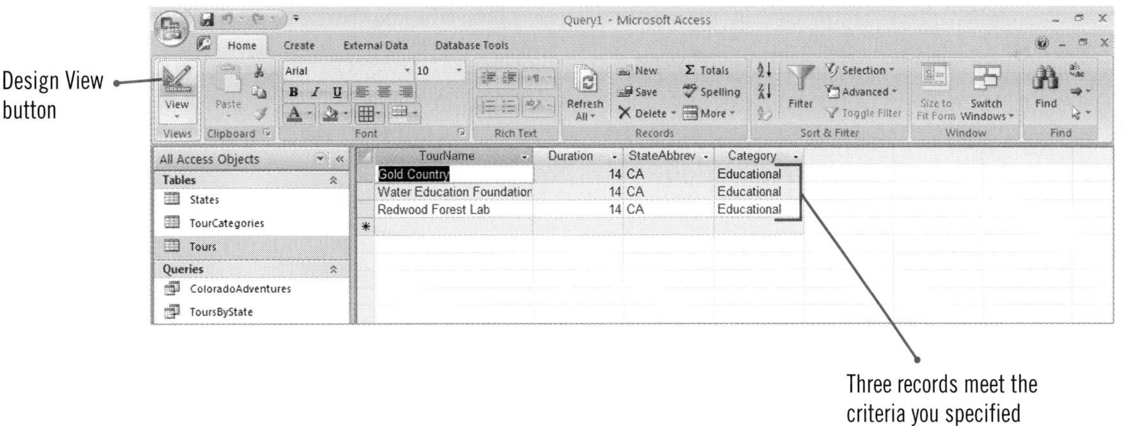

Three records meet the criteria you specified

TABLE B-4: Comparison operators

operator	description	expression	meaning
>	Greater than	>500	Numbers greater than 500
>=	Greater than or equal to	>=500	Numbers greater than or equal to 500
<	Less than	<"Braveheart"	Names from A to Braveheart, but not Braveheart
<=	Less than or equal to	<="Bridgewater"	Names from A through Bridgewater, inclusive
<>	Not equal to	<>"Fontanelle"	Any name except for Fontanelle

UNIT B
Access 2007

Applying OR Criteria

To create **OR criteria**, which means that *any one* criterion must be true in order for the record to be selected, enter two or more criteria on the *different* Criteria rows of the query design grid. To create OR criteria for the *same field*, enter the two criteria in the same Criteria cell separated by the OR operator. As you add rows of OR criteria to the query design grid, you *increase* the number of records selected for the resulting datasheet because the record needs to be true for *only one* of the criteria rows in order to be selected for the datasheet. Mark Rock asks you to add Cultural tours longer than seven days in duration from the state of California to the previous query. To do this, you can modify the query to employ OR criteria to add the records.

STEPS

1. **Click the Design View button on the Home tab, click the second Criteria cell in the Category field, type cultural, then click the Datasheet View button on the Design tab**

   The query added all of the tours with "Cultural" in the Category field to the datasheet, as specified by the second row of the query grid in Query Design View. Because each row of the query grid is evaluated separately, the fact that three criteria were entered in the first row is of no consequence to the second row. In order for the second row to also apply three criteria—Cultural, California, and duration of greater than 7—three criteria must be entered in the second row. In other words, the criteria in one row have no effect on the criteria of other rows.

2. **Click the Design View button on the Home tab, click the second Criteria cell in the Duration field, type >7, click the second Criteria cell in the StateAbbrev field, then type CA**

   Query Design View should look like Figure B-14.

3. **Click the Datasheet View button on the Design tab**

   Five records were selected that meet all three criteria as entered in row one OR row two of the query grid, as shown in Figure B-15.

4. **Edit the Gold Country record to be your last name Country, then save, print, and close the datasheet**

   Because the CaliforniaEducational query now selects both educational and cultural records, you rename it.

5. **Right-click CaliforniaEducational in the Navigation Pane, click Rename on the shortcut menu, type CaliforniaEducationalCultural to rename the query, then press [Enter]**

FIGURE B-14: Query Design View with criteria on two rows (OR criteria)

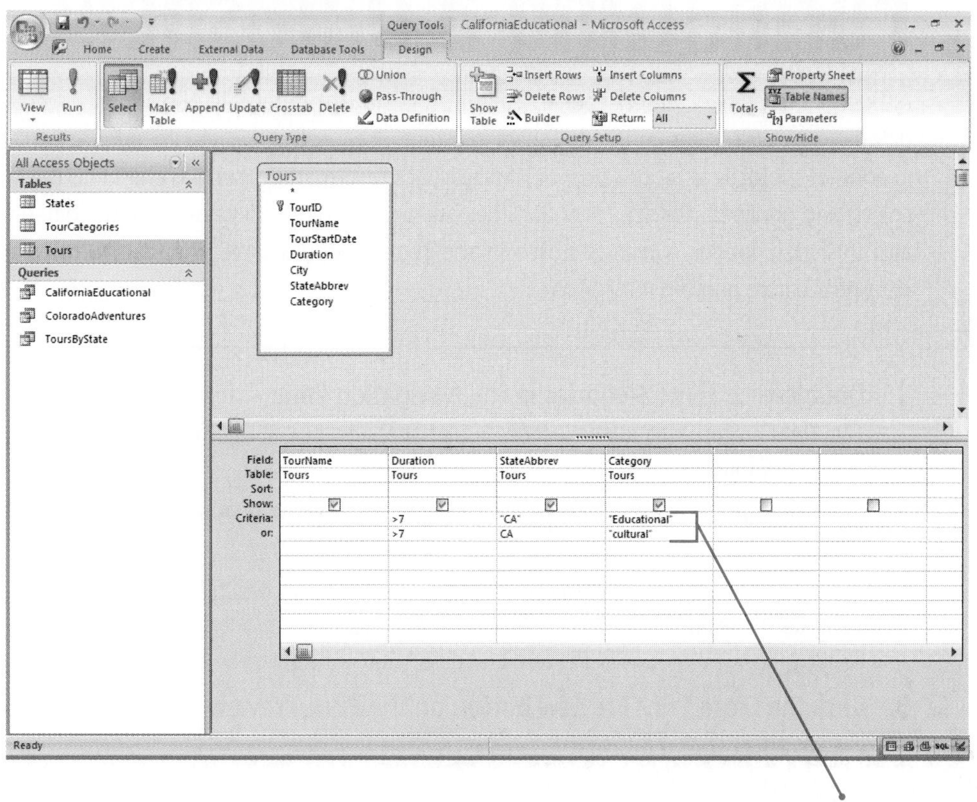

Access 2007

FIGURE B-15: Datasheet of CaliforniaEducationalCultural query

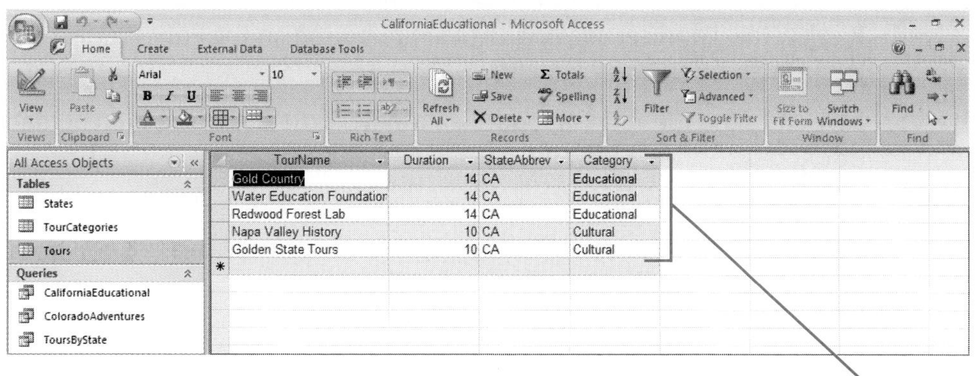

UNIT B

Access 2007

Formatting a Datasheet

Although the primary Access tool to create professional printouts is the report object, you can print a datasheet as well. Although a datasheet printout does not allow you to add custom headers, footers, images, or subtotals as reports do, you can apply some formatting, such as changing the font size, font face, colors, and gridlines. Mark Rock has asked you to create a printout of the different tour categories and their descriptions, which is stored in the TourCategories table. You can format the TourCategories datasheet before printing it for Mark.

STEPS

1. **Double-click TourCategories in the Navigation Pane**

   The TourCategories datasheet opens. Before applying new formatting enhancements, you preview the default printout.

2. **Click the Office button, point to Print, click Print Preview, then click the top edge of the paper to zoom in**

   The preview window displays the layout of the printout, as shown in Figure B-16. By default, the printout of a datasheet contains the object name and current date in the header. The page number is in the footer. You decide to increase the size of the font and data before printing.

3. **Click the Close Print Preview button on the Print Preview tab, click the Font Size list arrow, then click 12**

   A larger font size often makes a printout easier to read. You also need to adjust the width of the Description column to its best fit.

4. **Double-click the column separator to the right of the Description field**

   Double-clicking the column (field) separator automatically adjusts the width of the column to the widest entry in the datasheet.

5. **Click the Alternate Fill/Back Color button arrow on the Home tab, then click Yellow**

   For datasheet printouts, alternating the background color of each row makes the printout easier to read, as shown in Figure B-17. You want to add one more new category, Sports, before printing the datasheet.

6. **Type Sports in the Category field for a new record, then type (any valid and unique description) for this category in the Description field**

7. **Preview the datasheet again, click the Print button on the Print Preview tab, then click OK in the Print dialog box**

8. **Save and close the TourCategories datasheet, close the Quest-B.accdb database, then exit Access**

FIGURE B-16: Default printout of a datasheet

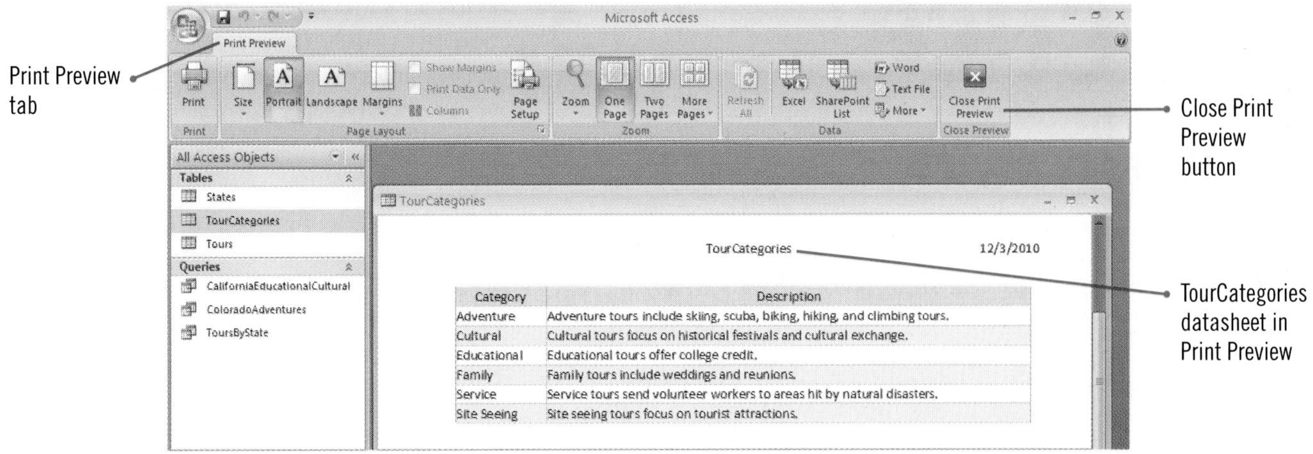
Print Preview tab
Close Print Preview button
TourCategories datasheet in Print Preview
Microsoft Access
TourCategories
12/3/2010
Category
Description
Adventure
Adventure tours include skiing, scuba, biking, hiking, and climbing tours.
Cultural
Cultural tours focus on historical festivals and cultural exchange.
Educational
Educational tours offer college credit.
Family
Family tours include weddings and reunions.
Service
Service tours send volunteer workers to areas hit by natural disasters.
Site Seeing
Site seeing tours focus on tourist attractions.

FIGURE B-17: Formatted datasheet

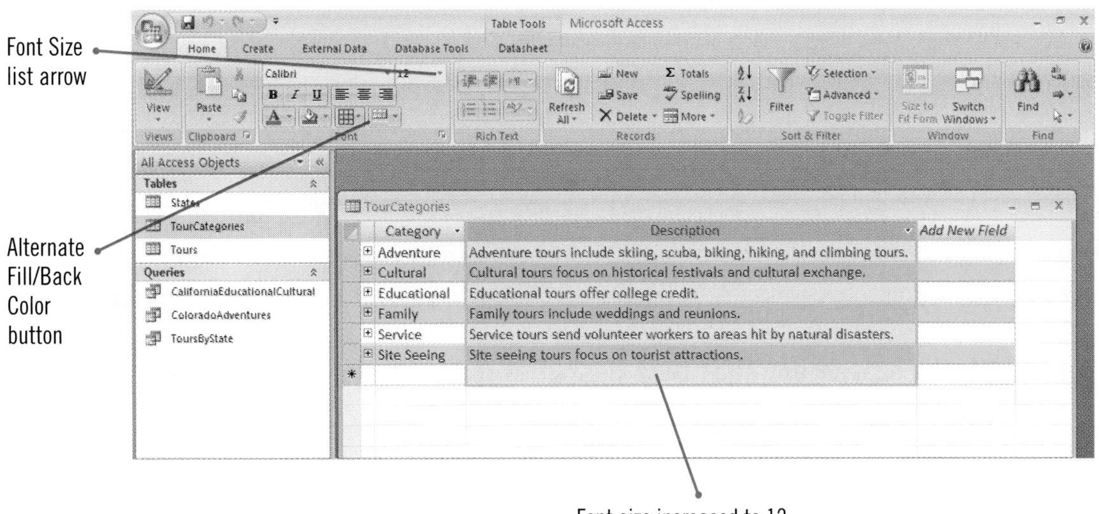
Font Size list arrow
Alternate Fill/Back Color button
Font size increased to 12, Description field resized, and Yellow alternate color applied

Practice

If you have a SAM user profile, you may have access to hands-on instruction, practice, and assessment of the skills covered in this unit. Log in to your SAM account (http://sam2007.course.com/) to launch any assigned training activities or exams that relate to the skills covered in this unit.

▼ CONCEPTS REVIEW

Label each element of the Access window shown in Figure B-18.

FIGURE B-18

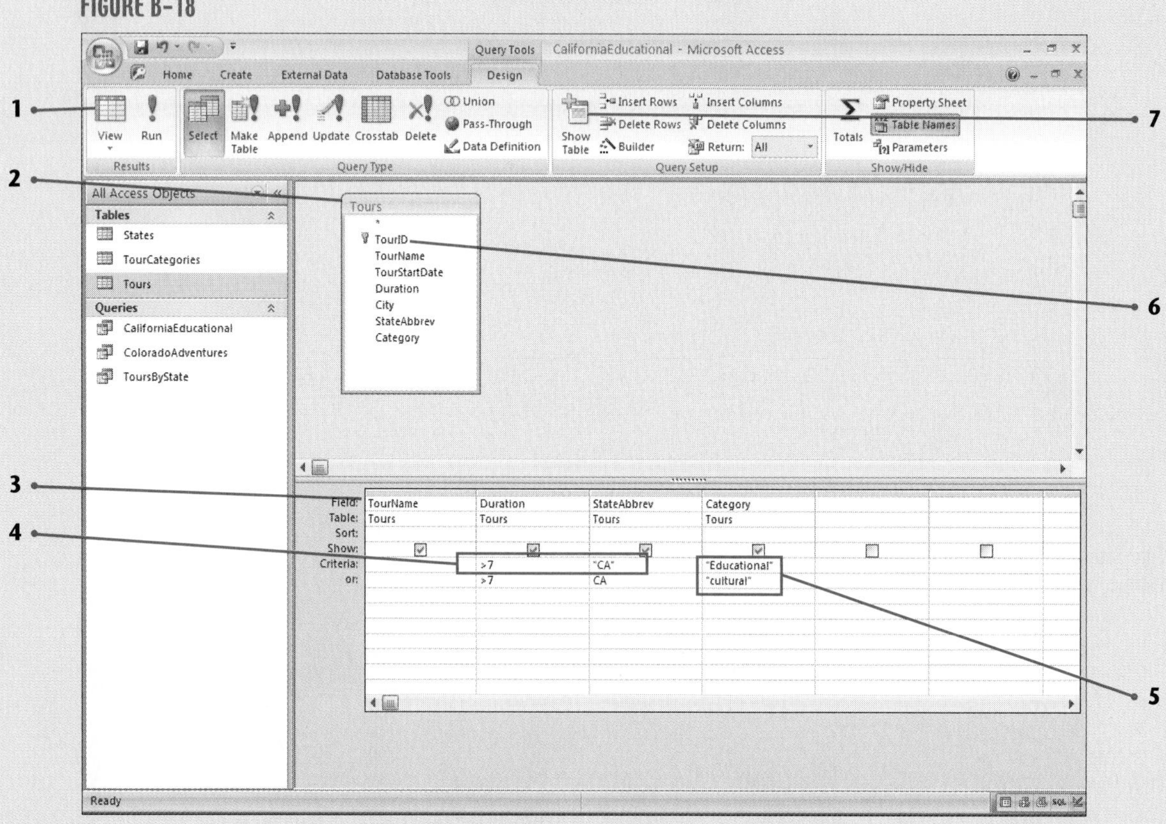

Match each term with the statement that best describes it.

8. Query grid
9. Criteria
10. Filter
11. Syntax
12. Query
13. Sorting
14. Wildcard
15. Is Null

a. Creates a datasheet of selected fields and records from one or more tables
b. Creates a temporary subset of records
c. Limiting conditions used to narrow the number of records that appear on a datasheet
d. Used to search for a pattern
e. Criterion that finds all records where no entry has been made in the field
f. The lower pane in Query Design View
g. Putting records in ascending or descending order based on the values of a field
h. Rules that determine how criteria is entered

Select the best answer from the list of choices.

16. The rules by which criteria need to be entered in the query grid are referred to as:

a. Syntax.
b. Hyperlink.
c. Field lists.
d. Formatting.

17. SQL stands for which of the following?

a. Standard Query Language
b. Structured Query Language
c. Special Query Listing
d. Simple Query Listing

18. A query is sometimes called a "logical view" of data because:

a. You can create queries with the Logical Query Wizard.
b. Queries contain logical criteria.
c. Query naming conventions are logical.
d. Queries do not store data, they only display a view of data.

19. Which of the following describes OR criteria?

a. Using two or more rows of the query grid to select only those records that meet given criteria
b. Selecting a subset of fields and/or records to view as a datasheet from one or more tables
c. Reorganizing the records in either ascending or descending order based on the contents of one or more fields
d. Using multiple fields in the query design grid

20. Which of the following is *not* true about a query?

a. A query is the same thing as a filter.
b. A query can be used to create calculated fields.
c. A query can be used to create summary statistics.
d. A query can be used to enter and edit data.

▼ SKILLS REVIEW

1. Create a query.

a. Open the **RealEstate-B.accdb** database from the drive and folder where you store your Data Files. Enable content if you are prompted with a Security Alert message.
b. Create a new query using the Simple Query Wizard. Select the AgentFirst and AgentLast names from the Agents table, and select the Type, SqFt, and Asking fields from the Listings table. Select all details, and title the query AgentListings.
c. Choose any record with Michelle Litten's name and change it to your own. As soon as you save the changes by moving to another record, all three of Michelle's records update to your name. Although Michelle Litten was entered only once in the database, her agent number was linked to three different listings in the Listings table, which selects her name three times out of the Agents table for this query.

2. Use Query Design View.

a. Open the AgentListings query in Query Design View.
b. Enter criteria to display only homes with an Asking price of greater than $200,000. (*Hint*: Enter the value in the criterion as 200000 without a comma. Also, don't forget the greater than operator, >.) Display the datasheet.
c. In Query Design View, sort the records in ascending order based on the AgentLast field, then display and print the datasheet.
d. Save and close the AgentListings query.

▼ SKILLS REVIEW (CONTINUED)

3. Modify queries.

- **a.** Open the ListingsMasterList query in Datasheet View.
- **b.** Switch to Query Design View, then add the AgencyName field from the Agencies table to the first column in the query grid.
- **c.** Add the AgentFirst field to the third column.
- **d.** Add ascending sort orders to the AgentLast and AgentFirst fields, then display the datasheet.
- **e.** Print, save, and close the ListingsMasterList query.

4. Sort and find data.

- **a.** Open the Listings table datasheet.
- **b.** Select both the SqFt and LakeFt fields, then sort the records in descending order.
- **c.** In the Area field, find all occurrences of Shell Knob, replace them with **Shell City**, then close the Find and Replace dialog box.
- **d.** Enter your own last name in the Area field of the first record, then print only the first page of the datasheet.

5. Filter data.

- **a.** Filter the Listings datasheet for only those records where the Type field equals Two Story.
- **b.** Apply an advanced filter by form to further narrow the records so that only the Two Story listings with an Asking Price of greater than or equal to $194,500 are selected.
- **c.** Print the datasheet, then close the Listings datasheet without saving changes.

6. Apply AND criteria.

- **a.** Open the ListingsMasterList query in Query Design View.
- **b.** Enter criteria to select all of the listings in the Shell City area with three or more baths. Display the datasheet and save the changes.
- **c.** Print the ListingsMasterList datasheet in landscape orientation.

7. Apply OR criteria.

- **a.** Open the ListingsMasterList query in Query Design View.
- **b.** In addition to the existing criteria, include criteria to select all listings in Kimberling City with three or more baths, so that both Shell City and Kimberling City records with three or more baths are selected. Display the datasheet, compare it to Figure B-19, and save the changes.

FIGURE B-19

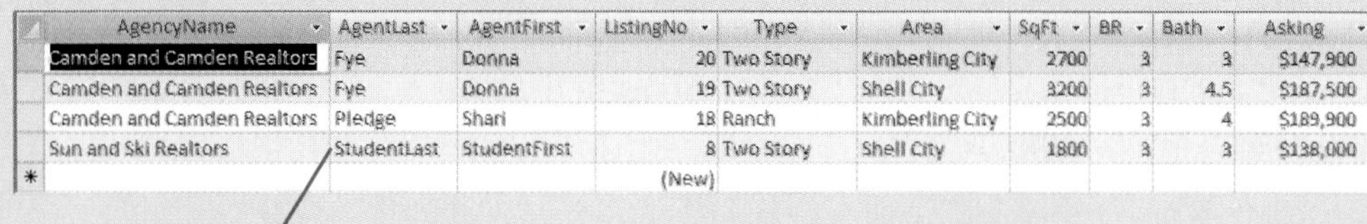

AgencyName	AgentLast	AgentFirst	ListingNo	Type	Area	SqFt	BR	Bath	Asking
Camden and Camden Realtors	Fye	Donna	20	Two Story	Kimberling City	2700	3	3	$147,900
Camden and Camden Realtors	Fye	Donna	19	Two Story	Shell City	3200	3	4.5	$187,500
Camden and Camden Realtors	Pledge	Shari	18	Ranch	Kimberling City	2500	3	4	$189,900
Sun and Ski Realtors	StudentLast	StudentFirst	8	Two Story	Shell City	1800	3	3	$138,000
*			(New)						

The order of the records might differ, depending on your name

- **c.** Print the ListingsMasterList datasheet in landscape orientation, then save and close the ListingsMasterList query.

8. Format a datasheet.

- **a.** Open the Agents table datasheet and apply the Arial Narrow font and a 14-point font size.
- **b.** Resize all columns so that all data and field names are visible.
- **c.** Apply a Light Gray 2 alternate fill/back color.
- **d.** Print the datasheet, then save and close the Agents datasheet.
- **e.** Close the RealEstate-B.accdb database, then exit Access.

▼ INDEPENDENT CHALLENGE 1

You have built an Access database to track the veterinarians and clinics where they work in your area.

a. Start Access, open the **Vet-B.accdb** database from the drive and folder where you store your Data Files, enable content if prompted, then open the Vets table datasheet.
b. Open the Clinics datasheet, review the data in both datasheets, then close them.
c. Using the Simple Query Wizard, select the Last and First fields from the Vets table, and select the ClinicName and Phone fields from the Clinics table. Title the query **ClinicListing**, then view and maximize the datasheet.
d. Sort the records in ascending order by Last name, then First name. Review the values in the Last field, and determine if the First sort order was needed.
e. Find Cooper in the Last field, and replace it with **Chen**.
f. Find any occurrence of Leawood Animal Clinic in the ClinicName field, and change Leawood to **Emergency**.
g. In Query Design View, add criteria to select only Emergency Animal Clinic or Animal Haven in the ClinicName field.
h. Display the datasheet, change Vicki Kowalewski's name to your own, then save and print the ClinicListing datasheet.
i. Close the ClinicListing datasheet and the Vet-B.accdb database, and exit Access.

▼ INDEPENDENT CHALLENGE 2

You have built an Access database to track membership in a community service club. The database tracks member names and addresses as well as their status in the club, which moves from rank to rank as the members contribute increased hours of service to the community.

a. Start Access, open the **Membership-B.accdb** database from the drive and folder where you store your Data Files, enable content if prompted, open the Members and Status table datasheets to review the data, then close them.
b. In Query Design View, build a query with the following fields: LName and FName from the Members table, and StatusLevel from the Status table.
c. View the datasheet, then return to Query Design View.
d. In Query Design View, add criteria to select only those members with a silver or gold StatusLevel. Apply an ascending sort order on the LName and FName fields, then view the datasheet.
e. Return to Query Design View, add an ascending sort order to StatusLevel, then rearrange the fields in the query grid so that the StatusLevel field is the first sort order, LName the second, and FName the third. View the datasheet.
f. Save the query with the name **GoldSilver**.
g. Return to Query Design View, then add the Phone field as the fourth field in the query. View the datasheet, shown in Figure B-20.
h. Enter your own name in the first record, widen all columns so that all data is visible, then print the datasheet.
i. Save and close the GoldSilver query, then close the Membership-B.accdb database, and exit Access.

FIGURE B-20

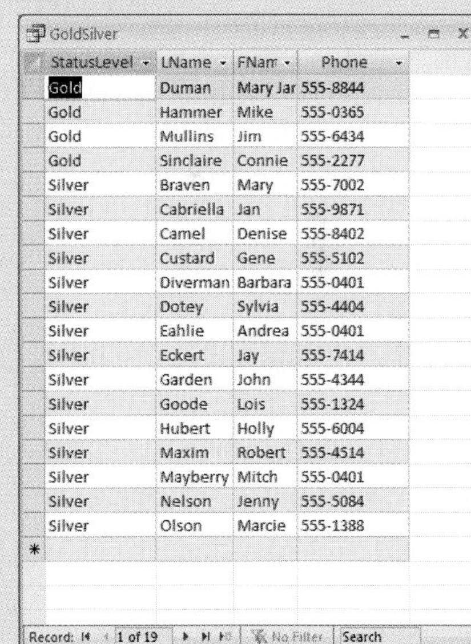

GoldSilver

StatusLevel	LName	FNam	Phone
Gold	Duman	Mary Jar	555-8844
Gold	Hammer	Mike	555-0365
Gold	Mullins	Jim	555-6434
Gold	Sinclaire	Connie	555-2277
Silver	Braven	Mary	555-7002
Silver	Cabriella	Jan	555-9871
Silver	Camel	Denise	555-8402
Silver	Custard	Gene	555-5102
Silver	Diverman	Barbara	555-0401
Silver	Dotey	Sylvia	555-4404
Silver	Eahlie	Andrea	555-0401
Silver	Eckert	Jay	555-7414
Silver	Garden	John	555-4344
Silver	Goode	Lois	555-1324
Silver	Hubert	Holly	555-6004
Silver	Maxim	Robert	555-4514
Silver	Mayberry	Mitch	555-0401
Silver	Nelson	Jenny	555-5084
Silver	Olson	Marcie	555-1388

Record: 1 of 19 No Filter Search

Access 2007

▼ INDEPENDENT CHALLENGE 3

You have built an Access database to organize the deposits at a recycling center. Various clubs regularly deposit recyclable material, which is measured in pounds when the deposits are made.

a. Start Access, open the **Recycle-B.accdb** database from the drive and folder where you store your Data Files, then enable content if prompted.

b. Open the Clubs table datasheet to review this data, then close it. Open the Centers table datasheet to review this data, then close it.

c. Review the Deposits datasheet, then filter the datasheet for records where the Weight value is greater than or equal to 100.

d. Apply an alternate light gray fill/back color of your choice, print the datasheet, then save and close the Deposits datasheet.

e. Using either the Query Wizard or Query Design View, create a query with the following fields: Deposit Number, Deposit Date, and Weight from the Deposits table; Name from the Centers table; and Name from the Clubs table. Note that in the Simple Query Wizard's field list and in the query datasheet, when two fields from different tables have the same name, the fields are distinguished by adding the table name and a period before the field name.

f. Name the query **DepositList**. Sort the records in ascending order by Deposit Number.

g. Change any occurrence of "Adair" in the "Adair County Landfill" entry in the Centers.Name field to your last name, then print the datasheet.

h. Save and close the DepositList query.

Advanced Challenge Exercise

- Compare the printout of the Deposits table datasheet and the DepositList query. In a document, answer the following questions:
  - What common field links the Deposits table to the Centers table? (*Hint*: Use the Relationships window if the answer is not apparent from the printouts.)
  - What common field links the Deposits table to the Clubs table? (*Hint*: Use the Relationships window if needed.)
  - Why do you think that number fields are often used as the common field to link two tables in a one-to-many relationship, as opposed to text fields?
  - How many times is each center name and each club name physically entered in the database?
  - Why do many center names and club names appear many times on the DepositList query?

i. Close the Recycle-B.accdb database, then exit Access.

▼ REAL LIFE INDEPENDENT CHALLENGE

You can use an Access database to record and track your experiences, such as places you've visited. Suppose that your passion for travel includes a plan to visit the capitals of all 50 states. A database is provided with your Data Files that includes one table listing each state and capital, and another table of people from each state that you can contact for more information about state information.

a. Start Access, open the **Capitals-B.accdb** database from the drive and folder where you store your Data Files, then enable content if prompted.

b. Open both the Contacts and States datasheets to review their data, then close them.

c. In the States table, add a new field to track information about each state that you are personally interested in. Options include recording the current state population, state bird, primary tourist attraction, largest city, or any other fact about each state you choose.

d. Research and enter correct data for the new field you created in step c, for both your home state and another state that you are interested in, then print the States datasheet.

e. Using either Query Design View or the Simple Query Wizard, create a query with the following fields: StateName and Capital from the States table, and LName and FName from the Contacts table. Save the query as **StateContacts**, then display the datasheet.

▼ REAL LIFE INDEPENDENT CHALLENGE (CONTINUED)

f. Use Query Design View to add three ascending sort orders on these fields—StateName, then LName, then FName—then display the datasheet.

g. Use Query Design View to add a criterion to select only records from the state of New York, then display the datasheet.

h. Edit Ablany to correct the spelling of New York's state capital, Albany. Navigate to a new record so that the edit is saved in the database.

i. Format the datasheet to a 14-point font size, Times New Roman font face, and a Light Blue 1 alternate fill/back color.

j. Save the revised query with the name **NewYorkContacts**.

k. Change the name of the first record to your name, then print the datasheet.

Advanced Challenge Exercise

This Advanced Challenge Exercise requires an Internet connection.

- Use the Web to research state mottos.
- Create a Text field in the States table called Motto and enter the motto for at least five different states, including New York.
- In Query Design View of the NewYorkContacts query, add the Motto field as the fifth column of the query.
- View the datasheet, widen the motto field as necessary, as shown in Figure B-21, then print the NewYorkContacts query.
- Close the NewYorkContacts query without saving changes.

l. Close the Capitals-B.accdb database, then exit Access.

FIGURE B-21

NewYorkContacts

StateName	Capital	LName	FName	Motto
New York	Albany	McCollum	Roman	Ever Upward!
New York	Albany	Oberstar	John	Ever Upward!
New York	Albany	Osborne	Mike	Ever Upward!
New York	Albany	Peterson	Hilda	Ever Upward!
New York	Albany	Pickering	Bob	Ever Upward!
New York	Albany	Porter	William	Ever Upward!
New York	Albany	Ramstad	Tammy	Ever Upward!
New York	Albany	Rehberg	Terry	Ever Upward!
New York	Albany	Sabo	Gary	Ever Upward!
New York	Albany	Schwarz	Paul	Ever Upward!
New York	Albany	Skelton	Randy	Ever Upward!
New York	Albany	Taylor	Corrine	Ever Upward!
New York	Albany	Terry	JoAnn	Ever Upward!
New York	Albany	Thompson	Ken	Ever Upward!
New York	Albany	Wicker	Luke	Ever Upward!
*				

Record: 1 of 27 No Filter Search

▼ VISUAL WORKSHOP

Open the **Basketball-B.accdb** database from the drive and folder where you store your Data Files, and enable content if prompted. Create a query based on the Players, Stats, and Games tables as shown in Figure B-22. Criteria has been added so that only those records where the Reb-O (offensive rebounds) and Reb-D (defensive rebounds) field values are equal to or greater than 1, and the 3P (three pointer) field values are equal to or greater than 2. The records are also sorted. A Light Gray 1 alternate fill/back color has been applied. Change the name of Kelsey Douglas to your own name before printing, save the query with the name HighPerformers, then close the query, the Basketball-B.accdb database, and Access.

FIGURE B-22

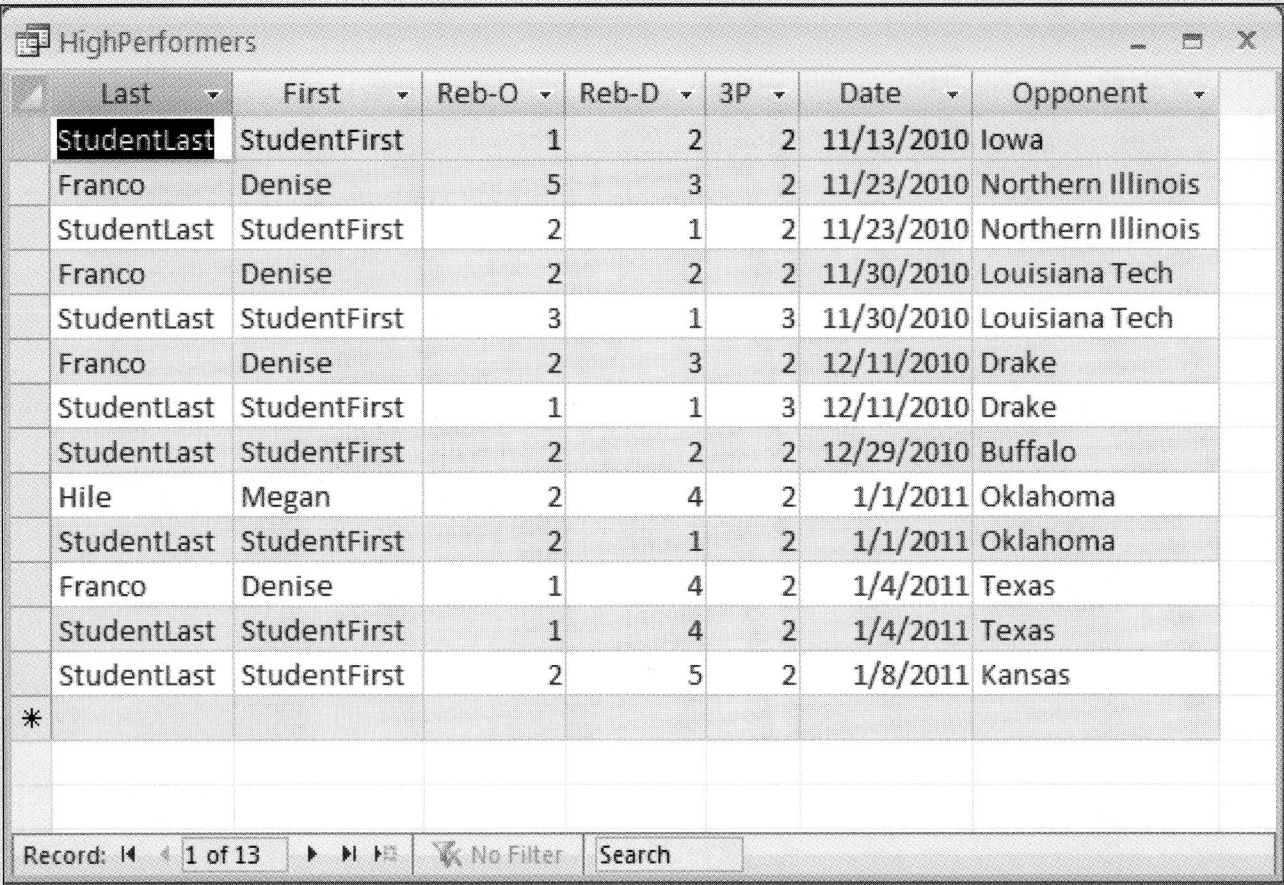

HighPerformers

Last	First	Reb-O	Reb-D	3P	Date	Opponent
StudentLast	StudentFirst	1	2	2	11/13/2010	Iowa
Franco	Denise	5	3	2	11/23/2010	Northern Illinois
StudentLast	StudentFirst	2	1	2	11/23/2010	Northern Illinois
Franco	Denise	2	2	2	11/30/2010	Louisiana Tech
StudentLast	StudentFirst	3	1	3	11/30/2010	Louisiana Tech
Franco	Denise	2	3	2	12/11/2010	Drake
StudentLast	StudentFirst	1	1	3	12/11/2010	Drake
StudentLast	StudentFirst	2	2	2	12/29/2010	Buffalo
Hile	Megan	2	4	2	1/1/2011	Oklahoma
StudentLast	StudentFirst	2	1	2	1/1/2011	Oklahoma
Franco	Denise	1	4	2	1/4/2011	Texas
StudentLast	StudentFirst	1	4	2	1/4/2011	Texas
StudentLast	StudentFirst	2	5	2	1/8/2011	Kansas

Record: 1 of 13 No Filter Search

UNIT C
Access 2007

Using Forms

Files You Will Need:

Quest-C.accdb
RealEstate-C.accdb
Vet-C.accdb
Membership-C.accdb
Recycle-C.accdb
States-C.accdb
Basketball-C.accdb
QSTLogo.jpg
house.jpg
dog.jpg

Although you can enter and edit data on datasheets, most database designers develop and build forms as the primary method for users to interact with a database. In a datasheet, sometimes you have to scroll left or right to see all of the fields, which is inconvenient and time consuming. A form solves these problems by allowing you to organize the fields on the screen in any arrangement. A form also supports graphical elements such as pictures, buttons, and tabs, which make data entry faster and more accurate. Mark Rock, a tour developer at Quest Specialty Travel, asks you to create forms to make tour information easier to access, enter, and update in the Quest Access database.

OBJECTIVES

- Create a form
- Use Form Layout View
- Use Form Design View
- Add fields to a form
- Modify form controls
- Create calculations
- Modify tab order
- Insert an image

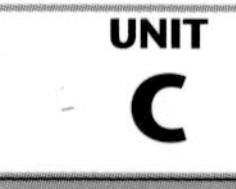

UNIT C

Access 2007

Creating a Form

A **form** is an Access database object that allows you to arrange the fields of a record in any layout so you can enter, edit, and delete records. A form provides an easy-to-use data entry and navigation screen. Forms provide many productivity and security benefits for the **user**, who is primarily interested in entering, editing, and analyzing the data in the database. As the **database designer**, the person responsible for building and maintaining tables, queries, forms, and reports, you also need direct access to all database objects, and use the Navigation Pane for this purpose. Users should not be able to access all the objects in a database—imagine how disastrous it would be if they accidentally deleted an entire table of data. You can prevent these types of problems by providing users with only the functionality they need in easy-to-use, well-designed forms. Mark Rock asks you to build a form to enter and maintain tour information.

STEPS

1. **Start Access, open the Quest-C.accdb database, then enable content if prompted**

   You can use many methods to create a new form, but the Form Wizard is a popular way to get started. The **Form Wizard** is an Access tool that prompts you for information it needs to create a new form, such as the layout, style, title, and record source for the form.

2. **Click the Create tab on the Ribbon, click the Tours table in the Navigation Pane, click the More Forms button, then click the Form Wizard**

   The Form Wizard starts, prompting you to select the fields for this form from the table you selected.

3. **Click the Select All Fields button [>>]**

   You could now select more fields from other tables. In this case, you can base the new form only on the fields of the Tours table.

TROUBLE

Your field values might appear with a different color border, or no border at all.

4. **Click Next, click the Columnar option button, click Next, click the Flow style, click Next, type Tours Entry Form as the title, click Finish, then maximize the form window**

   The Tours Entry Form opens in **Form View**, as shown in Figure C-1. The field names are shown as labels in the first column, and text boxes that display data from the underlying record source appear in the second column. You can enter, edit, find, sort, and filter records using Form View.

QUICK TIP

Always click a value in a field to identify which field you want to sort or filter before clicking the sort or filter buttons.

5. **Click Cyclone Ski Club in the TourName text box, click the Ascending button on the Home tab, then click the Next record button on the navigation bar to move to the second record**

   Numbers sort before letters in a Text field, so the tour named *5 Days in Paradise* appears before *American Heritage Tour.* Information about the current record number and total number of records appears in the navigation bar, just as it does in a datasheet.

6. **Click the New (blank) record button on the navigation bar, then enter the record shown in Figure C-2**

   Note that when you click in the TourStartDate text box, a small calendar icon appears to the right of the record. You can type a date directly into a date text box or click the **calendar icon** to select a date from a pop-up calendar. Similarly, when you work in the Category field, you can either type a value directly into the text box or click the list arrow to select an option from the drop-down list. Every item on the form, such as a label or text box, is called a **control**. Table C-1 summarizes the most common form controls as well as whether they are **bound** (display data) or **unbound** (do not display data).

FIGURE C-1: Tours Entry Form in Form View

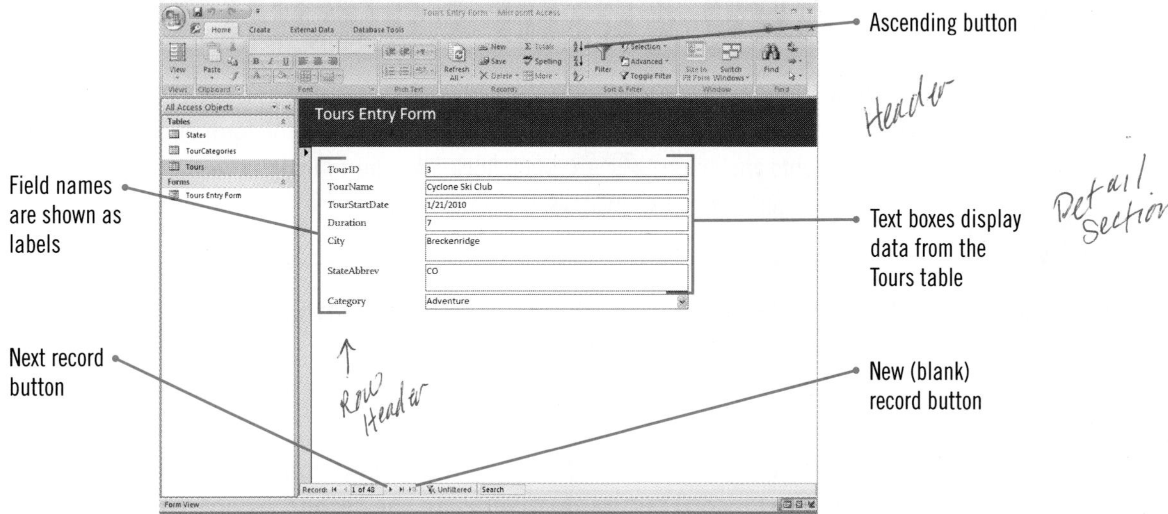

FIGURE C-2: Adding a new record in the Tours Entry Form

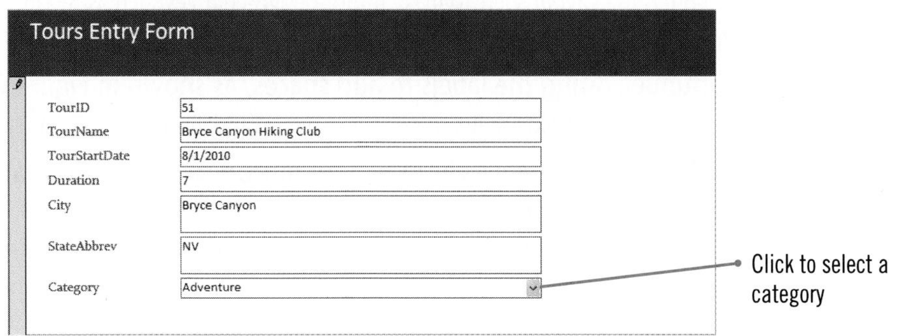

Access 2007

TABLE C-1: Form controls

name	used to	bound	unbound
Label	Provide consistent descriptive text as you navigate from record to record; the label is the most common type of unbound control and can also be used as a hyperlink to another database object, external file, or Web page		x
Text box	Display, edit, or enter data for each record from an underlying record source; the text box is the most common type of bound control	x	
List box	Display a list of possible data entries	x	
Combo box	Display a list of possible data entries for a field, and provide a text box for an entry from the keyboard; combines the list box and text box controls	x	
Tab control	Create a three-dimensional aspect to a form		x
Check box	Display "yes" or "no" answers for a field; if the box is checked, it means "yes"	x	
Toggle button	Display "yes" or "no" answers for a field; if the button is pressed, it means "yes"	x	
Option button	Display a choice for a field	x	
Option group	Display and organize choices (usually presented as option buttons) for a field	x	
Bound object frame	Display data stored by an OLE (object linking and embedding) field, such as a picture	x	
Unbound object frame	Display a picture or clip art image that doesn't change from record to record		x
Line and Rectangle	Draw lines and rectangles on the form		x
Command button	Provide an easy way to initiate a command or run a macro		x

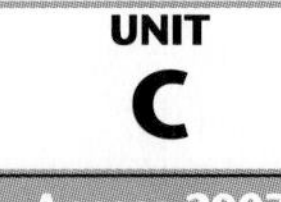

Using Form Layout View

Layout View, new to Access 2007, lets you make some design changes to the form while you are browsing the data. For example, you can add or delete a field to the form or change formatting characteristics such as fonts and colors. Mark Rock asks you to make several design changes to the Tours Entry Form. You can make these changes in Layout View.

STEPS

QUICK TIP

Click the Home tab on the Ribbon to display the frequently used View button.

1. **Click the TourID value, click the Ascending button on the Home tab, click the View button arrow, then click Layout View**

   In Layout View, you can move through the records, but you cannot enter or edit the data as you can in Form View.

2. **Click the First record button on the navigation bar to move to the first record, click the Next record button to move to the second record, click the TourID label to select it, then click between the words Tour and ID and press [Spacebar]**

   You often use Layout View to make minor design changes such as revising labels and changing formatting characteristics.

TROUBLE

Be sure to modify the *labels in the left column* instead of the text boxes on the right.

3. **Continue editing the labels to add spaces, as shown in Figure C-3**

   You also want to bold the first two labels, Tour ID and Tour Name, to make them more visible.

4. **Click the Tour ID label, click the Bold button on the Format tab, click the Tour Name label, then click**

   Often, you want to apply the same formatting enhancement to multiple controls. For example, you decide to narrow all of the text boxes. You select all the text boxes at the same time before applying the change.

TROUBLE

If you make an unintended change, click the Undo button on the Quick Access toolbar to undo your last action.

5. **Click the Tour ID text box (it currently displays 2), then press and hold [Shift] while clicking each of the other five text boxes and one combo box in that column**

   With all seven controls selected, any change you make to one control is made to all.

6. **Drag the right edge of the controls to the left to make them approximately half as wide**

   Your Layout View for the Tours Entry Form should look like Figure C-4.

FIGURE C-3: Using Layout View to modify form labels

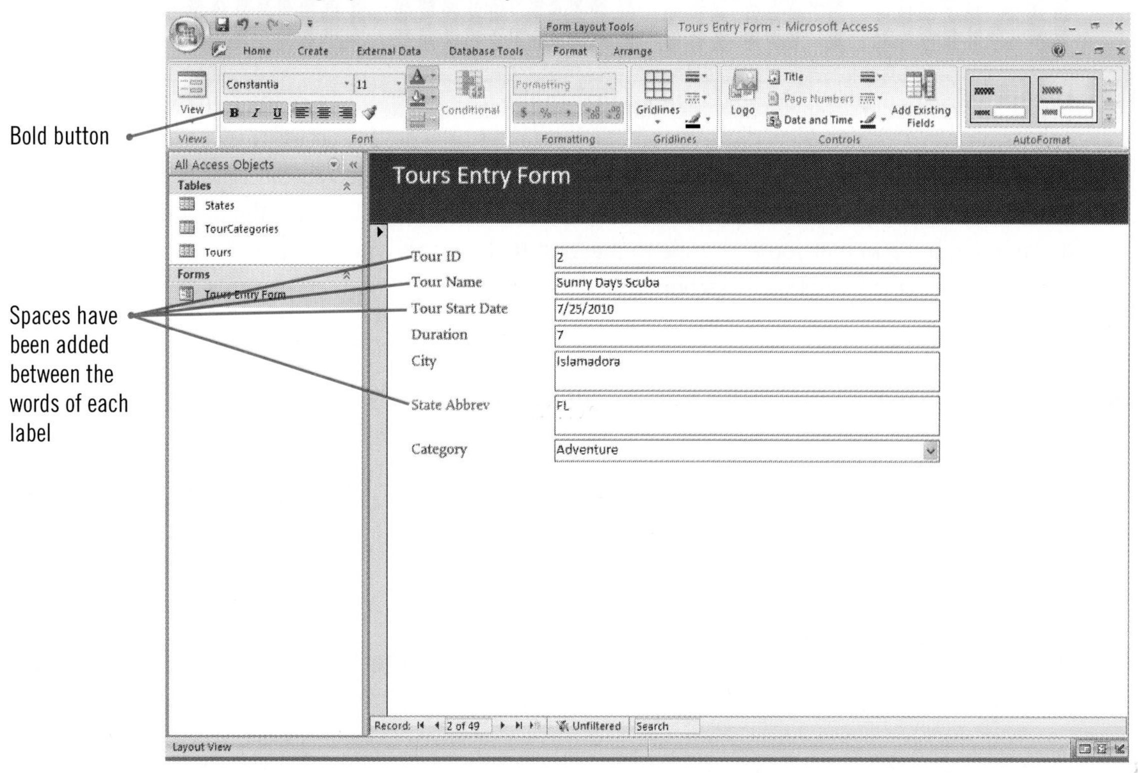

FIGURE C-4: Final Layout View for the Tours Entry Form

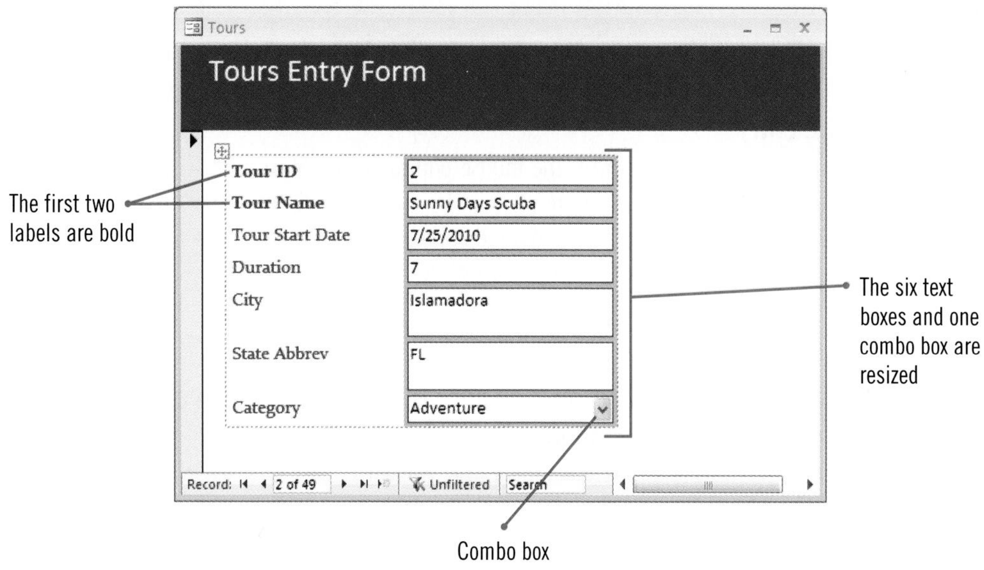

Access 2007

UNIT C

Access 2007

Using Form Design View

Design View of a form is devoted to working with the detailed structure of the form. Unlike Form View and Layout View, Design View displays no data, but rather provides full access to all of a form's structural and design modifications. In fact, Design View is the only place where you can modify certain structural elements such as the Form Header and Footer sections. Mark Rock likes the design changes you've made so far, but asks that you add a title to the form that appears when it is printed. To do so, you add a title as a label in the Form Header section in Design View.

STEPS

QUICK TIP

Another way to open an object in Design View is to right-click it in the Navigation Pane, then click Design View on the shortcut menu.

TROUBLE

If you do not see sizing handles on the Tours Entry Form label, click the label to select it.

1. **Click the View button arrow on the Home tab, then click Design View**

   In Design View, you can work with additional form sections such as the Form Header and Form Footer. The vertical and horizontal **rulers** help you position controls on the form. In Design View, you can add new controls to the form such as labels, combo boxes, and check boxes that are found on the Design tab of the Ribbon.

2. **Click the Label button on the Design tab, click below the Tours Entry Form label in the Form Header, type Quest Specialty Travel, then press [Enter]**

   With the label in position, as shown in Figure C-5, you change the font color and size so it is more visible. **Sizing handles**, small squares that surround the label, identify which control is currently selected.

3. **With the Quest Specialty Travel label still selected, click the Font Color button arrow, then click the white box**

   The white font color is more readable, but the label would be easier to read if it were larger, so you decide to increase the font size.

4. **With the Quest Specialty Travel label still selected, click the Font Size list arrow, click 18, then double-click a sizing handle to expand the label to automatically fit the entire entry**

   When you work with controls, the mouse pointer shape is very important. The shapes indicate whether dragging the mouse will select, move, or resize controls. Pointer shapes are summarized in Table C-2. With the Quest Specialty Travel label formatted appropriately, it's time to save your changes and review the form in Form View, where the users will work with it.

5. **Click the Save button on the Quick Access toolbar, then click the Form View button on the Design tab**

   The updated Tours Entry Form is shown in Figure C-6.

FIGURE C-5: Modifying controls in Form Design View

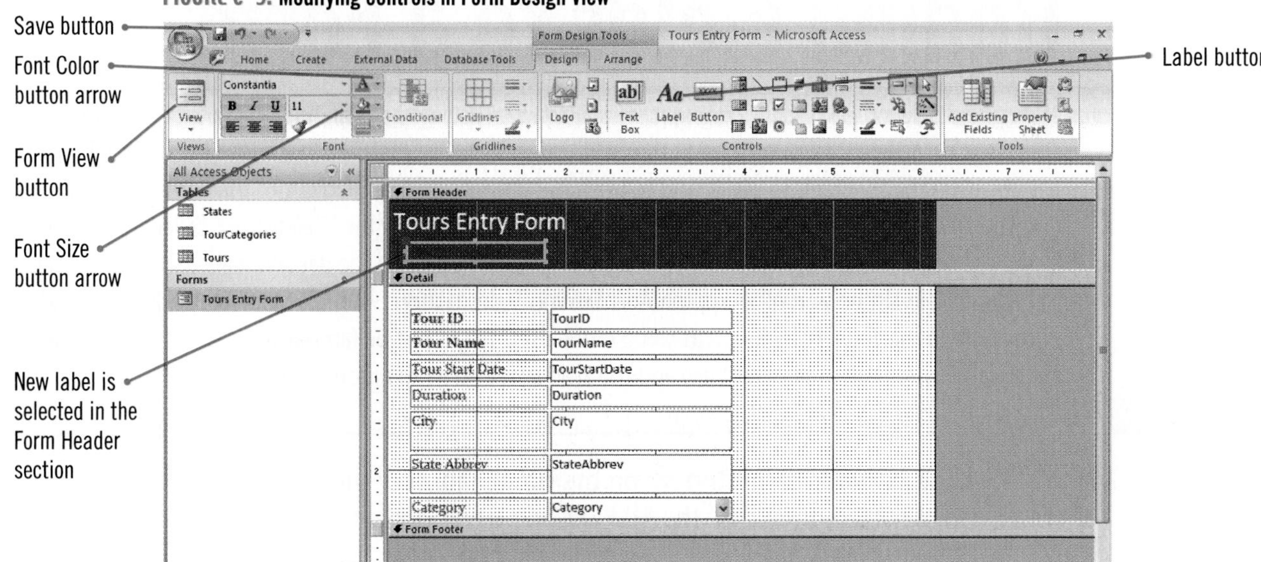

FIGURE C-6: Updated Tours Entry Form in Form View

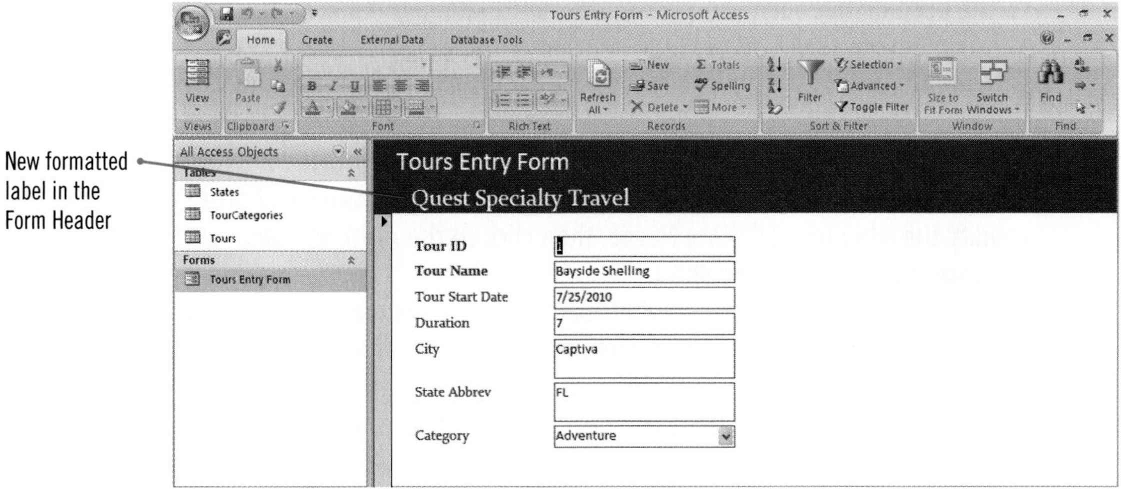

Access 2007

TABLE C-2: Mouse pointer shapes in Form Design View

shape	when does this shape appear?	action
↖	When you point to any unselected control on the form (the default mouse pointer)	Single-clicking with this mouse pointer *selects* a control
✥	When you point to the edge of a selected control (but not when you are pointing to a sizing handle)	Dragging one control with this mouse pointer moves all selected controls
✥	When you point to the larger sizing handle in the upper-left corner of a selected control	Dragging the larger sizing handle moves *only the single control* where the pointer is currently positioned, not other controls that may also be selected
↕ ↔ ↗ ↘	When you point to any sizing handle (except the larger one in the upper-left corner)	Dragging with one of these mouse pointers *resizes* the control

UNIT
C
Access 2007

Adding Fields to a Form

Adding and deleting fields to an existing form is a common activity. You can add or delete fields from a form in either Layout View or Design View using the Field List window. The **Field List** window lists the database tables and the fields they contain. To add a field to the form, drag it from the Field List to the desired location on the form. To delete a field on a form, click the field to select it, then press the [Delete] key. Deleting a field from a form does not delete it from the underlying table or have any effect on the data contained in the field. You can toggle the Field List on and off using the Add Existing Fields button. Mark Rock asks you to add the state name to the Tours Entry Form, as some of the users might not be familiar with all of the two-letter state abbreviations. You can use Layout View and the Field List window to accomplish this goal.

STEPS

TROUBLE

Click the Show all tables link at the bottom of the Field List if the States table is not visible in the Field List window.

1. **Click the Layout View button on the Home tab, click the Format tab if it is not already selected, then click the Add Existing Fields button**

   The Field List pane opens in Layout View, as shown in Figure C-7. Notice that the Field List is divided into an upper section, which shows the tables and fields within those tables that are used for the form, and the lower section, which shows related tables. The expand/collapse button to the left of the table names allows you to expand (show) the fields within the table or collapse (hide) them. The StateName field is in the States table in the lower section of the Field List.

2. **Click the expand button ⊞ to the left of the States table, then drag the StateName field to the position between the StateAbbrev and Category fields on the form**

   The form expands to accommodate the addition of the StateName label and text box by moving the Category label and text box down. When you add a new field to a form, two controls are generated: a label to describe the data that shows the field name, and a text box to display the contents of the field. With the field in place, you modify the label to be consistent with the other labels on the form.

3. **Click the StateName label to select it, click between the words and press [Spacebar] to modify the label to read State Name, then click to the right of Name: and press [Backspace] to delete the colon (:)**

   You also decide to delete the TourID field from the form. Because the TourID field has been defined as an AutoNumber field in the Tours table, it automatically increments as new tour records are entered and does not need to be displayed on this form.

4. **Click the text box that contains the TourID value, then press [Delete]**

   Deleting a field's text box automatically deletes its associated label control.

5. **Click the Save button on the Quick Access toolbar, then click the Form View button on the Design tab**

6. **Click the New (blank) record button in the navigation bar, then enter a new record in the updated form, as shown in Figure C-8**

   Note that after you enter MO in the StateAbbrev text box, the value in the StateName text box will automatically populate with the full state name, Missouri. Because the Tours table is related to the States table through the common State Abbrev field, the state name is automatically selected, or "pulled" out of the State table after you enter the state abbreviation into the Tour record.

FIGURE C-7: Adding controls in Form Layout View

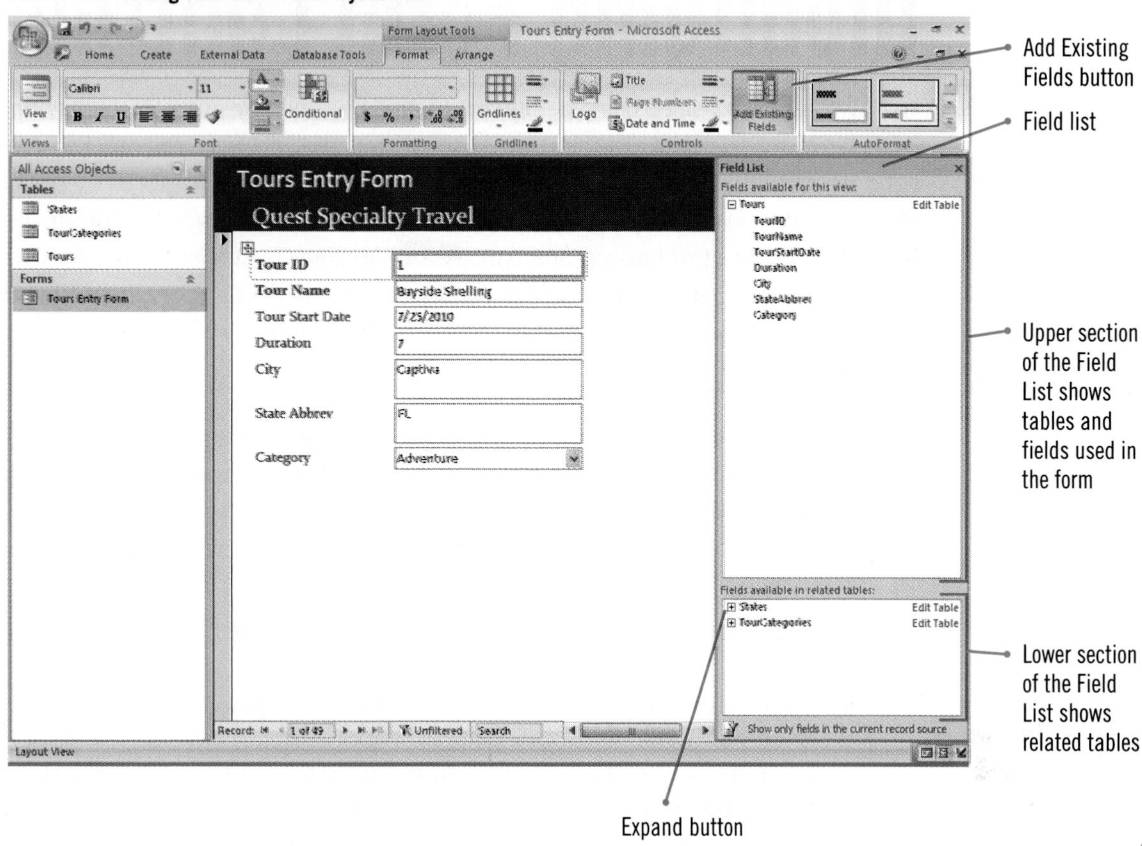

FIGURE C-8: Updated Tours Entry Form in Form View

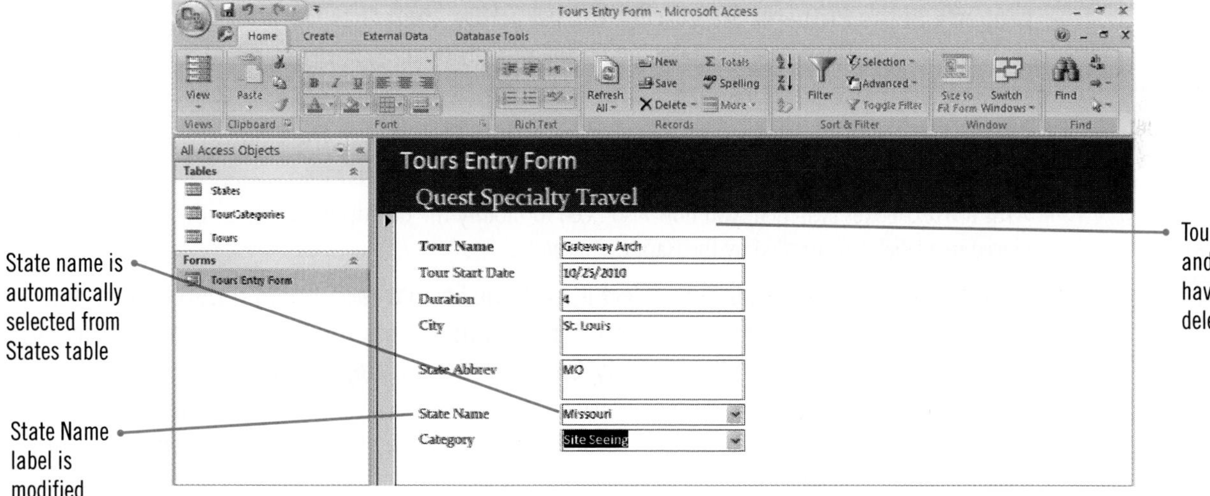

Bound versus unbound controls

Controls are said to be either bound or unbound. **Bound controls** are controls that display values from a field such as text boxes and combo boxes. **Unbound controls** do not display data, but rather serve to describe data or enhance the appearance of the form. Labels are the most common type of unbound control, but other types include lines, images, tabs, and command buttons. Another way to distinguish bound from unbound controls is to observe the form as you move from record to record. Because bound controls display data, their contents change as you move through the records, displaying the entry in the field of the current record. Unbound controls such as labels and lines do not change as you move through the records in a form.

UNIT C

Access 2007

Modifying Form Controls

You have already modified one type of form control, the label, by using the formatting buttons on the Ribbon to change font size and color. Some control properties, however, can only be viewed and modified using the control's **Property Sheet**, a comprehensive listing of all **properties** (characteristics) for the selected control. One such property is the **Control Source property**, which determines field **binding** (the field to which a text box is connected). Because Quest offers more adventure tours than any other type of tour, you decide to modify the default value of the Category field to be "Adventure." You work with the control's Property Sheet to modify the default value.

STEPS

1. **Click the View button arrow on the Home tab, click Design View, click the Design tab on the Ribbon if it is not already selected, then click the Property Sheet button**
   The Property Sheet opens, showing you all of the properties for the selected item, which is currently the entire form. The Category field is bound to a **combo box**, which is a combination of a text box and a list of values commonly entered for that field.

2. **Click the Category combo box, click the Data tab in the Property Sheet, click the Default Value box, type Adventure, then press [Enter]**
   The Property Sheet should look like Figure C-9. Access often helps you with the rules, or syntax, of entering property values. In this case, it entered quotation marks around "Adventure" to indicate that the default entry is text. You can also use the Property Sheet window to modify the most important property of a text box, its Control Source property, to bind the text box to a field. In the Tours Entry Form, each text box and combo box is already bound to the field name shown in the control. To change this binding, use the Control Source property in the Property Sheet. In this case, you want to switch the order of the Duration and TourStartDate text boxes. You could either move the controls on the form or change their bindings.

QUICK TIP

If you know the field name, you can change a field's Control Source property by directly typing the field name into the text box on the form. You must know the exact field name to use this method.

3. **Click the TourStartDate text box to select it, click TourStartDate in the Control Source property of the Property Sheet, click the list arrow, then click Duration**
   At this point, you have two text boxes bound to the Duration field. Change the second one to bind it to the TourStartDate field.

TROUBLE

Be sure to modify the text boxes on the right, not the labels on the left. If the Expression Builder dialog box opens, click Cancel.

4. **Click the second Duration text box to select it, click Duration in the Control Source property of the Property Sheet, click the list arrow, then click TourStartDate**
   With the text boxes switched, you now also need to modify the descriptive labels on the left. The text displayed in a label is controlled by the Caption property.

5. **Click the Tour Start Date label to select it, click the Format tab in the Property Sheet, select Tour Start Date in the Caption property, type Duration, click the Duration label to select it, select Duration in the Caption property, type Tour Start Date, then press [Enter]**
   Don't be overwhelmed by the number of properties available for each control on the form or the number of ways to modify each property. Over time, you will learn about most of these properties, but at first you can make most property changes directly in Form or Layout View, rather than using the Property Sheet itself.

6. **Click the Save button on the Quick Access toolbar, then click the Form View button on the Design tab**
   The modified Tours Entry Form is shown in Figure C-10.

FIGURE C-9: Using the Property Sheet

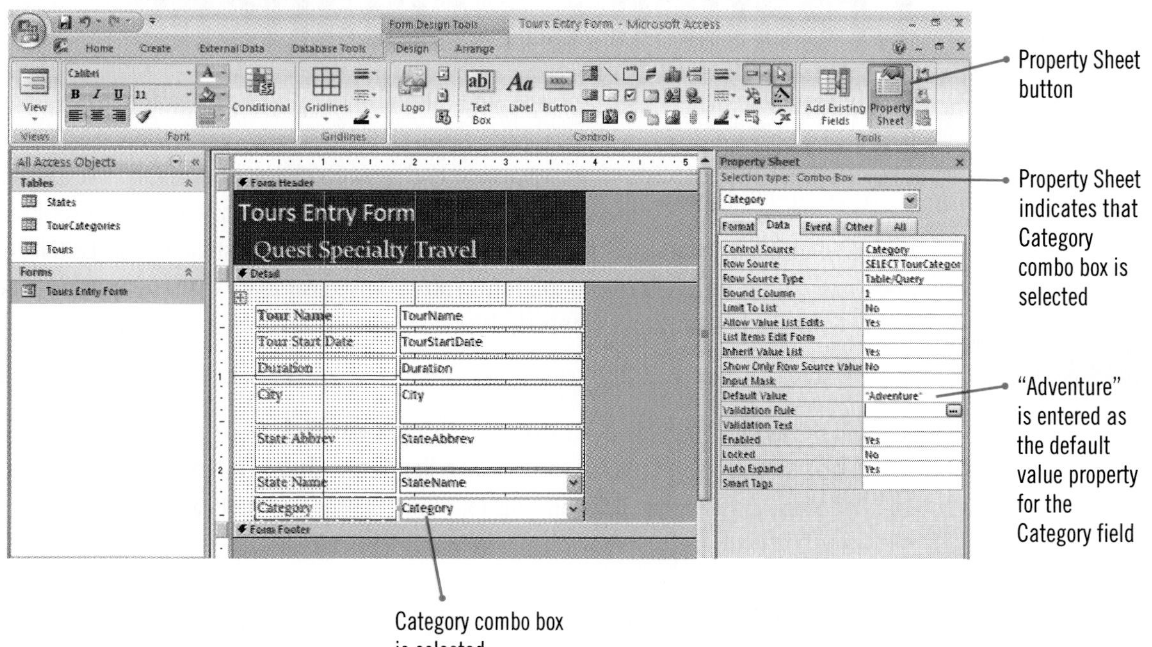

FIGURE C-10: Modified Tours Entry Form

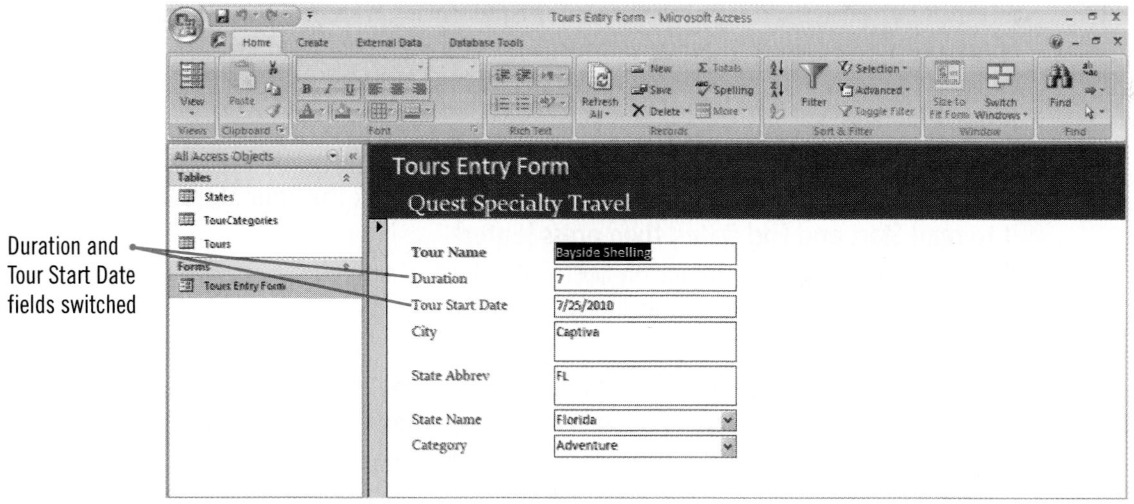

Access 2007

UNIT C

Access 2007

Creating Calculations

Text boxes are generally used to display data from underlying fields and are therefore *bound* to those fields. A text box control can also display a calculation. To create a calculation in a text box, you enter an **expression**, which consists of an equal sign and a combination of symbols that calculates a result. For example, you could use a text box to calculate sales tax or commission. Or, you could use a text box to combine, or concatenate, the values of two Text fields such as FirstName and LastName. Mark Rock asks you to add a text box to the Tours Entry Form to calculate the tour end date. You can add a text box in Form Design View to accomplish this.

STEPS

1. **Click the View button arrow on the Home tab, click Design View, click the Design tab if it is not already selected, then click the Property Sheet button to close the Property Sheet**

   To add the calculation to determine the tour end date (the tour start date plus the duration), start by adding a text box to the form.

2. **Click the Text Box button on the Design tab, then click to the right of the TourStartDate text box on the form**

   Adding a new text box automatically adds a new label to the left of the new text box. The form also widens to accommodate new controls. The number in the default caption of the label identifies how many controls you have previously added to the form. You don't need this label, so you can delete it.

> **TROUBLE**
> The number in your label might vary, based on previous work done to the form.

3. **Click the Text17 label to the left of the new text box, then press [Delete]**

> **QUICK TIP**
> You can resize controls one **pixel** (picture element) at a time by pressing [Shift] and an arrow key.

4. **Click the new text box to select it, click Unbound, type =[TourStartDate]+[Duration], press [Enter], then drag the middle-right sizing handle to the right far enough to view the entire expression, as shown in Figure C-11**

   All expressions entered into a text box start with an equal sign (=). When referencing a field name within an expression, [square brackets]—(not parentheses) and not {curly braces}—surround the field name. In an expression, you must type the field name exactly as it was created in Table Design View, but you do not need to match the capitalization.

> **TROUBLE**
> Move the Start and End Dates label, the TourStartDate text box, and the calculated text box as necessary so that they do not overlap.

5. **Click the Tour Start Date label on the left to select it, click the Tour Start Date text, edit it to read Start and End Dates, then press [Enter]**

   With the new calculation in place and the label modified, a final step before previewing the form is to align the top edges of the two text boxes that display dates.

6. **Click the TourStartDate text box, press [Shift], click the expression text box to add it to the selection, click the Arrange tab on the Ribbon, then click the Align Top button**

   Now the top edges of the text boxes are perfectly aligned. The Control Alignment buttons on the Layout tab (To Grid, Left, Right, Top, and Bottom) control alignment of two or more controls with respect to one another. Table C-3 shows techniques on how to select more than one control at the same time. The alignment buttons on the Design tab, , and align text within the edges of the control itself.

7. **Click the Save button on the Quick Access toolbar, click the Home tab on the Ribbon, click the Form View button, then press [Page Down] to navigate to the Fullington Family Reunion tour, viewing the calculated field as you move through the records**

   The updated Tours Entry Form with the tour date end calculation for the Fullington Family Reunion is shown in Figure C-12.

FIGURE C-11: Adding a text box to calculate a value

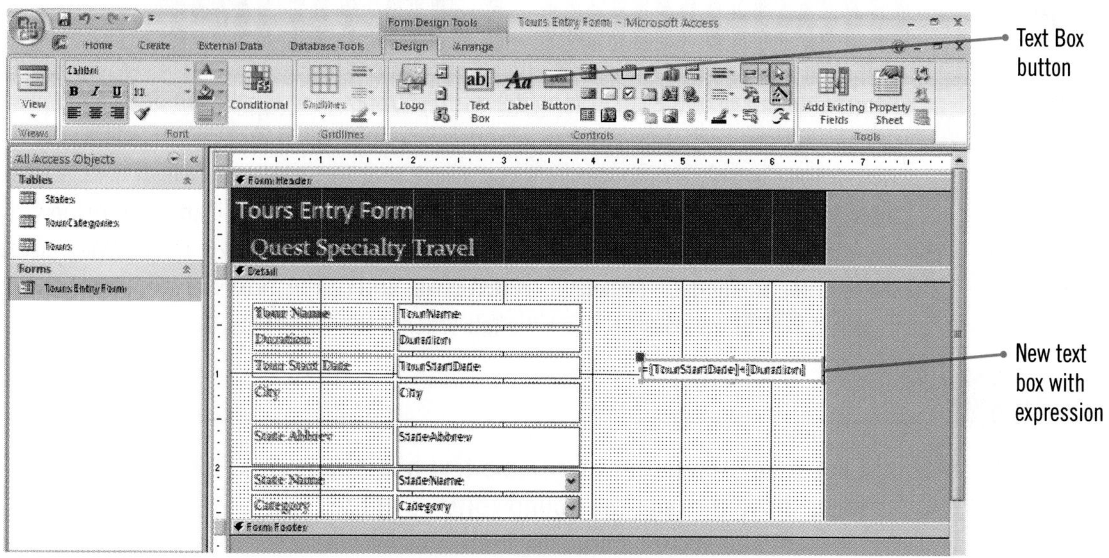

FIGURE C-12: Displaying the results of a calculation in Form View

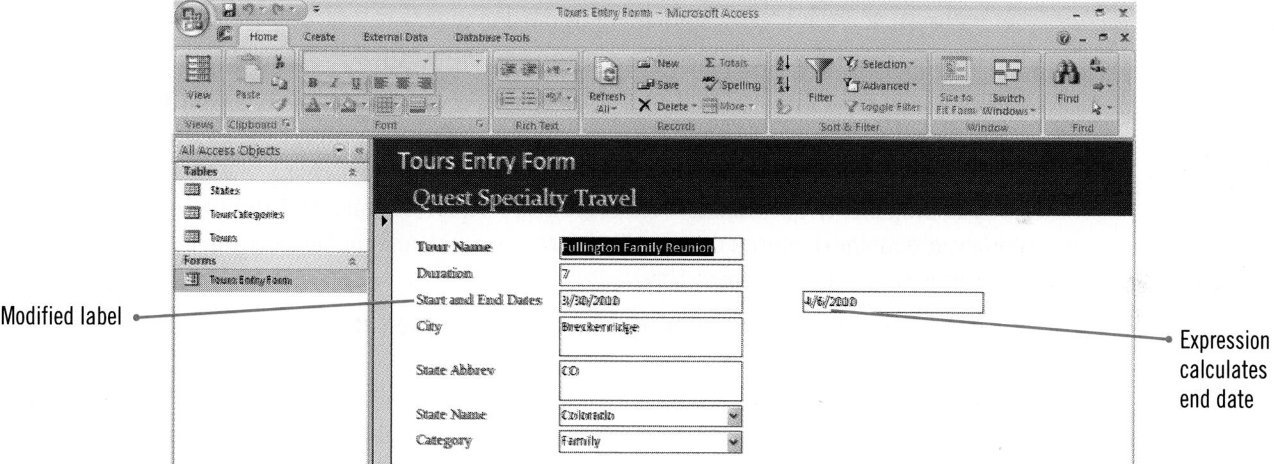

TABLE C-3: Selecting more than one control at a time

technique	description
Click, [Shift]+click	Click a control, then press and hold [Shift] while clicking other controls; each one is selected
Drag a selection box	Drag a selection box (an outline box you create by dragging the pointer in Form Design View); every control that is in or is touched by the edges of the box is selected
Click in the ruler	Click in either the horizontal or vertical ruler to select all controls that intersect the selection line
Drag in the ruler	Drag through either the horizontal or vertical ruler to select all controls that intersect the selection line as it is dragged through the ruler

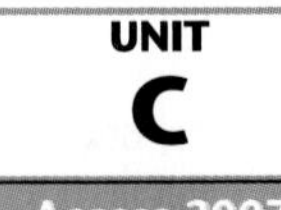

Modifying Tab Order

After positioning all of the controls on the form, you should check the tab order and tab stops. A **tab stop** in Access refers to whether you can tab into a control when entering or editing data, in other words, whether the control can receive the focus. Recall that focus refers to which field would be edited if you started typing. **Tab order** is the order the focus moves as you press [Tab] in Form View. Controls that cannot be bound to fields such as labels and lines cannot have the focus in Form View because they are not used to enter or edit data. By default, all text boxes and combo boxes have a tab stop and are placed in the tab order. You plan to check the tab order of the Tours Entry Form, then change tab stops and tab order as necessary in Design View.

STEPS

1. **Click Fullington in the Tour Name text box, then press [Tab] eight times, watching the focus move through the bound controls of the form**

   Currently, focus moves through the first column to the tour end date text box and then to the next record. Because the tour end date text box is a calculated field, you don't want it to receive the focus, as this date is automatically calculated based on the tour start date plus the duration. To remove the tour end date text box from receiving the focus, you remove its tab stop. You also review the tab order before and after this change to observe the difference.

> **TROUBLE**
> If the order of your fields does not match those in Figure C-13, move a field by clicking the row selector and then dragging the field.

2. **Click the View button arrow on the Home tab, click Design View, click the Arrange tab, click the Tab Order button, then click Detail in the Section box**

   The Tab Order dialog box allows you to change the tab order of controls by dragging the **row selector**, the box to the left of the field name, up or down. Text17 in Figure C-13 is the name of the text box you added that contains the expression. It can appear anywhere in the list, depending on how you added the field.

3. **Click Cancel, click the new text box with the expression to select it, click the Design tab, then click the Property Sheet button to open the Property Sheet**

   The Other tab of the Property Sheet contains the properties you need to change the tab stop and tab order. The **Tab Stop** property determines whether the field accepts focus, and the **Tab Index** property indicates the tab order for the control on the form. Therefore, you can change the tab order property in either the Tab Order dialog box or in the Property Sheet.

4. **Click the Other tab in the Property Sheet, then double-click the Tab Stop property to change the value from Yes to No**

   While working in this control's Property Sheet, you also decide to rename the text box from Text17 to something more descriptive so that when you reference this control, it also has a meaningful name.

> **TROUBLE**
> The name of the text box, Text17, might appear with a different number on your screen. The number identifies how many controls have been added to the form.

5. **Double-click Text17 in the Name property box, then type TourEndDate**

   Your form should look like Figure C-14. With the tab stop modified for the TourEndDate calculation, you're ready to test the new form.

> **QUICK TIP**
> In Form Design View, press [Ctrl][.] to switch to Form View. In Form View, press [Ctrl][,] to switch to Form Design View.

6. **Click the Form View button on the Design tab**
7. **Press [Tab] seven times, noticing that you no longer tab into the TourEndDate text box**
8. **Save the Tours Entry Form**

FIGURE C-13: Tab Order dialog box

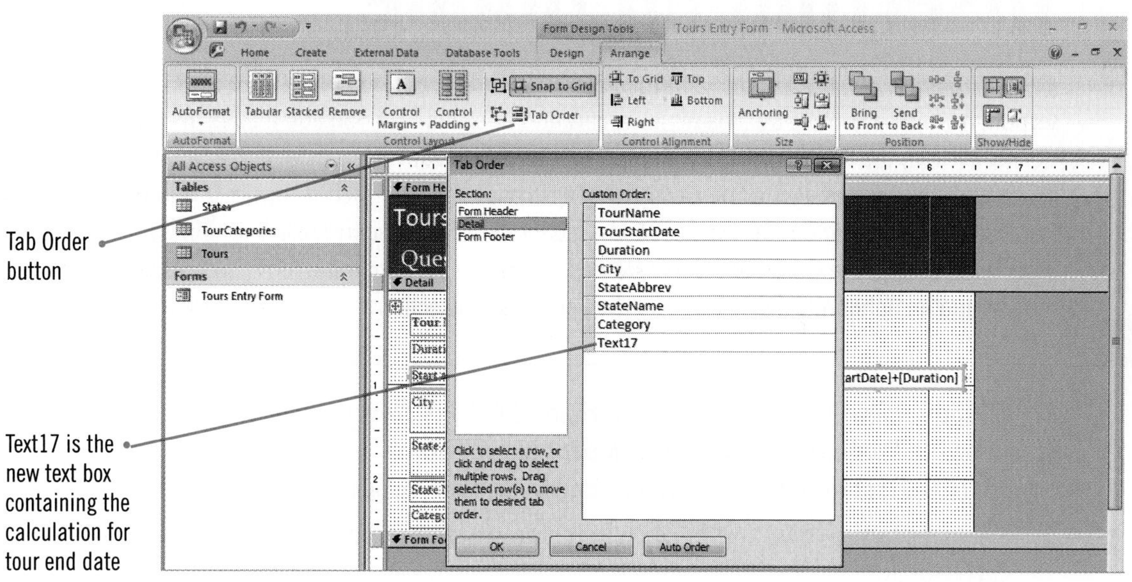

FIGURE C-14: Modifying tab properties for the selected field

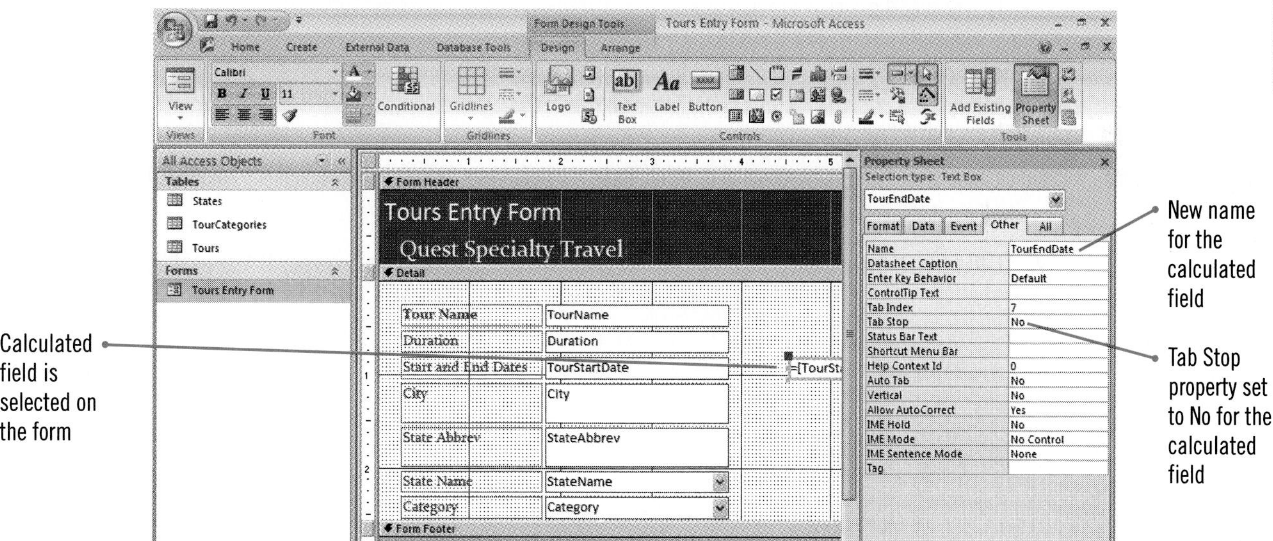

Inserting an Image

Graphic images, such as pictures, logos, or clip art, can add style and professionalism to a form. The form section in which you place the images is significant. For example, if you add a company logo to the Form Header section, the image appears at the top of the form in Form View as well as at the top of a printout. If you add the same image to the Detail section, it prints next to each record in a printout because the Detail section is printed for every record. Form sections are described in Table C-4. Mark Rock suggests that you add the Quest logo and a descriptive title to the top of the form. You plan to add the logo by inserting an unbound image control in the Form Header section.

STEPS

1. **Click the View button arrow on the Home tab, click Design View, click the Design tab, close the Property Sheet, then click the Logo button**

   The Insert Picture dialog box opens, prompting you for the location of the image.

2. **Navigate to the drive and folder where you store your Data Files, then double-click QSTLogo.jpg**

   The Quest logo image is added to the left side of the Form Header. You need to move it to the right so that the two labels are still clearly visible.

3. **With the Quest logo still selected, drag the logo to the right, so that the labels and logo in the Form Header section are clearly visible, then drag a sizing handle on the logo to display it clearly**

   The Quest logo is inserted into the Form Header in an image control, as shown in Figure C-15. Table C-5 summarizes other types of multimedia controls that you can add to a form. With the form completed, you open it in Form View to observe the changes.

4. **Click the Save button on the Quick Access toolbar, then click the Form View button on the Design tab**

   You decide to add one more record.

5. **Enter the new record shown in Figure C-16, using your name in the TourName field**

   Now print only this new record.

6. **Click the Office button, click Print, click the Selected Record(s) option button, then click OK**

7. **Close the Tours Entry Form, close the Quest-C.accdb database, then exit Access**

FIGURE C-15: Adding an image to the Form Header section

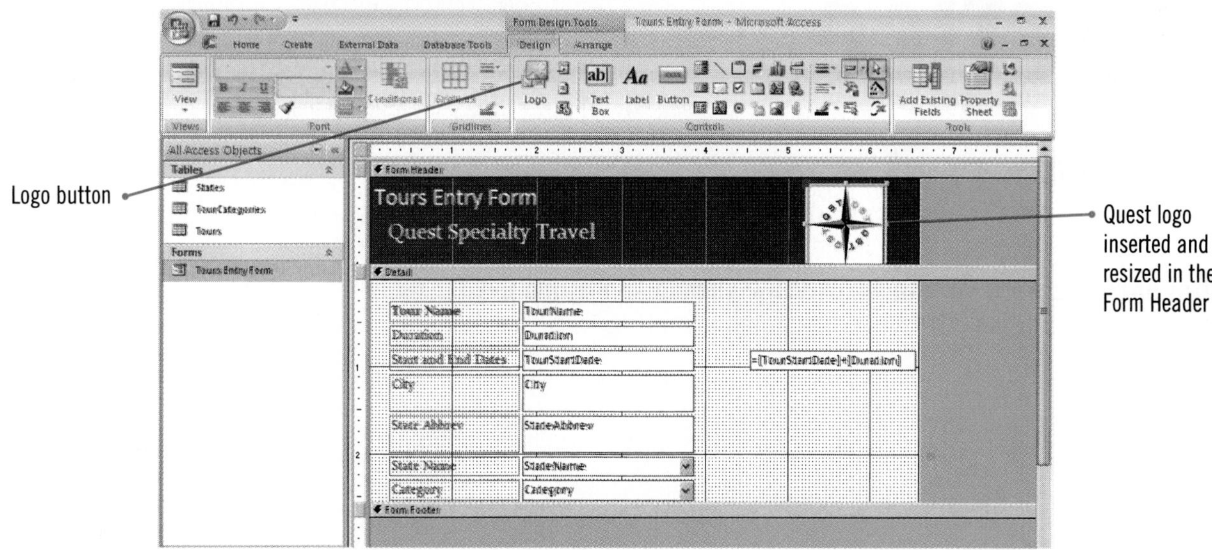

FIGURE C-16: Final Tours Entry Form

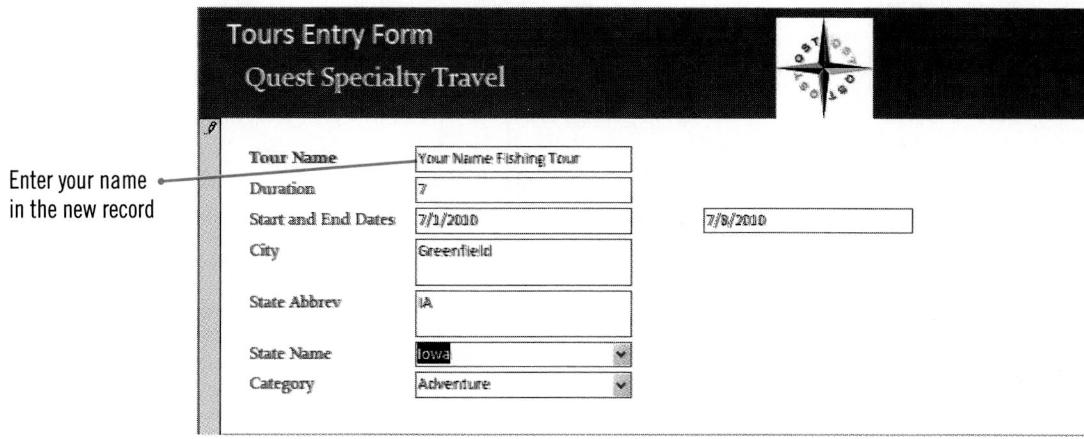

Access 2007

TABLE C-4: Form sections

section	description
Form Header	Controls placed in the Form Header section print only once at the top of the printout
Detail	Controls placed in the Detail section appear in Form View and print once for every record in the underlying table or query object
Form Footer	Controls placed in the Form Footer section print only once at the end of the printout

TABLE C-5: Multimedia controls

control	button	description
Image		Adds a single piece of clip art, a photo, or a logo to a form
Unbound object frame		Adds a sound clip, movie clip, document, or other type of unbound data (data that isn't stored in a table of the database) to a form
Bound object frame		Displays the contents of a field with an **OLE Object** (object linking and embedding) data type; an OLE Object field might contain pictures, sound clips, documents, or other data created by other software applications

Practice

If you have a SAM user profile, you may have access to hands-on instruction, practice, and assessment of the skills covered in this unit. Log in to your SAM account (http://sam2007.course.com/) to launch any assigned training activities or exams that relate to the skills covered in this unit.

▼ CONCEPTS REVIEW

Label each element of the Form View shown in Figure C-17.

FIGURE C-17

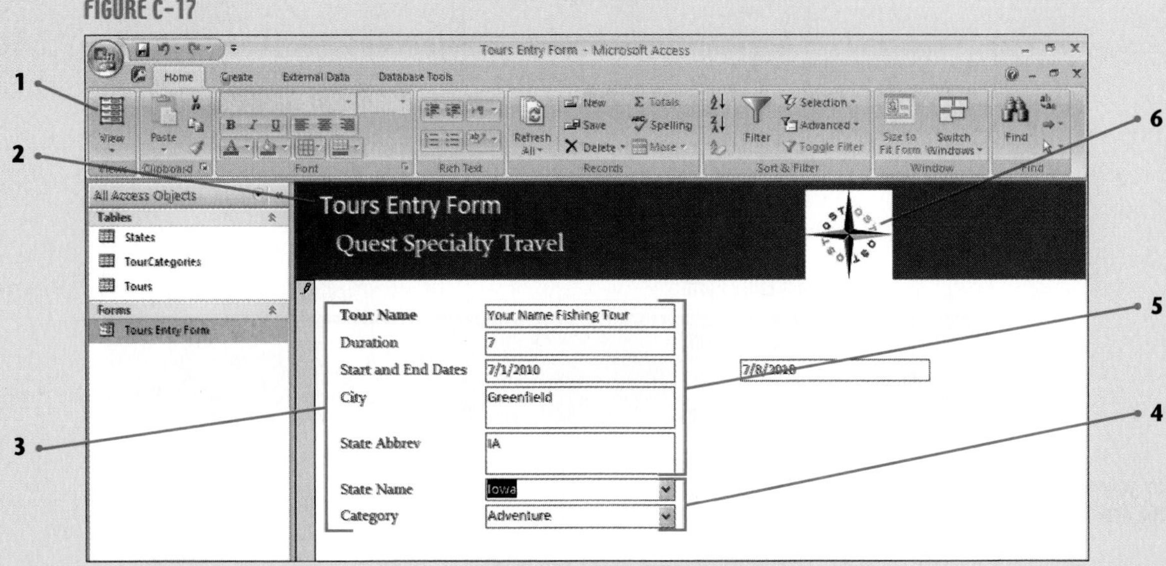

Match each term with the statement that best describes it.

7. Bound control
8. Calculated control
9. Detail section
10. Form
11. Tab order
12. Form Footer section

a. An Access database object that allows you to arrange the fields of a record in any layout and which is used to enter, edit, and delete records
b. The way the focus moves from one bound control to the next in Form View
c. Created by entering an expression in a text box
d. Controls placed here print once for every record in the underlying record source
e. Controls placed here print only once at the end of the printout
f. Used on a form to display data from a field

Select the best answer from the list of choices.

13. Every element on a form is called a(n):

a. Property.
b. Tool.
c. Item.
d. Control.

14. Which of the following is probably *not* a graphic image?

a. Logo
b. Calculation
c. Clip art
d. Picture

15. The most common bound control is the:

a. Text box.
b. List box.
c. Combo box.
d. Label.

16. The most common unbound control is the:

a. Command button.
b. Text box.
c. Label.
d. Combo box.

17. Which view *cannot* be used to view data?

a. Layout
b. Design
c. Preview
d. Datasheet

18. Which property helps you bind a text box to a field?

a. Control Source
b. Name
c. Bindings
d. Bound

19. When you enter a calculation in a text box, the first character is a(n):

a. Equal sign, =
b. Left parenthesis, (
c. Left square bracket, [
d. Asterisk, *

▼ SKILLS REVIEW

1. Create a form with the Form Wizard.

a. Start Access and open the **RealEstate-C.accdb** database from the drive and folder where you store your Data Files. Enable content if prompted.

b. Click the Create tab, then use the Form Wizard to create a form based on all of the fields in the Agents table. Use a Columnar layout and an Equity style. Title the form **Agent Entry Form**.

c. Add a new record with your name. Note that the AgentNo field is an AutoNumber field and automatically increments as you enter your first and last names. Enter your school's telephone number for the AgentPhone field value, and 4 as the AgencyNo field value.

2. Use Layout View.

a. Switch to Layout View.

b. Modify each of the labels in Layout View by adding a space between the words in the labels.

c. Modify the text color of the labels to be black.

d. Modify the font size of each label to be 14 points.

e. Save the form and view it in Form View.

3. Use Form Design View.

a. Open the Agent Entry Form in Design View.

b. Add a label with your name to the Form Header section, below the Agent Entry Form label.

c. Format both labels so that the font size is 22, the font color is white, and they are bold.

d. Resize the label with your name to display its complete text.

e. Position the labels so that the left edges are aligned and all text is clearly visible.

f. Save the form and view it in Form View.

4. Add fields to a form.

a. Open the form in Layout View.

b. Open the Field List window if it is not already displayed, then expand the field list for the Agencies table.

c. Drag the AgencyName field directly under the AgencyNo field on the form.

d. Delete the AgencyNo label and text box.

e. Modify the AgencyName: label to add a space between the words and to delete the colon.

f. Save the form and display it in Form View.

5. Modify form controls.

a. Open the form in Design View, then open the Property Sheet.

b. Change the order of the first three controls to **AgencyName**, **AgentLast**, and **AgentFirst** by using their Control Source properties. Change the Name property of the AgentLast text box to TemporaryName, change the Name property of the AgentFirst text box to AgentFirst, and then change the Name property of the AgentLast text box to AgentLast.

c. Change the text of the first three labels to Agency Name, Agent Last, and Agent First by using their Caption properties.

d. Save the form, then view it in Form View.

6. Create calculations.

a. Switch to Design View, then drag the top edge of the Form Footer down about 0.5 inch to make room for a new text box.

b. Add a text box to the Form Footer section, then delete the accompanying label.

c. Widen the text box to be almost as wide as the entire form, then enter the following expression into the text box, which will add the words "Agent information for" to the agent's first name, a space, and then the agent's last name.
="Agent information for "&[AgentFirst]&" "&[AgentLast]

d. Save the form, then view it in Form View.

▼ SKILLS REVIEW (CONTINUED)

7. Modify tab order.

a. Switch to Form Design View, then open the Property Sheet.

b. Select the new text box with the expression, change the Name property to **AgentInfo** and change the Tab Stop property to **No**.

c. Save the form and view it in Form View. Tab through the form to make sure that the tab order is sequential. Use the Tab Order button on the Arrange tab in Form Design View to modify tab order, if necessary.

8. Insert an image.

a. Switch to Form Design or Layout View, then close the Property Sheet.

b. Add the **house.jpg** image to the right side of the Form Header, then resize the image and labels as necessary.

c. Save, then display the form in Form View. It should look similar to Figure C-18. Display the record with your name in it, then print only that record.

d. Close the Agent Entry Form, close the RealEstate-C.accdb database, then exit Access.

FIGURE C-18

Access 2007

▼ INDEPENDENT CHALLENGE 1

As the office manager of a veterinary association, you need to create a data entry form for new veterinarians.

a. Start Access, then open the **Vet-C.accdb** database from the drive and folder where you store your Data Files. Enable content if prompted.

b. Using the Form Wizard, create a form that includes all the fields in the Vets table, using the Columnar layout and Solstice style. Title the form **Vet Entry Form**.

c. Add a record with your own name. Note that the VetNo field is an AutoNumber field and automatically increments. Add yourself to ClinicNo 1.

d. In Form Design View, add a label with your name to the Form Header, below the Vet Entry Form label, in a font color and size that is easily visible.

e. Right-align the text within the four labels in the Detail section so that they are closer to the text boxes they describe. (*Hint*: Use the Align Text Right button on the Design tab.)

f. Add the **dog.jpg** image to the Form Header section. Move and resize the image so that the entire image as well as both labels are clearly visible.

g. Save the form, then display it in Form View. Print only the record that includes your name, as shown in Figure C-19.

h. Close the Vet Entry Form, close the Vet-C.accdb database, then exit Access.

FIGURE C-19

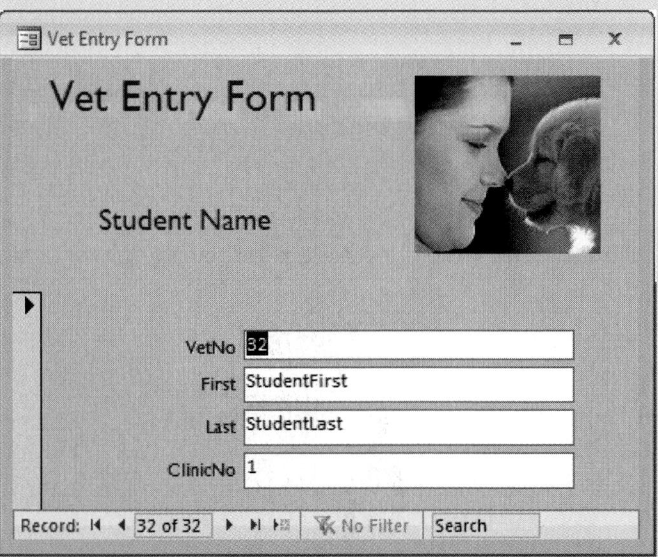

▼ INDEPENDENT CHALLENGE 2

You have built an Access database to track membership in a community service club. The database tracks member names and addresses as well as their status in the club, which moves from rank to rank as the members contribute increased hours of service to the community.

a. Start Access, then open the **Membership-C.accdb** database from the drive and folder where you store your Data Files. Enable content if prompted.

b. Using the Form Wizard, create a form based on all of the fields of the Members table and only the DuesOwed field in the Status table.

c. View the data by Members, use a Columnar layout and a Trek style, then title the form **Membership Entry Form**.

d. Enter a new record with your name and the address of your school. Give yourself a StatusNo entry of **1**. In the DuesPaid field, enter **75**. DuesOwed automatically displays 100 because that value is pulled from the Status table and is based on the entry in the StatusNo field, which links the Members table to the Status table.

e. In Design View, expand the Detail section down about 0.5 inches, then add a text box below DuesOwed with an expression that calculates the balance between DuesOwed and DuesPaid. Change the label for the calculated field to **Balance**.

f. Right-align all of the labels.

g. Set the Tab Stop property for the calculated field to **No**, and enter **Balance** for the Name property.

▼ INDEPENDENT CHALLENGE 2 (CONTINUED)

Advanced Challenge Exercise

- Drag the top edge of the Form Footer down about 0.5 inch to make more room for the form's Detail section.
- Open the field list, then drag the Status field from the Status table in the field list to below the Balance field in the form. Edit the label to delete the colon (:).
- Check the tab order to make sure that the fields receive focus in a logical order.
- If the calculated field or Status text boxes or labels aren't sized or aligned similarly to the rest of the controls on the form, return to Layout or Design View to resize and align them. (*Hint*: Use the Size to Widest button on the Arrange tab to size several selected controls to the widest selection. Use the Align Left and Align Right buttons on the Arrange tab to align the edges of several selected controls.)
- View the form in Form View. It should look like Figure C-20.

h. Save the form, find the record with your name, then print only that record.

i. Close the Membership Entry Form, then close the Membership-C.accdb database and exit Access.

FIGURE C-20

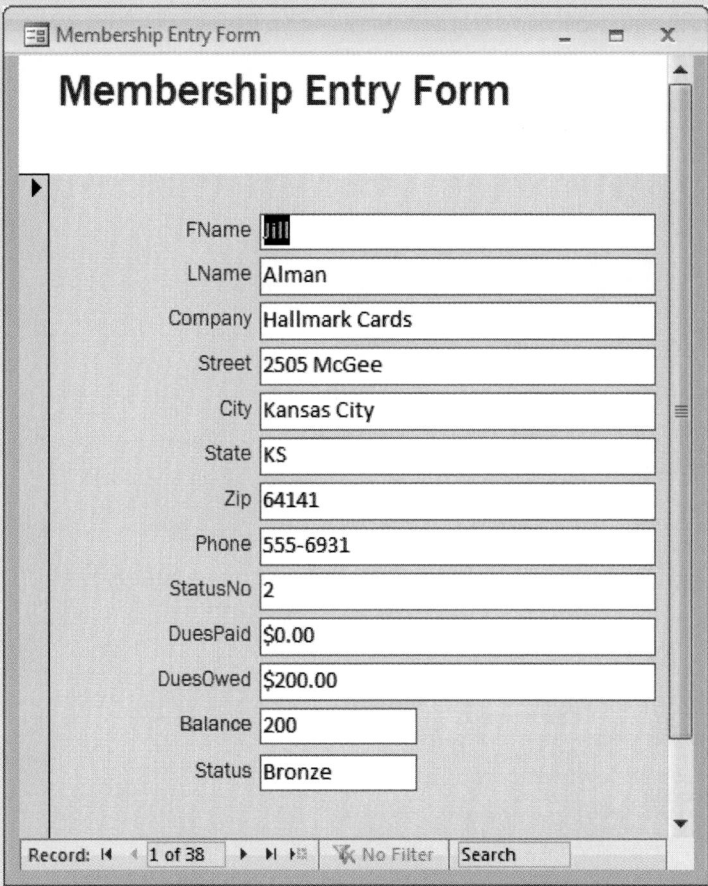

Access 2007

▼ INDEPENDENT CHALLENGE 3

You have built an Access database to organize the deposits at a recycling center. Various clubs regularly deposit recyclable material, which is measured in pounds when the deposits are made.

a. Open the **Recycle-C.accdb** database from the drive and folder where you store your Data Files. Enable content if prompted.

b. Using the Form Wizard, create a form based on all of the fields in the DepositList query. Use the Tabular layout and Urban style, then enter **Deposit List Form** as the title.

c. Bold each label. Resize the labels and text boxes to be sure they are all wide enough to accommodate all entries in the fields and display the entire label at the top of each column.

d. Modify the Centers_Name and Clubs_Name labels so they read Center Name and Club Name.

e. Continue to work in Layout View to drag the bottom edge of the text boxes up, so that they are tall enough to accommodate all of the entries, as shown in Figure C-21, but do not waste any vertical space.

f. In Form View, change any entry of Jaycees in the Clubs Name to your last name, then print the first page of the form.

Advanced Challenge Exercise

- Using Form View of the Deposit List Form, filter for all records with your name in the Clubs Name field.
- Using Form View of the Deposit List Form, sort the filtered records in ascending order on the Deposit Date field.
- Preview, then print the filtered and sorted records.

g. Save and close the Deposit List Form, close the Recycle-C.accdb database, then exit Access.

FIGURE C-21

▼ REAL LIFE INDEPENDENT CHALLENGE

One way you can use an Access database on your own is to record and track your experiences, such as places you've visited. Suppose that your passion for travel includes a dream to visit all 50 states. A database with information about all 50 states is provided with your Data Files, and you can use it to develop a form to help you enter more travel information.

This Independent Challenge requires an Internet connection.

- **a.** Start Access and open the **States-C.accdb** database from the drive and folder where you store your Data Files. Enable content if prompted.
- **b.** Open the States table datasheet to view the existing information on each state.
- **c.** Add a field to the States table with the name **Attractions** and a data type of Memo.
- **d.** Create a form based on all of the fields of the States table. Title the form **State Entry Form**.
- **e.** Using any search engine such as *www.google.com* or *www.yahoo.com*, research two states that you'd like to visit.
- **f.** Make entries in the Attractions field of each of your two selected states to store information about the attractions that you'd like to visit in each of those states.
- **g.** Make any other formatting embellishments on the State Entry Form that you desire, then print the record for each of the two states that you updated with information in the Attractions field.
- **h.** Save and close the State Entry Form, close the States-C.accdb database, then exit Access.

▼ VISUAL WORKSHOP

Open the **Basketball-C.accdb** database, then use the Form Wizard to create the form as shown in Figure C-22 based on all of the fields in the Games table. Use a Columnar layout and a Foundry style. The label in the Form Header, Basketball Scores, is a font size of 22. The Margin of Victory label and calculation were added in Form Design View. The margin of victory is calculated as the Home Score minus the Opponent Score. Also notice that the labels are right-aligned. Enter the record shown in Figure C-22, using your name as the name of the school. Print only that record.

FIGURE C-22

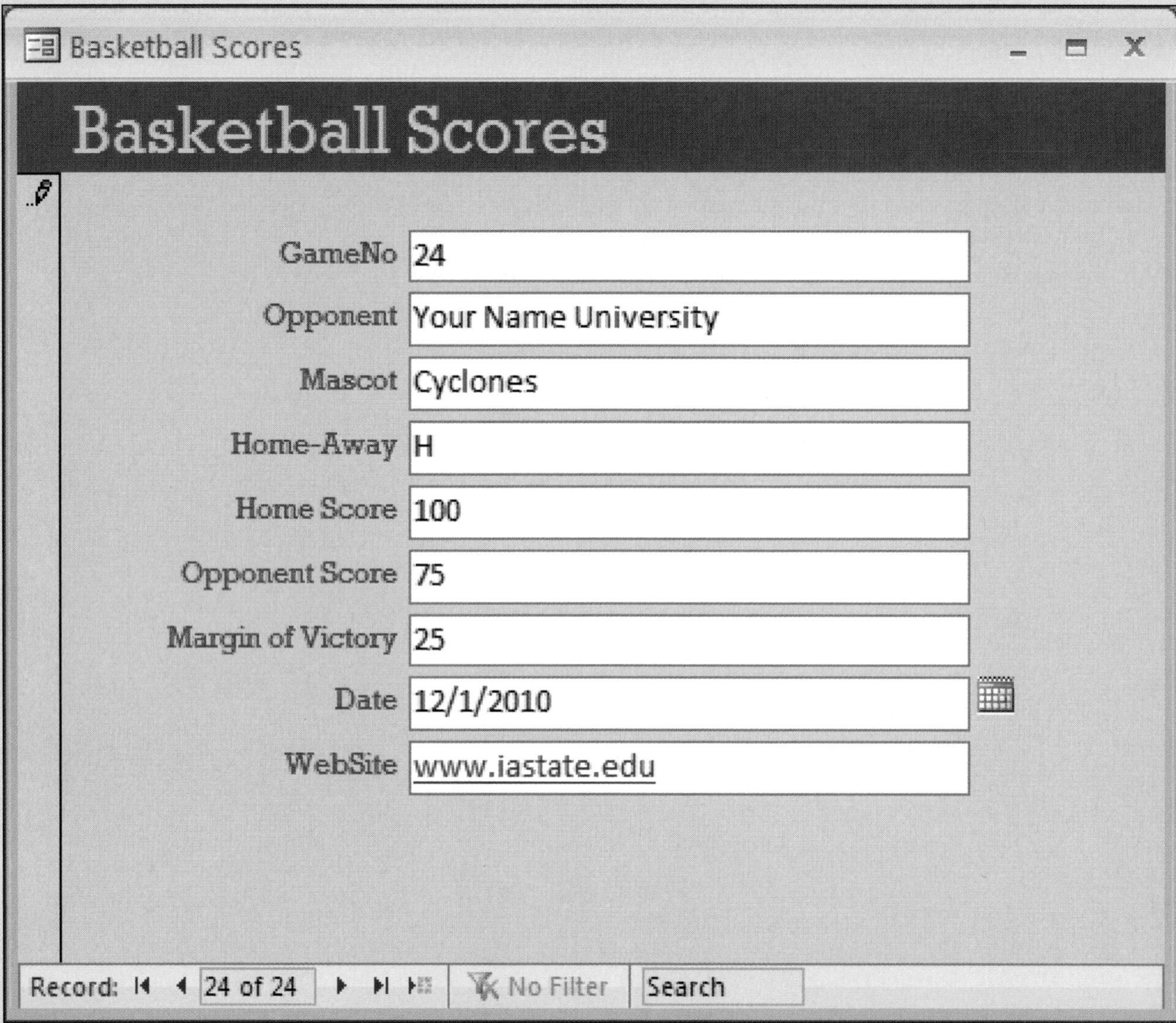

UNIT

D

Access 2007

Using Reports

Files You Will Need:

Quest-D.accdb

RealEstate-D.accdb

Vet-D.accdb

Membership-D.accdb

Recycle-D.accdb

States-D.accdb

Basketball-D.accdb

A **report** is an Access object used to create professional-looking printouts. Although you can print a datasheet or form, reports are the primary object you use to print database content because they provide many more data layout options. For example, a report might include formatting embellishments such as multiple fonts and colors, extra graphical elements such as clip art and lines, and multiple headers and footers. Reports are also very powerful data analysis tools. A report can calculate subtotals, averages, counts, or other statistics for groups of records. However, you cannot enter or edit data through a report. Mark Rock, a tour developer at Quest Specialty Travel, asks you to produce some reports to analyze data for Quest meetings.

OBJECTIVES

- Preview a report
- Use the Report Wizard
- Use Report Design View
- Use report sections
- Add subtotals and counts
- Resize and align controls
- Format a report
- Change page layout

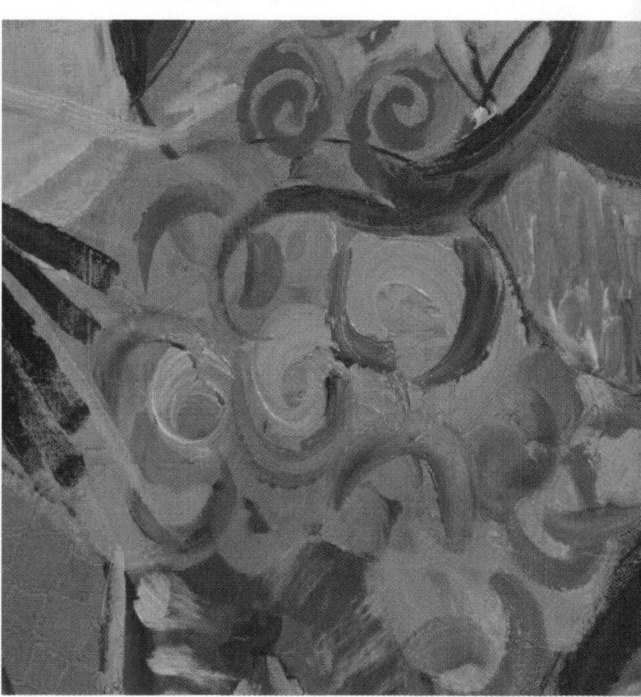

UNIT
D
Access 2007

Previewing a Report

When you want to communicate Access information at internal meetings or with customers, the report object helps you professionally format and summarize the data. Creating a report is similar to creating a form—you work with bound, unbound, and calculated controls in Report Design View just as you do in Form Design View. Reports, however, have more sections than forms. A **section** determines where and how often controls in that section print in the final report. Table D-1 shows more information on report sections. You and Mark Rock preview a completed report that illustrates many features of Access reports.

STEPS

1. **Start Access, open the Quest-D.accdb database, then enable content if prompted**
   The Quest-D database already contains two reports named Tour Descriptions and Tours By Category. You'll open the Tours By Category report in **Report View**, a view that maximizes the amount of data you can see on the screen.

TROUBLE
If you do not see any reports in the Navigation Pane, click the Reports button in the Navigation Pane.

2. **Double-click the Tours By Category report in the Navigation Pane, then double-click the title bar of the report to maximize it**
   The Tours By Category report appears in Report View, as shown in Figure D-1. The Tours By Category report shows all of the tours for each state within each category. In the Adventure category, four tours are in California and five tours are in Colorado.
3. **Double-click California in the State column, then attempt to type Oregon**
   Reports are **read-only** objects, meaning that they read and display data, but cannot be used to change (write to) data. Like forms, a report always displays the most up-to-date data that is stored in only one type of Access object, tables. Switching to **Print Preview** shows you how the report prints on a sheet of paper.
4. **Click the View button arrow on the Home tab, then click Print Preview**
   Print Preview shows you the report as it appears on a full sheet of paper, including margins. You can zoom in and out to increase or decrease the magnification of the image by clicking the report.
5. **Click the report once to view an entire sheet of paper, then click the Next Page button on the navigation bar to advance to the second page of the report**
   The second page of the Tours By Category report appears in Print Preview, as shown in Figure D-2. On the second page, you can clearly see how the records are grouped together by the value in the Category field, then by State, and finally sorted in ascending order on the Start Date field.
6. **Click the Close Print Preview button, then close the Tours By Category report**

FIGURE D-1: Tours By Category report in Report View

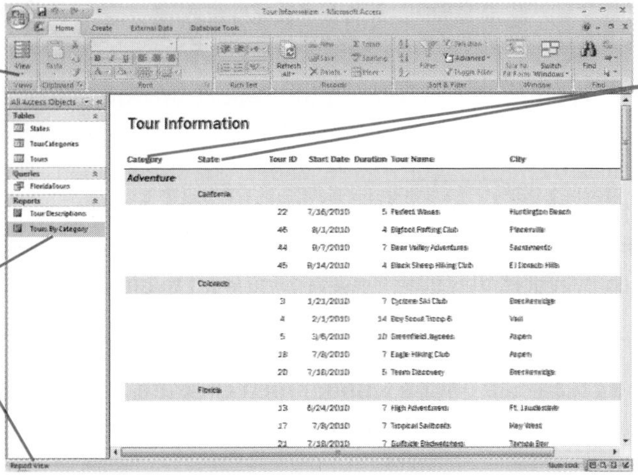

FIGURE D-2: Second page of the Tours By Category report in Print Preview

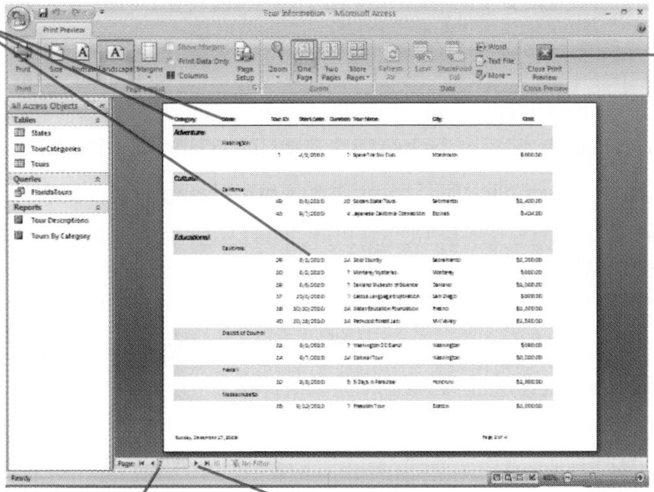

TABLE D-1: Report sections

section	where does this section print?	which controls are most commonly placed in this section?
Report Header	At the top of the first page of the report	Label controls containing the report title; can also include clip art, a logo image, or a line separating the title from the rest of the report
Page Header	At the top of every page (but below the Report Header on page one)	Text box controls containing a page number or date expression
Group Header	Before every group of records	Text box controls for the field by which the records are grouped
Detail	Once for every record	Text box controls for the rest of the fields in the recordset (the table or query upon which the report is built)
Group Footer	After every group of records	Text box controls containing calculated expressions, such as subtotals or counts, for the records in that group
Page Footer	At the bottom of every page	Text box controls containing a page number or date expression
Report Footer	At the end of the entire report	Text box controls containing expressions such as grand totals or counts that calculate a value for all of the records in the report

UNIT
D
Access 2007

Using the Report Wizard

You can create reports in Access by using the **Report Wizard**, a tool that asks questions to guide you through the initial development of the report, similar to the Form Wizard. Your responses to the Report Wizard determine the record source, style, and layout of the report. The **record source** is the table or query that defines the fields and records displayed on the report. The Report Wizard also helps you sort, group, and analyze the records. You plan to use the Report Wizard to create a report similar to the Tours By Category report. This time, however, you want to group the tours by state.

STEPS

1. **Click the Create tab on the Ribbon, then click the Report Wizard button**
   The Report Wizard starts, prompting you to select the fields you want on the report. You can select fields from one or more tables or queries.
2. **Click the Tables/Queries list arrow, click Table: States, double-click the StateName field, click the Tables/Queries list arrow, click Table: Tours, click the Select All Fields button [>>], click StateAbbrev in the Selected Fields list, then click the Remove Field button [<]**
   By selecting the StateName field from the States table, and all fields from the Tours table except the StateAbbrev field, you have all of the fields you need for the report—including the full state name stored in the States table, instead of the two-letter state abbreviation used in the Tours table—as shown in Figure D-3.
3. **Click Next, then click by States if it is not already selected**
   Choosing "by States" groups the records together within each state. In addition to record-grouping options, the Report Wizard asks if you want to sort the records within each group. You can use the Report Wizard to specify up to four fields to sort in either ascending or descending order.

> **TROUBLE**
> Click Back to review previous dialog boxes within a wizard.

4. **Click Next, click Next again to add no grouping levels, click the first sort list arrow, click TourName, then click Next**
   The last questions in the wizard deal with report appearance and creating a report title.

> **TROUBLE**
> Depending on how you installed Access 2007, the appearance of your report might differ slightly.

5. **Click the Stepped option button, click the Portrait option button, click Next, click the Apex style, click Next, type Tours By State for the report title, click Finish, then maximize the Print Preview window**
   The Tours By State report opens in Print Preview, as shown in Figure D-4. The records are grouped by state, the first state being California, and then sorted in ascending order by the TourName field within each state.
6. **Scroll down to see the second grouping section on the report for the state of Colorado, click the Close Print Preview button on the Print Preview tab, then save and close the report**
   Closing Print Preview displays the report in either Report View, Layout View, or Design View, depending upon which view you used last.

FIGURE D-3: Selecting fields for a report using the Report Wizard

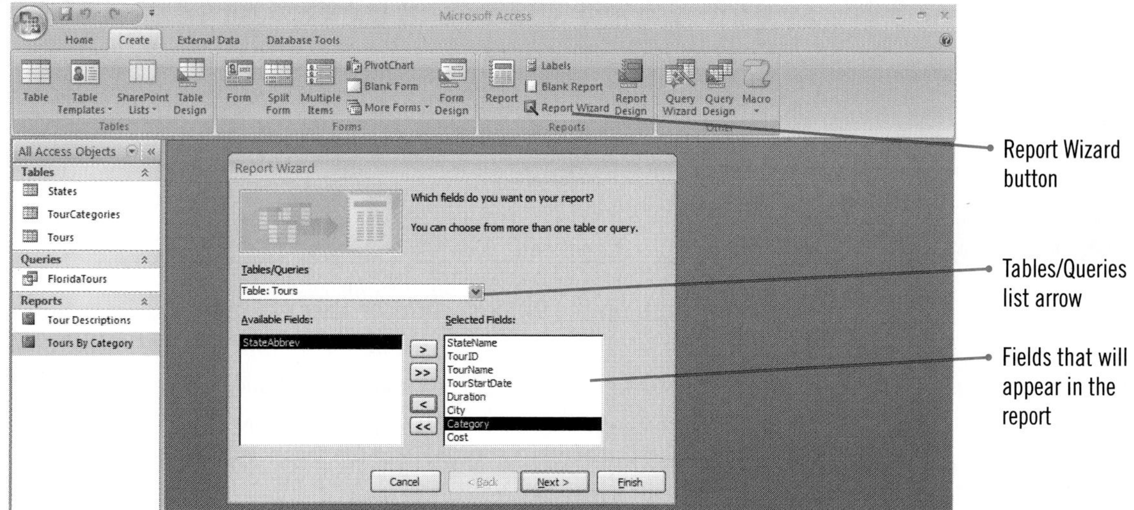

FIGURE D-4: Tours By State report in Print Preview

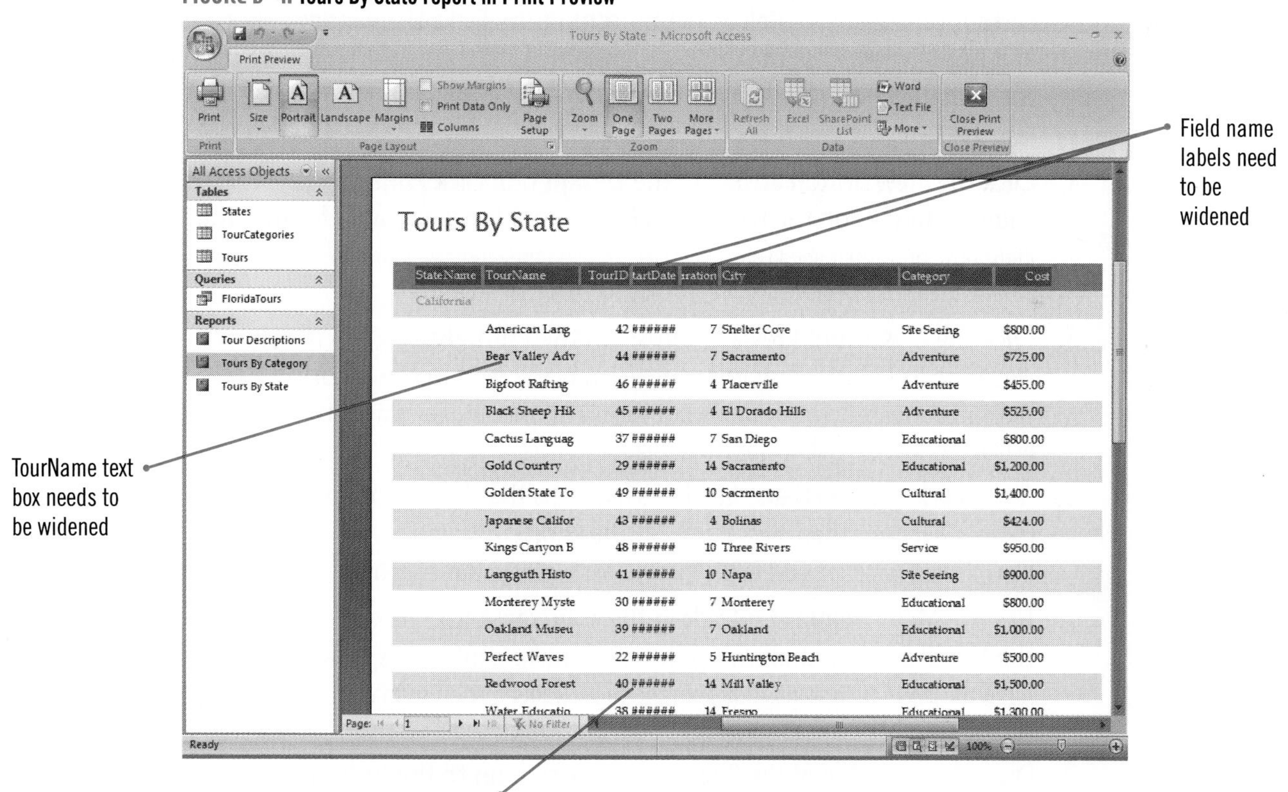

Using Report Design View

Like forms, reports have multiple views—including Report View, Layout View, Design View, and Print Preview—that you can use for various activities. Design View is the most complicated view because it allows you to make the most changes to the report. Mark Rock asks you to create a new report that lists all of the tours from Florida.

STEPS

1. **Click the Create tab on the Ribbon, click the Report Design button, then maximize the window**

   Design View opens with a blank report design surface. When building a report from scratch in Report Design View, the first task is to select the object (table or query) on which to base the report. The **Record Source** property of the report determines the object that the report is based on, which provides the fields and records displayed on the report.

2. **Click the Property Sheet button on the Design tab, click the Data tab, click the Record Source list arrow, then click FloridaTours**

   The FloridaTours query contains all of the fields in the Tours table as well as criteria to select only those records from the state of Florida. By choosing this query for the Record Source property, the report will display only Florida tours. Now add the fields from the FloridaTours query to the report.

3. **Click the Add Existing Fields button on the Design tab, click the Show only fields in the current record source link at the bottom of the Field List window, click TourName, press and hold [Shift], click the Cost field, release [Shift], then drag the fields to the middle of the Detail section**

   Report Design View should look similar to Figure D-5.

4. **Click the View button arrow on the Design tab, click Print Preview, then click the Next Page button ▶ on the navigation bar several times to page through the report**

   Right now, only one record prints per page, making the report very long. You can return to Design View and modify the report to make it more compact.

5. **Click the Close Print Preview button on the Print Preview tab to return to Design View, close the Field List window, then click a blank spot in the report**

   You can save space by arranging the fields across the page in a row (instead of in a vertical column), with the field labels appearing above the text boxes.

6. **Right-click the TourName label, click Cut on the shortcut menu, right-click the Page Header section, then click Paste on the shortcut menu**

   Moving the TourName label to the Page Header section means it prints once per page.

7. **Use the Move pointer ✥ to drag the TourName text box under the TourName label in the Detail section, then cut, paste, and move controls as shown in Figure D-6**

   All of the labels are now positioned in the Page Header section so that they appear only once per page, and all of the text box controls are positioned in the Detail section.

8. **Drag the top edge of the Page Footer section up to the bottom edge of the text boxes, click the Save button on the Quick Access toolbar, type Tours In Florida, click OK, click the View button arrow on the Design tab, then click Print Preview**

   Because the Detail section prints once per record, eliminating blank space in this section removes extra blank space in the report overall.

9. **Click the Close Print Preview button on the Print Preview tab, then close the Tours In Florida report**

FIGURE D-5: Adding fields to Report Design View

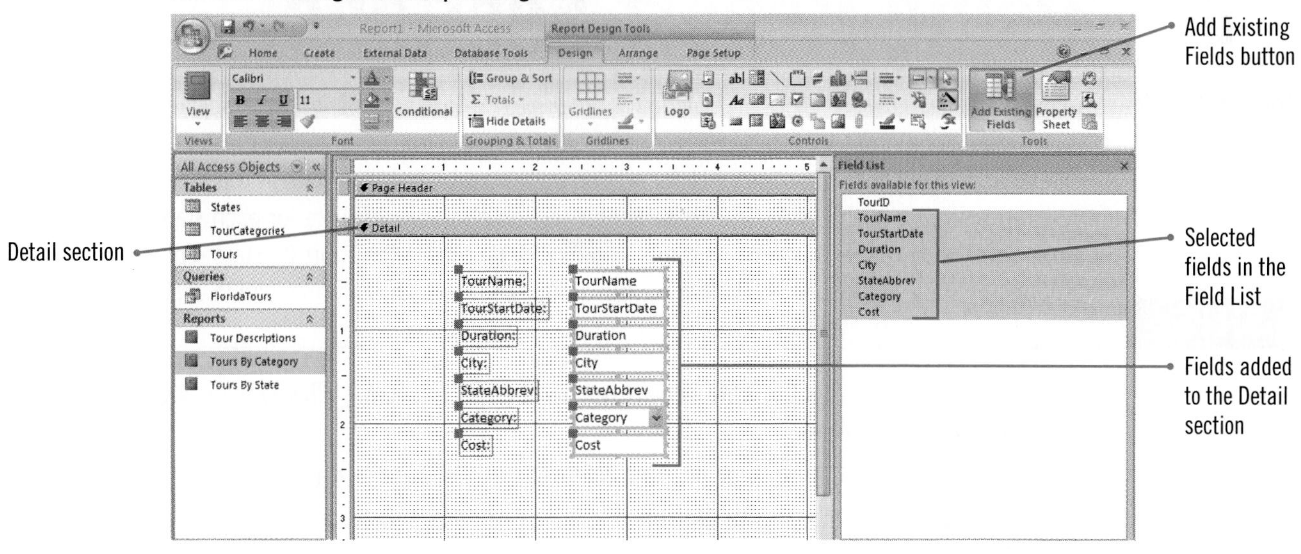

FIGURE D-6: Redesigning a report in Report Design View

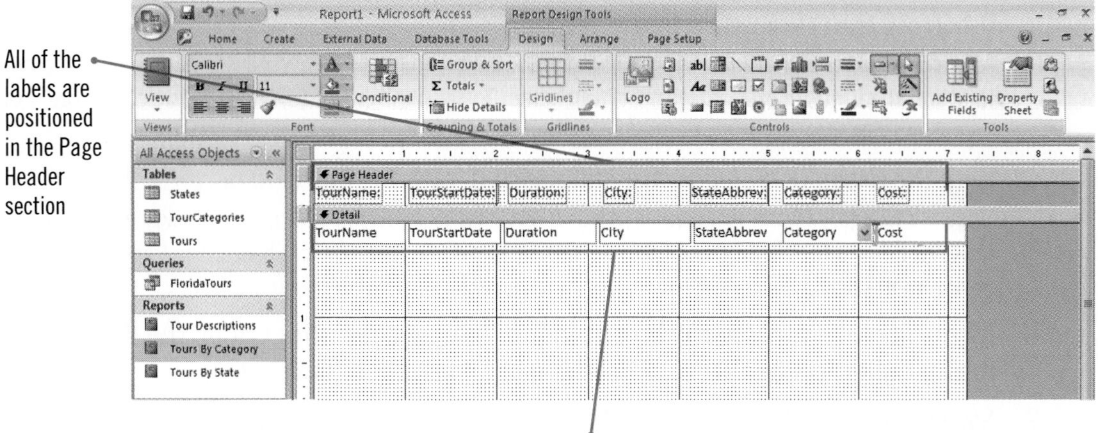

Access 2007

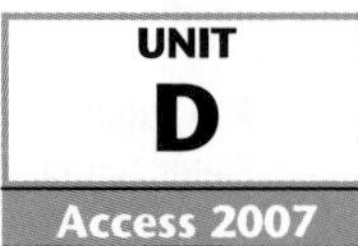

Using Report Sections

Grouping means to sort records in a particular order *plus* provide a header or footer section before or after each group. For example, if you group records by the State field, the grouping sections are called the State Header and State Footer. The State Header section appears once for each state in the report, immediately before the records in that state. The State Footer section also appears once for each state in the report, immediately after the records for that state. The records in the Tours By State report are currently grouped by state. Mark Rock asks you to further group the records by category within each state.

STEPS

1. **Right-click the Tours By State report in the Navigation Pane, click Design View, then maximize the report**

   To change sorting or grouping options for a report, you need to work in Report Design View.

2. **Click the Design tab on the Ribbon if it is not already selected, then click the Group & Sort button**

   The Group, Sort, and Total pane opens, as shown in Figure D-7. Currently, the records are grouped by the StateAbbreviation field and further sorted by the TourName field. To add the Category field as a grouping field within each state, you work with the Group, Sort, and Total pane.

3. **Click the Add a group button in the Group, Sort, and Total pane; click the select field list arrow if the field list window doesn't automatically appear; then click Category**

   A Category Header section appears on the report. In addition to grouping the records by both the StateAbbreviation and Category fields, you want to count the number of records in each group later so that, as an example, you can find out how many Adventure tours are in California. You open the Category Footer section and then add an expression to calculate this information to the Category Footer section.

4. **Click the More button on the Group on Category bar, click the without a footer section list arrow, then click with a footer section**

   A Category Footer section is added to the report. You want to group the records by state, then category, and then sort them within each category by TourName. To accomplish this you need to switch the order of the TourName and Category fields in the Group, Sort, and Total pane.

5. **With the Group on Category bar still selected, click the Move up button**

   With the Category Header and Footer sections open and in correct position, you're ready to add controls to those sections to further enhance the report. First, move the Category text box to the Category Header section so that it displays once per new category, rather than once for every record.

6. **Right-click the Category combo box in the Detail section, click Cut on the shortcut menu, right-click the Category Header section bar, then click Paste**

7. **Save the report, click the View button arrow, then click Print Preview**

   The Tours By State report should look similar to Figure D-8. Notice that the values in the Category field now appear once per category, before the records in each category are listed.

FIGURE D-7: Group, Sort, and Total pane

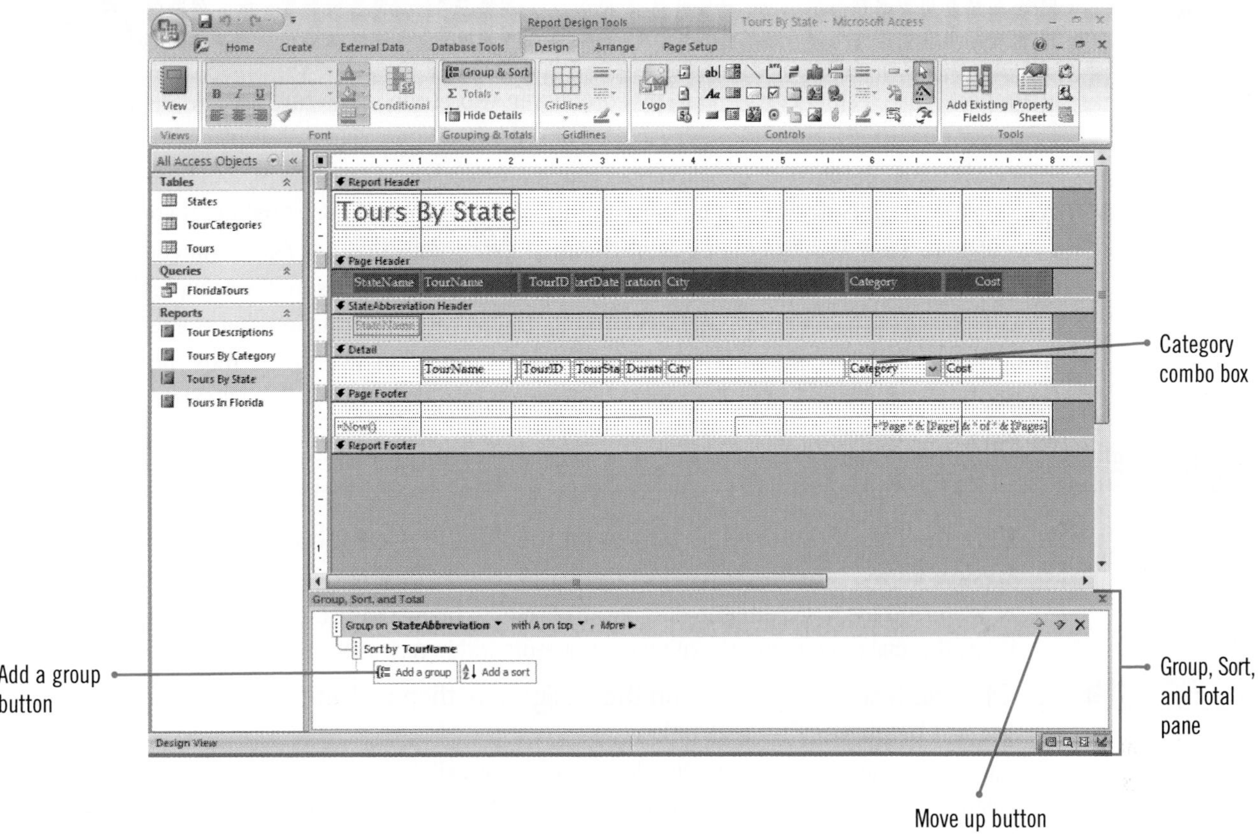

FIGURE D-8: Tours By State report with Category Header and Footer sections

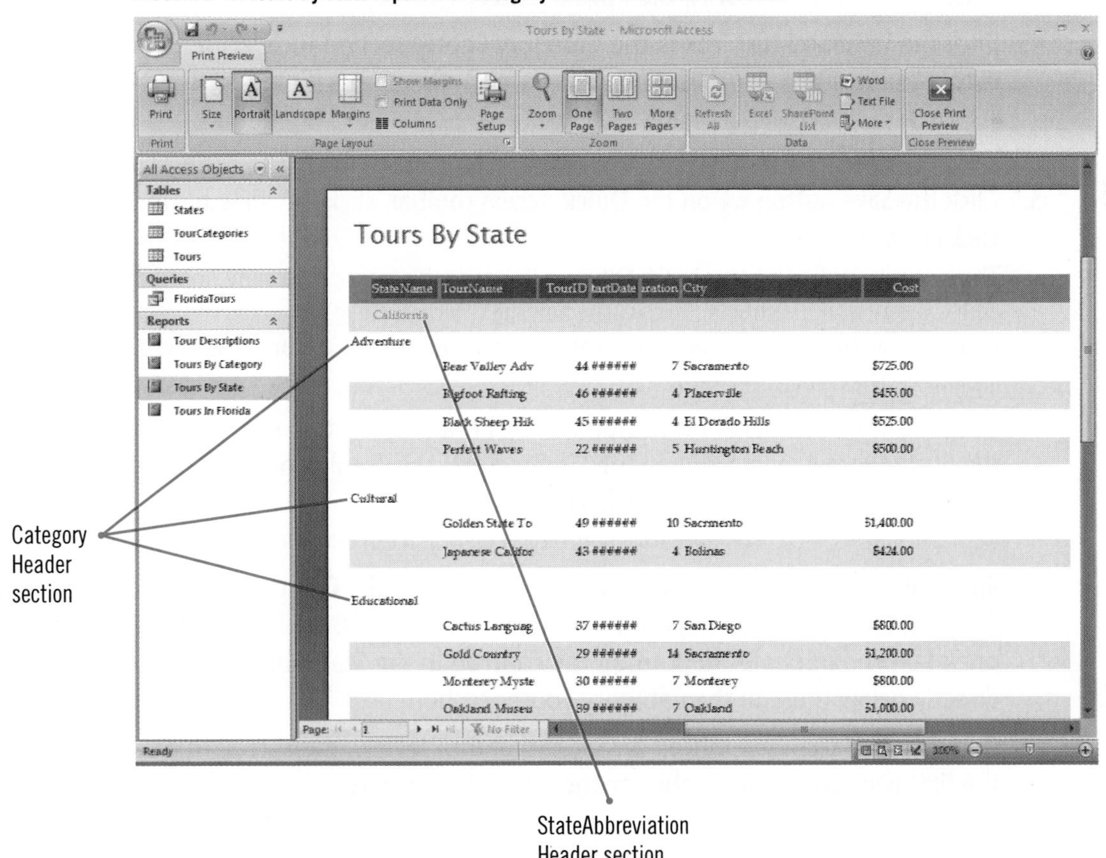

Access 2007

UNIT
D
Access 2007

Adding Subtotals and Counts

In a report, you create a **calculation** by entering an expression into a text box. When a report is previewed or printed, the expression is evaluated and the resulting calculation is placed on the report. An **expression** is a combination of field names, operators (such as +, –, /, and *), and functions that result in a single value. A **function** is a built-in formula, such as Sum or Count, that helps you quickly create a calculation. Table D-2 lists examples of common expressions that use Access functions. Notice that every expression starts with an equal sign (=), and when it uses a function, the arguments for the function are placed in (parentheses). **Arguments** are the pieces of information that the function needs to create the final answer. When an argument is a field name, the field name must be surrounded by [square brackets]. Mark Rock asks you to add a calculation to the Tours By State report to count the number of records in each category within each state.

STEPS

1. **Click the Close Print Preview button on the Print Preview tab to return to Report Design View**

   Now you can add two controls to the Category Footer section—a label and a text box—to describe and calculate the total count of records within each category within each state.

2. **Click the Text Box button on the Design tab, then click in the Category Footer section below the City text box**

   Adding a new text box automatically adds a new label as well. First, you modify the label to identify the calculation you want to add to the text box, then you enter the appropriate expression to count the records in the text box.

3. **Click the new Text19 label to select the label, double-click the Text19 entry to select the text, type Count of records, then press [Enter]**

4. **Click the Unbound text box in the Category Footer section to select it, click Unbound within the text box, type =Count([TourName]), then press [Enter]**

   The Count function counts the values in the TourName field, as shown in Figure D-9. To add numeric values in a Number or Currency field, you use the Sum function, as in =Sum([Price]).

5. **Click the Save button on the Quick Access toolbar, click the View button arrow, then click Print Preview**

   The new label and calculation in the Category Footer section correctly identify how many records are in each category within each state. To calculate how many records are in each state, you can copy the controls from the Category Footer section to the StateAbbreviation Footer section. First, you need to open the StateAbbreviation Footer section.

6. **Click the Close Print Preview button on the Print Preview tab; click the More button for the StateAbbreviation group in the Group, Sort, and Total pane; click the without a footer section list arrow; then click with a footer section**

   With the State Footer section open in Report Design View, you can now add controls to this section.

7. **Right-click the text box with the Count expression in the Category Footer section, click Copy on the shortcut menu, right-click the StateAbbreviation Footer, click Paste, then press [→] enough times to position the controls in the StateAbbreviation Footer section directly below those in the Category Footer section**

8. **Click, click the View button arrow, click Print Preview, then scroll to the bottom of the first page to see the footer for the state of California**

   As shown in Figure D-10, 16 records were counted for the California group, but some of the data is not displayed correctly. You widen and align controls in the next lesson.

QUICK TIP

To add only a descriptive label to the report, use the Label button on the Design tab.

TROUBLE

Depending on your activity in Report Design View, you may get a different number in the Text##: label. The number corresponds to the number of controls that have been added to this report.

TROUBLE

Click the Next Page button to view page 2 if the footer for the state of California doesn't appear at the bottom of page 1.

FIGURE D-9: Counting records in the Category Footer

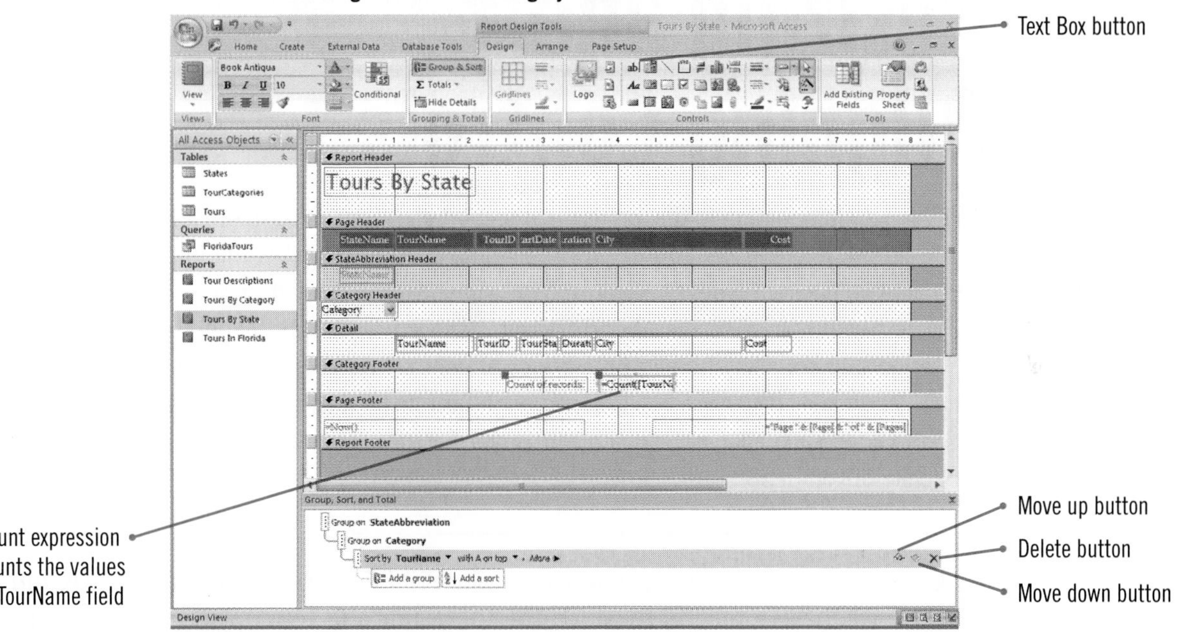

FIGURE D-10: Previewing the new group footer calculations

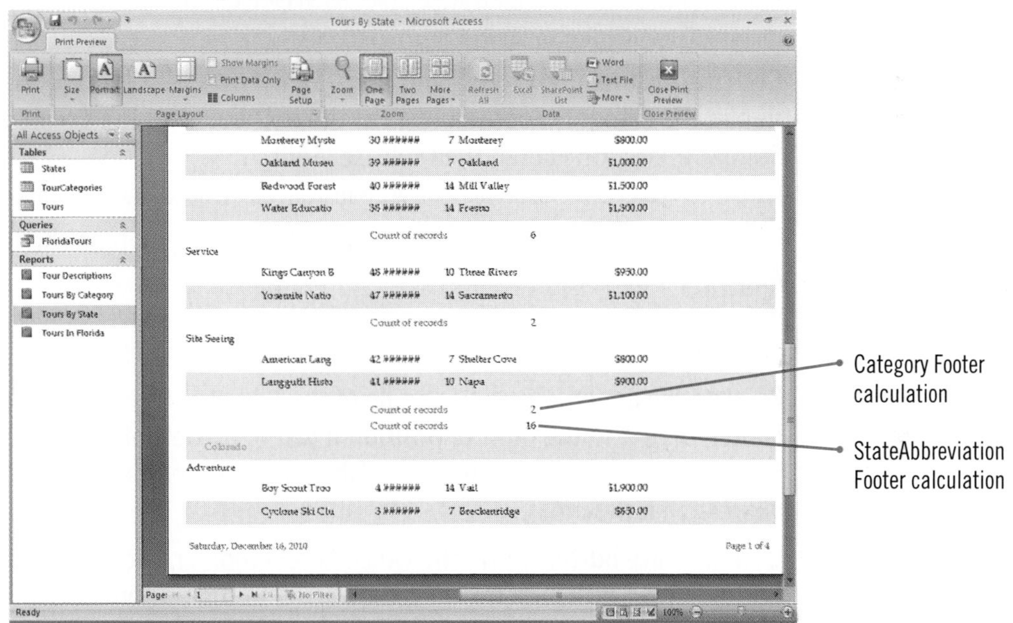

Access 2007

TABLE D-2: Sample Access expressions

sample expression	description
=Sum([Salary])	Uses the **Sum function** to add up the values in the Salary field
=[Price] * 1.05	Multiplies the Price field by 1.05 (adds 5% to the Price field)
=[Subtotal] + [Shipping]	Adds the value of the Subtotal field to the value of the Shipping field
=Avg([Freight])	Uses the **Avg function** to display an average of the values in the Freight field
=Date()	Uses the **Date function** to display the current date in the form of mm-dd-yy
="Page " &[Page]	Displays the word Page, a space, and the result of the [Page] field, an Access field that contains the current page number
=[FirstName]& " " &[LastName]	Displays the value of the FirstName and LastName fields in one control, separated by a space
=Left([ProductNumber],2)	Uses the **Left function** to display the first two characters in the ProductNumber field

UNIT
D
Access 2007

Resizing and Aligning Controls

After you add information to the appropriate section of a report, you might also want to align the data on the report. Aligning controls in precise columns and rows makes the information easier to read. There are two different types of **alignment** commands. You can left-, right-, or center-align a control *within its own border* using the Align Text Left, Center, and Align Text Right buttons on the Design tab. You can also align the edges of controls *with respect to one another* using the Align Left, Align Right, Align Top, and Align Bottom buttons on the Arrange tab. You decide to widen and align several controls in the Category and State Footer sections to improve the readability of your report.

STEPS

TROUBLE

If you make a mistake, click the Undo button on the Quick Access toolbar.

TROUBLE

Be sure to select the text boxes that contain expressions, and not the labels.

QUICK TIP

You can also click or drag through the horizontal or vertical rulers to select all controls that intersect with the selection line.

TROUBLE

If the entire state name is not displayed, return to Report Design View and widen the StateName field in the StateAbbreviation Header section.

1. **Click the Close Print Preview button on the Print Preview tab to return to Design View, then use the ⟷ pointer to widen the TourName and TourStartDate fields as shown in Figure D-11**

   When you add, move, or resize controls, they often need to be realigned. You decide to align the expressions that count records directly under the Cost text box.

2. **Click the Cost text box, press and hold [Shift], click the text box with the Count expression in the Category Footer as well as the text box with the Count expression in the StateAbbreviation Footer, then release [Shift]**

   With these three controls selected, you want to align the right edge of the controls *with respect to each other*.

3. **With the three controls still selected, click the Arrange tab on the Ribbon, then click the Align Right button**

   With the expressions aligned, you want to move the labels in the footer sections below the City text box in the Detail section.

4. **Point to the upper-left sizing handle of the Count of records label in the Category Footer, drag it to the right to position it just to the left of the expression it describes, then repeat this action to move the label in the StateAbbreviation Footer closer to the expression it describes**

5. **Click the Save button on the Quick Access toolbar, click the Home tab, click the View button arrow, click Print Preview, then scroll to the bottom of the first page to see the footer for the state of California as shown in Figure D-12**

6. **Click the Close Print Preview button on the Print Preview toolbar, then close the Tours By State report**

FIGURE D-11: Widening controls

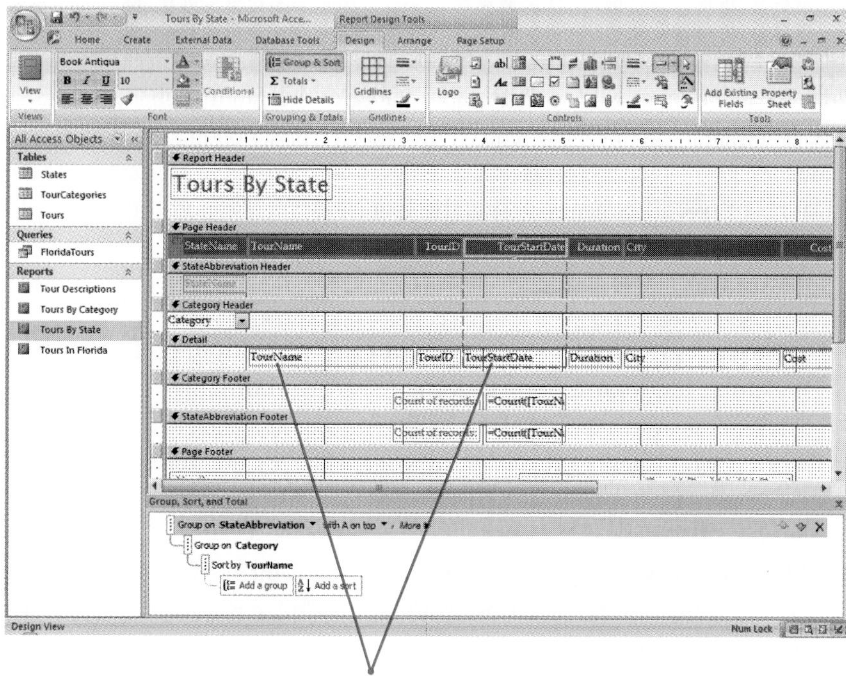
Widening the TourName and TourStartDate fields

FIGURE D-12: Previewing the widened and aligned controls

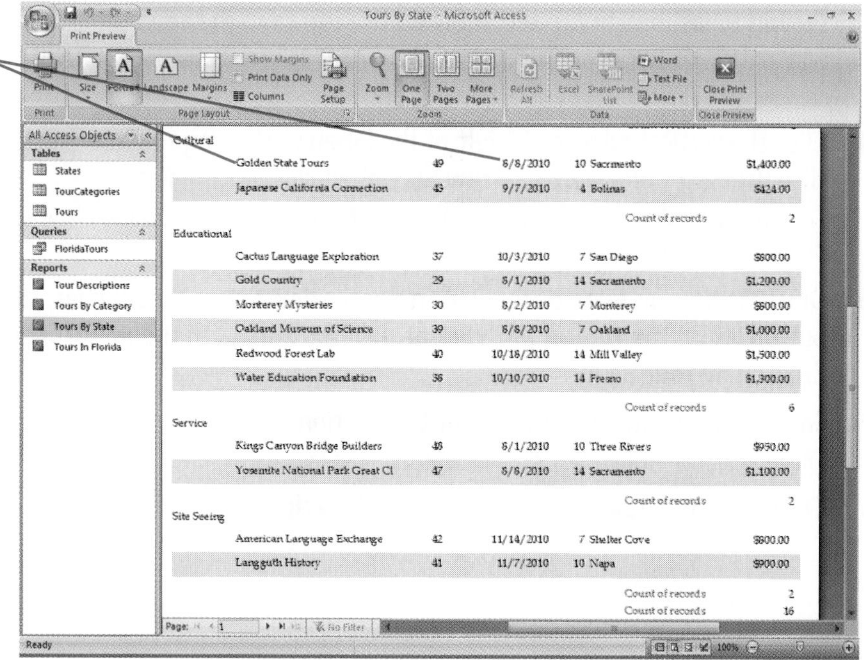
TourName and TourStartDate fields are wide enough to show field values

Precisely moving and resizing controls

You can move and resize controls using the mouse, but precise movements are often easier to accomplish using the keyboard. Pressing the arrow keys while holding [Ctrl] moves selected controls one **pixel** (picture element) at a time in the direction of the arrow. Pressing the arrow keys while holding [Shift] resizes selected controls one pixel at a time.

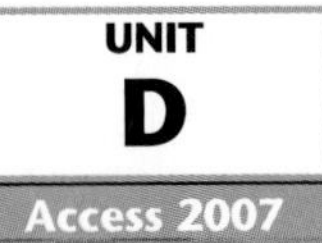

UNIT D
Access 2007

Formatting a Report

Formatting refers to enhancing the appearance of the information. Table D-3 lists several of the most popular formatting commands found on the Design tab. Although the Report Wizard automatically applies many formatting embellishments, you often want to improve the appearance of the report to fit your particular needs. When reviewing the Tour Descriptions report with Mark, you decide to format several sections to improve the appearance of the report.

STEPS

1. **Right-click the Tour Descriptions report in the Navigation Pane, click Print Preview, maximize the report, then click the report to zoom in**

   You decide to lighten the background of the Page Header section to the same shade as the Category Header section. You also want to darken the text color of the Page Header section to black. You can make some formatting changes in Layout View, which shows data, but Report Design View provides the best access to formatting and other design changes.

2. **Click the Close Print Preview button on the Print Preview toolbar, right-click the Tour Descriptions report, click Design View, maximize the report, then click the Page Header section bar to select it**

   The **Back Color** property determines the color of the section background. It is represented as a hexadecimal number (which uses both numbers 0–9 and letters A–F) in the Back Color property on the Format tab of the property sheet, or you can modify it using the Fill/Back Color button on the Ribbon. Avoid relying too heavily on color formatting. Background shades often become solid black boxes when printed on a black-and-white printer or fax machine.

QUICK TIP

When the color on the Fill/Back Color, Font Color, or Line Color button displays the color you want, click the button to apply that color.

3. **Click the Fill/Back Color button arrow on the Design tab, then click Aqua Blue 1 (the second to last box in the second from the top row) in the Standard Colors list**

   With the background color of the Page Header section lightened, the white labels in the Page Header section are now very difficult to read.

4. **Click the vertical ruler to the left of the labels in the Page Header section to select them, click the Font Color button arrow, then click Automatic**

   The report in Design View should look like Figure D-13. You also want to add a label to the Report Footer section to identify yourself.

QUICK TIP

The quick keystroke for Undo is [Ctrl][Z]. The quick keystroke for Redo is [Ctrl][Y].

5. **Drag the bottom edge of the Report Footer down about 0.5 inches, click the Label button on the Design tab, click at the 1-inch mark in the Report Footer, then type Created by your name**

6. **Save, preview, then print the Tour Descriptions report**

   The final formatted Tour Descriptions report should look like Figure D-14.

7. **Close Print Preview, then close the Tour Descriptions report**

FIGURE D-13: Formatting a report

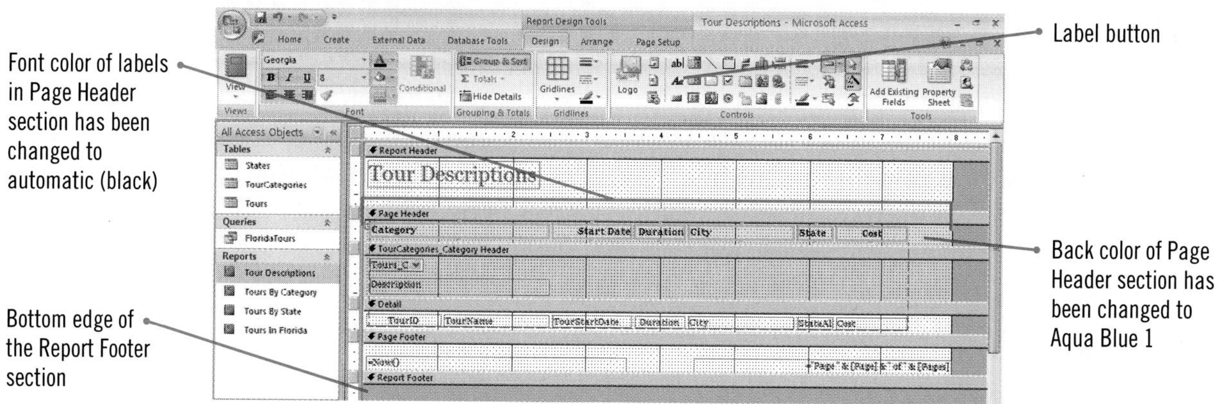
Font color of labels in Page Header section has been changed to automatic (black)
Bottom edge of the Report Footer section
Label button
Back color of Page Header section has been changed to Aqua Blue 1

FIGURE D-14: Formatted Tour Descriptions report

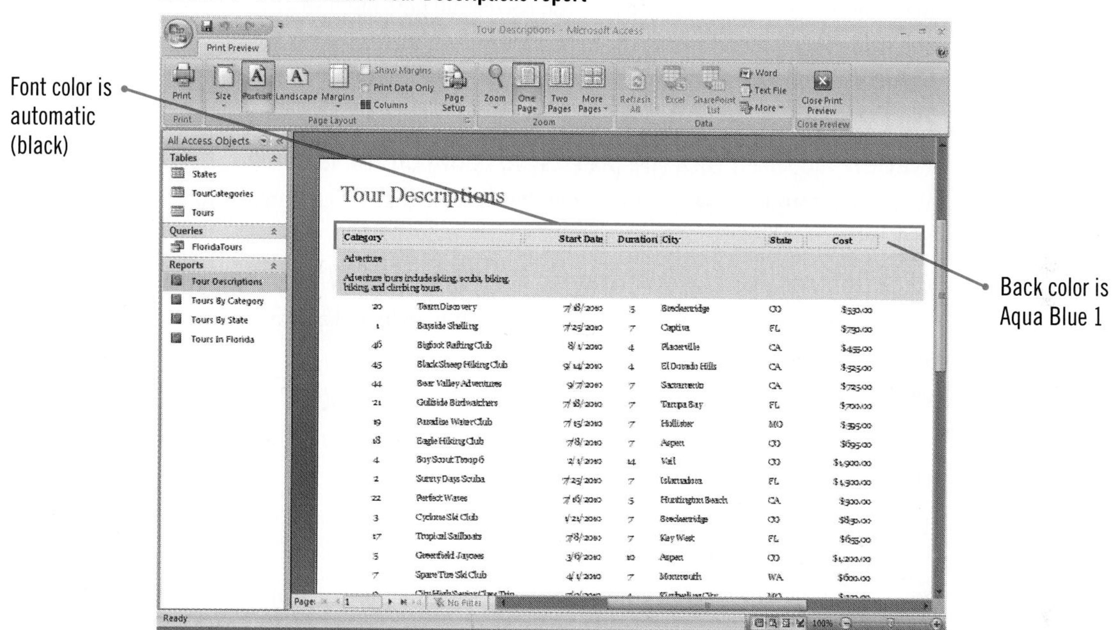
Font color is automatic (black)
Back color is Aqua Blue 1

Access 2007

TABLE D-3: Useful formatting commands

button	button name	description
B	Bold	Toggles bold on or off for the selected control(s)
I	Italic	Toggles italics on or off for the selected control(s)
U	Underline	Toggles underline on or off for the selected control(s)
	Align Text Left	Left-aligns the selected control(s) within its own border
	Center	Centers the selected control(s) within its own border
	Align Text Right	Right-aligns the selected control(s) within its own border
	Fill/Back Color	Changes the background color of the selected control(s)
	Alternate Fill/Back Color	Changes the background color of alternate records in the selected section
A	Font Color	Changes the text color of the selected control(s)
	Line Color	Changes the border color of the selected control(s)
	Line Thickness	Changes the border style of the selected control(s)
	Line Type	Changes the special visual effect of the selected control(s)

UNIT
D
Access 2007

Changing Page Layout

To fit all of the information on a report on a sheet of paper, you might need to change page layout options such as margins or page orientation. If a report contains many columns, for example, you might want to expand the print area by narrowing the margins. **Page orientation** refers to printing the report in either a **portrait** (8.5 inches wide by 11 inches tall) or **landscape** (11 inches wide by 8.5 inches tall) direction. Most of the page layout options such as paper size, paper orientation, and margins are accessible in Print Preview. Mark Rock asks you to print the Tours By State report. You preview it and make any page layout changes needed before printing it.

STEPS

1. **In the Navigation Pane, double-click the Tours By State report to open it in Report View, then maximize the report**

   In examining the report, you see that you need more horizontal space on the page to display all of the labels and field values properly. One way to provide more horizontal space on the report is to switch from portrait to landscape orientation.

2. **Click the View button arrow, click Print Preview, click the Landscape button on the Print Preview tab, then click the preview to zoom out to see an entire page**

   With the report in landscape orientation, you decide that wider margins would center the data to make it look better.

3. **Click the Margins button arrow on the Print Preview tab, then click Wide**

   Wide margins provide a one-inch top and bottom margin and at least a 0.75-inch left and right margin, as shown in Figure D-15.

4. **Close Print Preview, then switch to Report Design View**

   Carefully view the labels in the Page Header section, noting which ones need to be widened to display the entire entry.

5. **Use your moving, resizing, aligning, and previewing skills to make the report look like Figure D-16 in Print Preview**

   Your report doesn't have to look exactly like Figure D-16, but make sure that all of the labels are wide enough to display the text within them. To increase your productivity, use the [Shift] key to click and select more than one control at a time before you move, resize, or align them. You might need to move between Report Design View and Print Preview, making several adjustments before you are satisfied with your report.

6. **When finished improving the layout, save it, click the Office button, click Print, click the From box, type 1, click the To box, type 1, then click OK**

7. **Close the Tours By State report, close the Quest-D.accdb database, then exit Access**

QUICK TIP

If you want your name on the printout, switch to Report Design View and add your name as a label to the Page Header section.

FIGURE D-15: Changing the margins of the Tours By State report

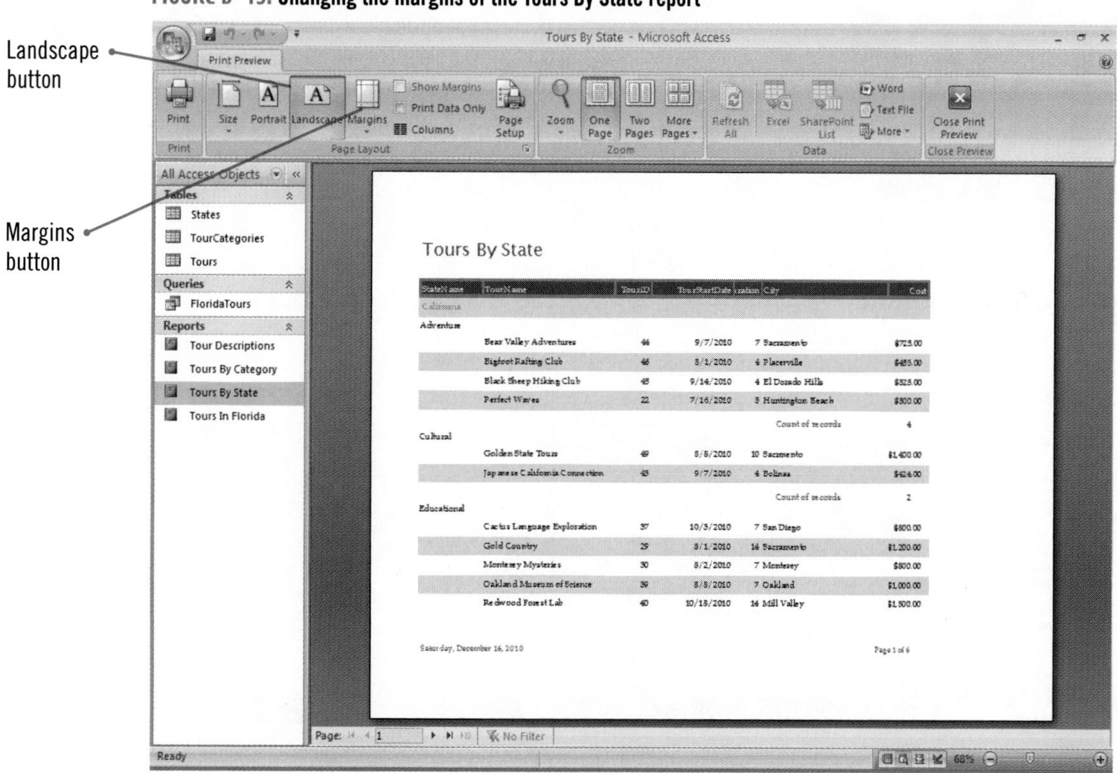

FIGURE D-16: Previewing the final Tours By State report

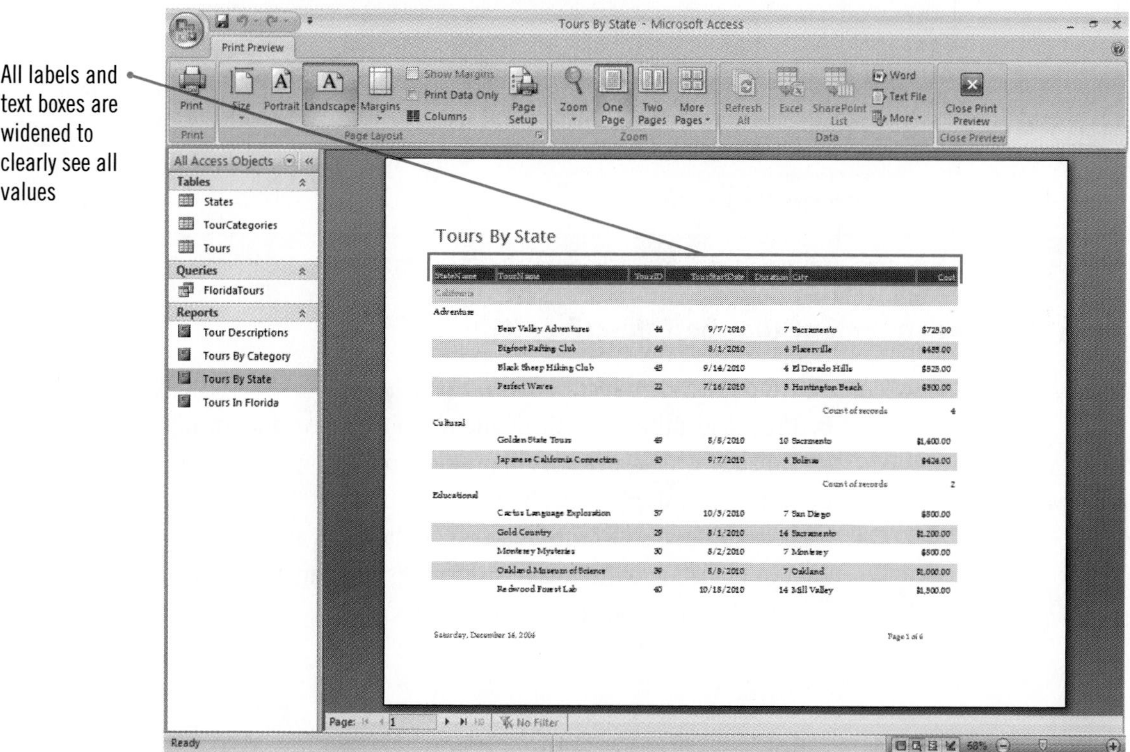

Access 2007

Practice

If you have a SAM user profile, you may have access to hands-on instruction, practice, and assessment of the skills covered in this unit. Log in to your SAM account (http://sam2007.course.com/) to launch any assigned training activities or exams that relate to the skills covered in this unit.

▼ CONCEPTS REVIEW

Label each element of the Report Design View window shown in Figure D-17.

FIGURE D-17

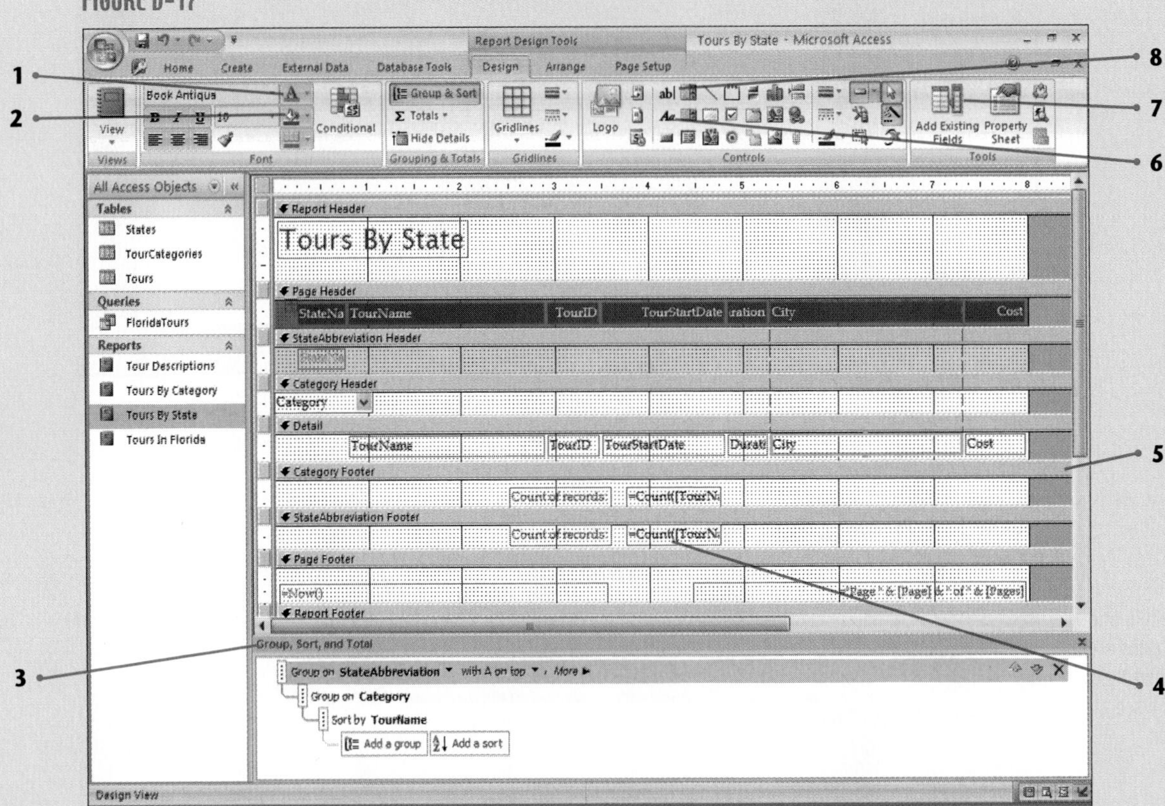

Match each term with the statement that best describes it.

9. Expression
10. Section
11. Detail section
12. Record Source property
13. Formatting
14. Grouping

a. Prints once for every record
b. Used to identify which fields and records are passed to the report
c. Enhancing the appearance of information displayed in the report
d. Sorting records *plus* providing a section
e. Determines where a control appears on the report and how often it prints
f. A combination of field names, operators, and functions that result in a single value before and after the group of records

Select the best answer from the list of choices.

15. You press and hold which key to select more than one control in Report Design View?

a. [Alt]

b. [Ctrl]

c. [Shift]

d. [Tab]

16. Which type of control is most commonly placed in the Detail section?

a. Combo box

b. Label

c. List box

d. Text box

17. Which type of control is most commonly placed in the Page Header section?

a. Bound image

b. Combo box

c. Command button

d. Label

18. A calculated expression is most often placed in which report section?

a. Layout

b. Formulas

c. Group Footer

d. Report Header

19. Which of the following would be the appropriate expression to count the number of records using the FirstName field?

a. =Count([FirstName])

b. =Count[FirstName]

c. =Count(FirstName)

d. =Count{FirstName}

20. To align the edges of several controls with respect to one another, you use the alignment commands on the:

a. Formatting tab.

b. Design tab.

c. Print Preview ribbon.

d. Arrange tab.

21. Which of the following *cannot* be changed in Print Preview?

a. Font size

b. Margins

c. Paper orientation

d. Paper size

▼ SKILLS REVIEW

1. Preview a report.

a. Start Access and open the **RealEstate-D.accdb** database from the drive and folder where you store your Data Files. Enable content if prompted.

b. Open the Agencies table and change A1 to your own last name in the A1 Realtors record, then close the Agencies table.

c. Open the Agency Listings report in Print Preview, then print the report.

d. On the printout, identify these sections:

- Report Header
- Page Header, Page Footer
- Detail

e. On the printout, identify the two Group Header sections as well as the field used to group the records. You can use Report Design View to confirm your answers, if needed.

f. Close the Agency Listings report.

2. Use the Report Wizard.

a. Use the Report Wizard to create a report based on the AgentLast and AgentPhone fields from the Agents table, and all the fields except the ListingNo, Pool, and AgentNo field from the Listings table.

b. View the data by Agents, then group it by the Type field. (*Hint*: Click Type, then click the > button.) Sort the records in descending order by the Asking field.

c. Use a Block layout and a Landscape orientation.

d. Use a Solstice style and title the report **Agent Listings by Type**.

e. Preview the first page of the new report. Notice which fields and field names are displayed completely and which need more space.

3. Use Report Design View.

a. In Report Design View, widen the AgentLast label in the Page Header section to begin at the left edge of the page. This automatically widens the AgentLast text box in the Detail section.

b. Modify the AgentLast label in the Page Header section to read Agent.

c. Narrow the Bath label and corresponding text box to be half as wide as they currently appear.

d. Switch between Print Preview and Report Design View to move and resize other labels in the Page Header section, so that the caption of each label is clearly visible. (*Hint*: If you make a mistake, click the Undo button.)

e. Preview the first page of the new report, switching between Report Design View and Print Preview to size all controls in a way that makes all data visible. Do not design the report to exceed the width of one landscape sheet of paper.

f. Save and close the Agent Listings by Type report, open the Agents table in Datasheet View, then enter your last name in place of Hughes in the Gordon Hughes record. Close the Agents table.

g. Reopen the Agent Listings by Type report, then print the first page.

4. Use report sections.

a. In Report Design View of the Agent Listings by Type report, expand the size of the Type Header section about 0.5 inches.

b. Cut the Type field from the Detail section, then paste it in the Type Header section.

c. Increase the font size of the Type text box to 14, then resize the control so that it is about three inches wide and tall enough for the larger text.

d. Open the Group, Sort, and Total pane by clicking the Group & Sort button, and remove the AgentNo grouping level by clicking the Delete button on the right edge of the Group on AgentNo bar.

e. Open a Group Footer section for the Type field.

f. Close the Group, Sort, and Total pane, then preview the report.

▼ SKILLS REVIEW (CONTINUED)

5. Add subtotals and counts.

- **a.** In Report Design View, add a text box control to the Type Footer section, just below the Asking text box in the Detail section. Change the label to read **Subtotal of Asking Price:** and enter the expression **=Sum([Asking])** in the text box.
- **b.** Copy and paste the text box that contains the =Sum([Asking]) expression, so that two copies of the text box and accompanying label appear in the Type Footer section.
- **c.** Modify the second text box to read **=Avg([Asking])**, and the second label to read **Average Asking Price:**.
- **d.** Open the Property Sheet for the =Avg([Asking]) expression, and on the Format tab, change the Format property to Currency and the Decimal Places property to 0.
- **e.** Open the Property Sheet for the =Sum([Asking]) expression, and on the Format tab, change the Format property to Currency and the Decimal Places property to 0.
- **f.** Open the Property Sheet for the Asking text box in the Detail section, and on the Format tab, change the Format property to Currency and the Decimal Places property to 0.
- **g.** Preview the report to view the new subtotals in the Type Footer section.

6. Resize and align controls.

- **a.** In Report Design View, right-align the right edges of the Asking, the =Sum([Asking]), and the =Avg([Asking]) text boxes.
- **b.** Right-align the text within the labels to the left of the expression text boxes in the Type Footer section, and also align the right edges of the labels with respect to one another.
- **c.** Save and preview the report.

7. Format a report.

- **a.** Switch to Report Design View and change the font of the label in the Report Header to Freestyle Script, 36 points.
- **b.** Double-click a sizing handle on the label in the Report Header to expand it to accommodate the entire label. Be sure to double-click a sizing handle of the label, not the label itself, which opens the property sheet.
- **c.** Change the background color of the Page Header section to Light Gray 1 on the Fill/Back Color palette.
- **d.** Click the Detail section bar, and apply a Light Gray 1 background color using the Alternate Fill/Back Color palette.
- **e.** Save and preview the report.

▼ SKILLS REVIEW (CONTINUED)

8. Change page layout.

- **a.** Use Report Design View to move the text box in the Page Footer section that calculates the page number to the left, so that no controls on the page extend beyond the 9-inch marker on the horizontal ruler.
- **b.** Drag the right edge of the report to the left, so that it is no wider than nine inches.
- **c.** Save the report, then switch to Print Preview. The first page of the report should look like Figure D-18. Your fonts and colors might look different.
- **d.** Change the margins to Normal (.75-inch top and bottom, .35-inch left and right), then print the first page of the report.
- **e.** Close and save the Agent Listings by Type report.
- **f.** Close the RealEstate-D.accdb database, then exit Access.

FIGURE D-18

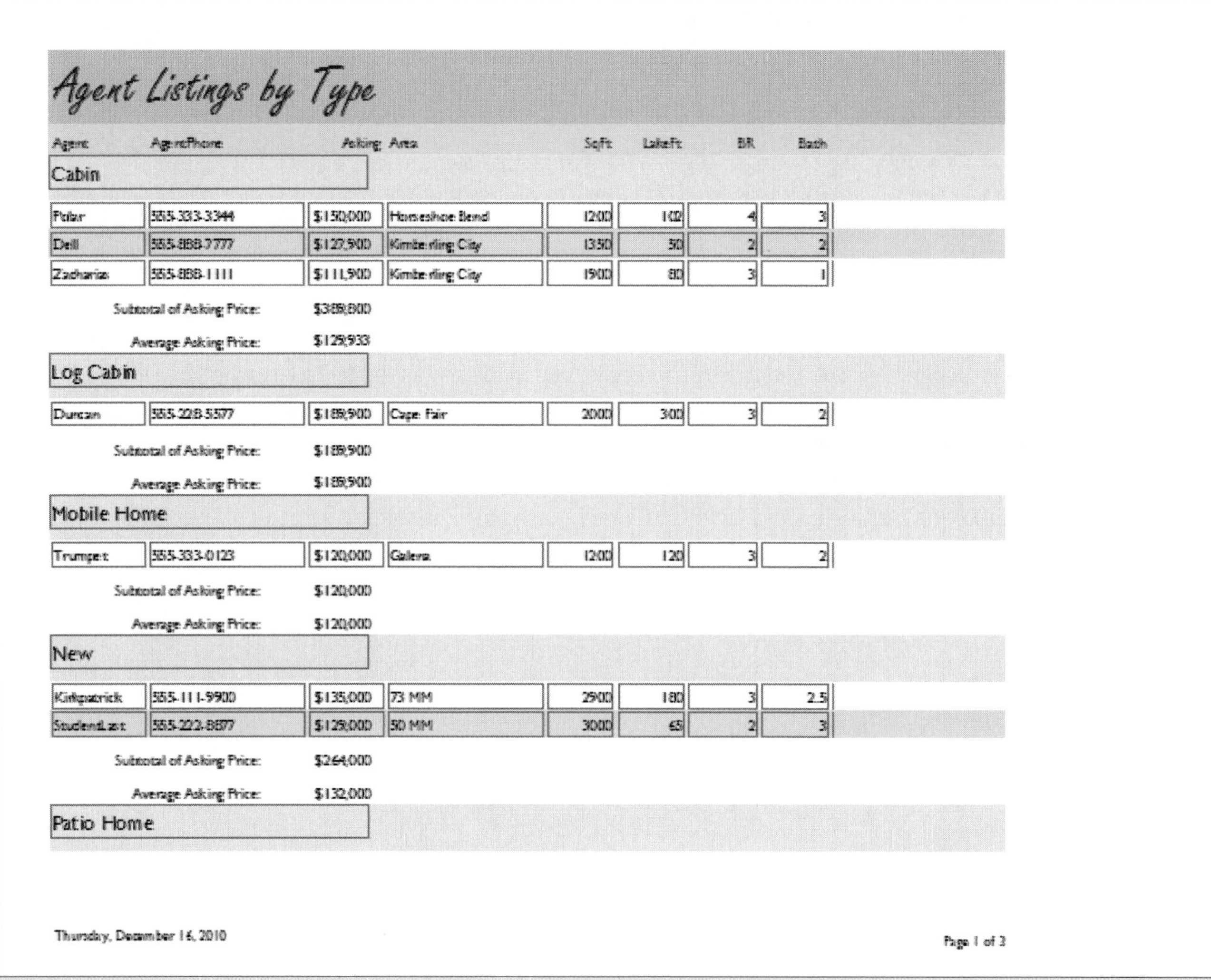

Agent Listings by Type

Agent	AgentPhone	Asking	Area	SqFt	LakeFt	BR	Bath
Cabin							
Pollar	555-333-3344	$150,000	Horseshoe Bend	1200	102	4	3
Dell	555-888-7777	$127,900	Kimberling City	1350	50	2	2
Zacharias	555-888-1111	$111,900	Kimberling City	1900	80	3	1
Subtotal of Asking Price:		$389,800					
Average Asking Price:		$129,933					
Log Cabin							
Duncan	555-228-5577	$189,900	Cape Fair	2000	300	3	2
Subtotal of Asking Price:		$189,900					
Average Asking Price:		$189,900					
Mobile Home							
Trumpet	555-333-0123	$120,000	Galena	1200	120	3	2
Subtotal of Asking Price:		$120,000					
Average Asking Price:		$120,000					
New							
Kirkpatrick	555-111-9900	$135,000	73 MM	2900	180	3	2.5
StudentLast	555-222-8877	$129,000	50 MM	3000	65	2	3
Subtotal of Asking Price:		$264,000					
Average Asking Price:		$132,000					
Patio Home							

Thursday, December 16, 2010 — Page 1 of 3

▼ INDEPENDENT CHALLENGE 1

As the office manager of a veterinary association, you need to create a report showing membership in the association.

a. Start Access, then open the **Vet-D.accdb** database from the drive and folder where you store your Data Files. Enable content if prompted.

b. Use the Report Wizard to create a report with the First and Last fields from the Vets table, and all the fields except for ClinicNo from the Clinics table.

c. View your data by Clinics, do not add any more grouping levels, and sort in ascending order by Last.

d. Use the Stepped layout, Portrait orientation, and Flow style.

e. Name the report **Clinic Membership**.

f. In Report Design View, expand the size of the Address1 label and text box to be about two inches wide. Be careful not to expand any controls beyond the 8-inch right edge of the report.

g. Open the Group, Sort, and Total pane, then add a ClinicNo Footer section.

h. Add a text box to the ClinicNo Footer section, just below the Last text box.

i. Modify the caption of the label to the left of the new text box in the ClinicNo Footer section to read **Count:**, move the label close to the text box, and right-align the text within the label.

j. Enter an expression in the new text box in the ClinicNo Footer section to count the values in the Last field, **=Count([Last])**, and left-align the values within the text box.

k. Add a label to the Report Header section to display your name. Format the label to be black text and 12 points, and expand the label to display your entire name as needed.

l. Using Report Design View to make modifications and Print Preview to review them, modify the controls as necessary to display all of the data clearly, then save the report and print the first page. Be careful not to expand beyond the 8-inch mark on the horizontal ruler in Report Design View, or the report will be wider than a sheet of paper in portrait orientation. The report should look similar to Figure D-19. Your fonts and colors might look different.

m. Close the Clinic Membership report, close the Vet-D.accdb database, then exit Access.

FIGURE D-19

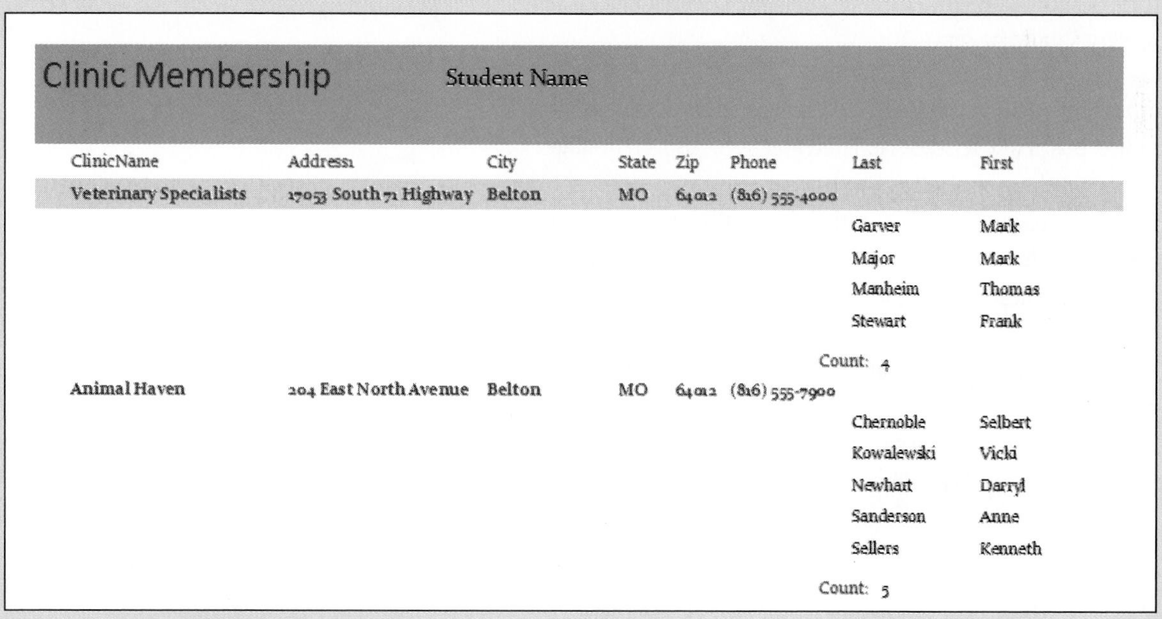

Clinic Membership   Student Name

ClinicName	Address1	City	State	Zip	Phone	Last	First
Veterinary Specialists	17053 South 71 Highway	Belton	MO	64012	(816) 555-4000		
						Garver	Mark
						Major	Mark
						Manheim	Thomas
						Stewart	Frank
					Count:	4	
Animal Haven	204 East North Avenue	Belton	MO	64012	(816) 555-7900		
						Chernoble	Selbert
						Kowalewski	Vicki
						Newhart	Darryl
						Sanderson	Anne
						Sellers	Kenneth
					Count:	5	

▼ INDEPENDENT CHALLENGE 2

You have built an Access database to track membership in a community service club. The database tracks member names and addresses as well as their status in the club, which moves from rank to rank as the members contribute increased hours of service to the community.

- **a.** Start Access and open the **Membership-D.accdb** database from the drive and folder where you store your Data Files. Enable content if prompted.
- **b.** Open the Members table and change the name of Traci Kalvert to your name, then close the Members table.
- **c.** Use the Report Wizard to create a report using the Status and DuesOwed fields from the Status table, and the FName, LName, and DuesPaid fields from the Members table.
- **d.** View the data by Status. Do not add any more grouping fields, and sort the records in ascending order by LName.
- **e.** Use an Outline layout, Portrait orientation, and Civic style.
- **f.** Title the report **Dues Analysis**, then preview the report.
- **g.** In Report Design View, use the Group, Sort, and Total pane to open the StatusNo Footer section.
- **h.** Add a text box to the StatusNo Footer section, just below the DuesPaid text box. Change the label to **Count:** and the expression in the text box to **=Count([DuesPaid])**.
- **i.** Expand the StatusNo Footer section as necessary, and add a second text box to the StatusNo Footer section, just below the first. Change the label to **Subtotal:** and the expression in the text box to **=Sum([DuesPaid])**.
- **j.** Apply two property changes to the =Sum([DuesPaid]) text box. The Format property should be set to Currency and the Decimal Places property should be set to 2.

Advanced Challenge Exercise

- Expand the StatusNo Footer section as necessary, and add a third text box to the StatusNo Footer section, just below the second. Change the label to **Dues Owed Less Dues Paid:**.
- Change the text box expression to **=Count([DuesPaid])*[DuesOwed]-Sum([DuesPaid])**.
- Apply two property changes to the new text box. The Format property should be set to Currency and the Decimal Places property should be set to 2.

- **k.** Align the right edges of the DuesPaid text box in the Detail section and all text boxes in the StatusNo Footer section. Also, right-align all data within these controls.
- **l.** Align the right edges of the labels in the StatusNo Footer section.
- **m.** Apply an Aqua Blue 1 Alternate Fill/Back color to the StatusNo Header, and a Dark Blue font color to the label in the Report Header.
- **n.** Save, then preview the Dues Analysis report. The report should look similar to Figure D-20. Your fonts and colors might look different.
- **o.** Print the first page of the Dues Analysis report, then close it.
- **p.** Close the Membership-D.accdb database, then exit Access.

FIGURE D-20

Dues Analysis

Status New
DuesOwed $100.00

LName	FName	DuesPaid
Lang	Brad	$50.00
Larson	Kristen	$50.00
Martin	Jerry	$50.00
Parton	Jeanette	$0.00
Student	StudentFirst	$100.00
Yode	Kathy	$100.00
	Count:	6
	Subtotal:	$350.00
	Dues Owed Less Dues Paid:	$250.00

▼ INDEPENDENT CHALLENGE 3

You have built an Access database to organize the deposits at a recycling center. Various clubs regularly deposit recyclable material, which is measured in pounds when the deposits are made.

- **a.** Start Access and open the **Recycle-D.accdb** database from the drive and folder where you store your Data Files. Enable content if prompted.
- **b.** Open the Centers table, change Johnson in Johnson County Landfill to your own last name, then close the table.
- **c.** Use the Report Wizard to create a report with the Name field from the Centers table, and the Deposit Date and Weight from the Deposits table.
- **d.** View the data by Centers, do not add any more grouping levels, and sort the records in ascending order by Deposit Date.
- **e.** Click the Summary Options button in the Report Wizard dialog box that also prompts for sort orders, and click the Sum check box for the Weight field.
- **f.** Use a Stepped layout, a Portrait orientation, and a Flow style. Title the report **Deposit Totals**.
- **g.** View the report in Print Preview, then switch to Report Design View and widen the Name text box. Switch between Print Preview and Report Design View to widen and then observe the Name text box. Widen it enough to make all trash center names visible.
- **h.** In Report Design View, delete the long, top text box in the Center Number Footer section that starts with ="Summary.
- **i.** Right-align the right edge of the Sum label in the Center Number Footer section with the Deposit Date text box in the Detail section.
- **j.** Left-align the left edge of the =Sum([Weight]) text box in the Center Number Footer section with the Weight text box in the Detail section.
- **k.** Save, preview, and then print the first page of the report. It should look similar to Figure D-21. Your fonts and colors might look different.

FIGURE D-21

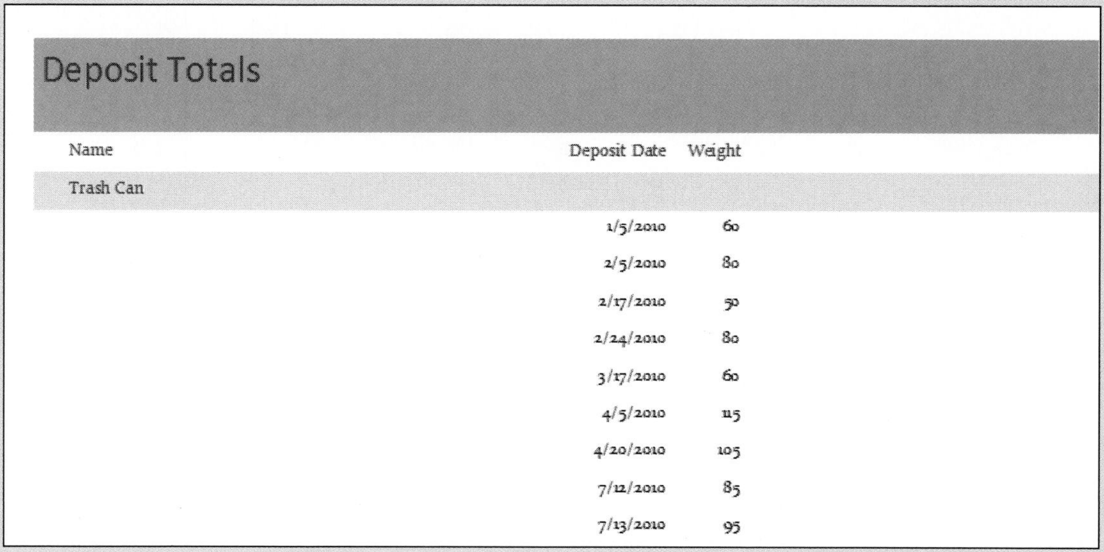

Deposit Totals

Name	Deposit Date	Weight
Trash Can		
	1/5/2010	60
	2/5/2010	80
	2/17/2010	50
	2/24/2010	80
	3/17/2010	60
	4/5/2010	115
	4/20/2010	105
	7/12/2010	85
	7/13/2010	95

Access 2007

▼ INDEPENDENT CHALLENGE 3 (CONTINUED)

Advanced Challenge Exercise

- In Report Design View, add Deposit Date as a grouping field, and move it above Deposit Date used as a sorting field.
- Open the Deposit Date Footer section, then change the by entire value option to by year.
- Add the Deposit Date field to the Deposit Date Header section, then change the Format property for the Deposit Date text box to **yyyy** (four-digit year format) and the Deposit Date label to **Year:**.
- Copy the controls from the Center Number Footer section, and paste them in the Deposit Date Footer section.
- Change the label in the Deposit Date Footer section from Sum to **Yearly Sum**. Change the label in the Center Number Footer section from Sum to **Center Sum**.
- Align the right edge of the label in the Deposit Date Footer section with the label in the Center Number Footer section, and the right edge of the text box in the Deposit Date Footer section with the right edge of the text box in the Center Number Footer section. Also, right-align the data within each of these four controls.
- Save and preview the report, then print the first page, a portion of which is shown in Figure D-22.

l. Close the Deposit Totals report, close the Recycle-D.accdb database, then exit Access.

FIGURE D-22

Deposit Totals

Name		Deposit Date	Weight
Trash Can			
Year:	2010		
		1/5/2010	60
		2/5/2010	80
		2/17/2010	50
		2/24/2010	80
		3/17/2010	60
		4/5/2010	115
		4/20/2010	105
		7/12/2010	85
		7/13/2010	95
		8/21/2010	205
		11/2/2010	80
		12/8/2010	80
		Yearly Sum	1095

▼ REAL LIFE INDEPENDENT CHALLENGE

One way you can use an Access database on your own is to help you study information. Suppose you have a passion for geography and want to memorize all 50 U.S. state capitals and mottos. A database with information about all 50 states is provided with your Data Files, and you can use it to develop a report to study this information.

- **a.** Start Access and open the **States-D.accdb** database from the drive and folder where you store your Data Files. Enable content if prompted.
- **b.** Use the Report Wizard to create a report that lists all four fields in the States table, sorted by StateName, using a Tabular layout, a Portrait orientation, and a None style. Title the report **State Trivia**.
- **c.** Widen all controls as necessary to display all of the data in each field, but do not extend the report beyond the width of the paper in portrait orientation.
- **d.** Add a line control to the top edge of the Detail section, just above the text boxes in the Detail section, to separate the states with a line, as shown in Figure D-23.
- **e.** Add your name as a label to the Report Header section.
- **f.** Save the report, then preview and print it.
- **g.** Close the State Trivia report, close the States.accdb database, then exit Access.

FIGURE D-23

State Trivia

StateName	StateAbbrev	Capital	Motto
Alabama	AL	Montgomery	We dare to defend our rights
Alaska	AK	Juneau	North to the future
Arizona	AZ	Phoenix	God enriches
Arkansas	AR	Little Rock	The people rule
California	CA	Sacramento	I have found it
Colorado	CO	Denver	Nothing without Providence
Connecticut	CT	Hartford	He who transplanted sustains
Delaware	DE	Dover	Liberty and independence
Florida	FL	Tallahassee	In God we trust
Georgia	GA	Atlanta	Wisdom, justice, and moderation
Hawaii	HI	Honolulu	The life of the land is perpetuated in righteousness
Idaho	ID	Boise	Let it be perpetual
Illinois	IL	Springfield	State sovereignty, national union

▼ VISUAL WORKSHOP

Open the **Basketball-D.accdb** database from the drive and folder where you store your Data Files and enable content if prompted. First, enter your own name instead of Heidi Harmon in the Players table. Your goal is to create the report shown in Figure D-24. Choose the First, Last, HomeTown, and HomeState fields from the Players table and the FG, 3P, and FT fields from the Stats table. View the data by Players, do not add any more grouping levels, and do not add any more sorting levels. When the Report Wizard prompts you for sort orders, click the Summary Options button and choose Sum for the FG, 3P, and FT fields. Use a Block layout, a Portrait orientation, a Solstice style, and title the report **Points per Player**. In Report Design View, delete the long text box calculation in the PlayerNo Footer section, and move and align the =Sum([FG]), =Sum([3P]), and =Sum([FT]) calculations in the PlayerNo Footer directly under the text boxes that they sum in the Detail section. Cut the First, Last, HomeTown, and HomeState text boxes from the Detail section, then paste them in the PlayerNoHeader section. Make sure that no Alternate Fill/Back color is applied to the Detail section. (Select the Detail section, then choose No Color for the Alternate Fill/Back color.) Move and resize all controls as needed.

FIGURE D-24

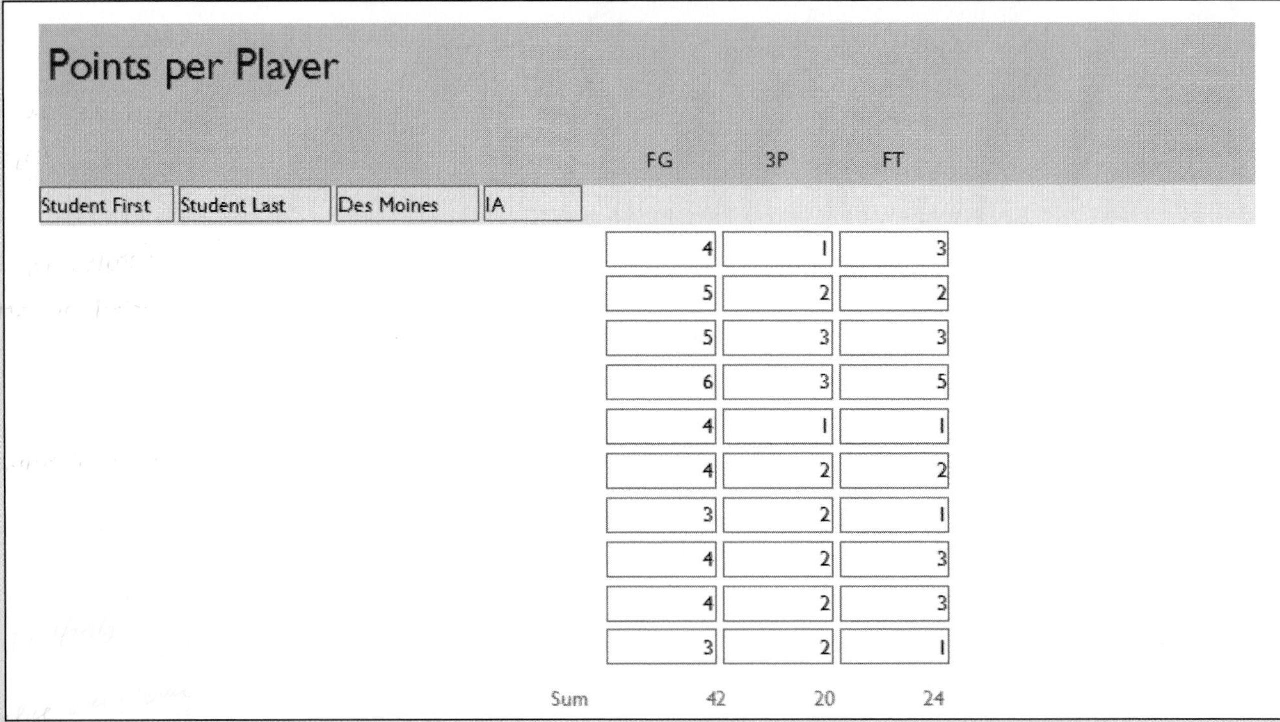

UNIT
E
Access 2007

Modifying the Database Structure

Files You Will Need:

Quest-E.accdb
Training-E.accdb
Member1.jpg
Sunset.jpg

In this unit, you refine a database by adding a new table to an existing database and linking tables using one-to-many relationships to create a relational database. You work with fields that have different data types, including Text, Number, Currency, Date/Time, and Yes/No, to define the data stored in the database. You create and use Attachment fields to store images. You also modify table and field properties to format and validate data. Working with Mark Rock, the tour developer for U.S. group travel at Quest Travel Services, you are developing an Access database to track the tours, customers, and sales for his division. The database consists of multiple tables that you can link, modify, and enhance to create a relational database.

OBJECTIVES

Examine relational databases
Design related tables
Create one-to-many relationships
Create Lookup fields
Modify Text fields
Modify Number and Currency fields
Modify Date/Time fields
Modify validation properties
Create Attachment fields

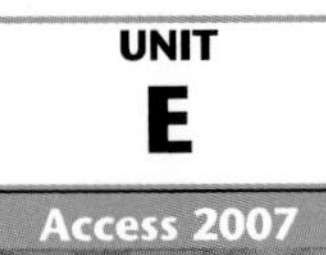

Examining Relational Databases

The purpose of a relational database is to organize and store data in a way that minimizes redundancy and maximizes your flexibility when querying and analyzing data. To accomplish these goals, a relational database uses related tables of data rather than a single large table. At one time, the Sales department at Quest Travel Services tracked information about their tour sales using a single Access table called Sales, shown in Figure E-1. You see a data redundancy problem because of the duplicate tour and customer information entered into a single table. You decide to study the principles of relational database design to help Quest Travel Services reorganize these fields into a correctly designed relational database.

DETAILS

To redesign a list into a properly structured relational database, follow these principles:

- **Design each table to contain fields that describe only one subject**
  Currently, the Sales table in Figure E-1 contains three subjects: tours, customers, and sales data. Putting multiple subjects in a single table creates redundant data. For example, the customer's name must be reentered every time that customer purchases a different tour. Redundant data causes extra data-entry work, a higher rate of data-entry inconsistencies and errors, and larger physical storage requirements. Moreover, it limits the user's ability to search for, analyze, and report on the data. These problems are minimized by implementing a properly designed relational database.

- **Identify a primary key field or key field combination for each table**
  A **primary key field** is a field that contains unique information for each record. An employee number field often serves this purpose in a table that stores employee data. A customer number field usually serves this purpose in a table that stores customer data. Although using the employee or customer's last name as the primary key field might work in a small database, it is generally a poor choice because it does not accommodate two employees or customers that have the same last name. A **key field combination** uses more than one field to uniquely identify each record.

- **Build one-to-many relationships between the tables of your database using a field common to each table**
  To tie the information from one table to another, a field must be common to each table. This linking field is the primary key field on the "one" side of the relationship and the **foreign key field** on the "many" side of the relationship. To create a one-to-many relationship between the tables, the primary key field contains a unique entry for each record in the "one" table, but the foreign key field can contain the same value in several records in the "many" table. Table E-1 describes common examples of one-to-many relationships. You are not required to give the linking field the same name in the "one" and "many" tables.

  The new design for the fields of the tour database is shown in Figure E-2. One customer can purchase many tours, so the Customers and Sales tables have a one-to-many relationship based on the linking CustNo field. One tour can have many sales, so the Tours and Sales tables also have a one-to-many relationship based on the common TourID field (named TourNo in the Tours table).

Using many-to-many relationships

As you design your database, you might find that two tables have a **many-to-many relationship**. To join them, you must establish a third table called a **junction table**, which contains two foreign key fields to serve on the "many" side of separate one-to-many relationships with the two original tables. The Customers and Tours tables have a many-to-many relationship because one customer can purchase many tours and one tour can have many customers purchase it. The Sales table serves as the junction table to link the three tables together.

FIGURE E-1: Sales as a single table

TourName	City	StateAbbrev	SaleDate	FName	LName
American Heritage Tour	Philadelphia	PA	6/2/2010	Cynthia	Browning
American Heritage Tour	Philadelphia	PA	7/10/2010	Jan	Cabriella
American Heritage Tour	Philadelphia	PA	6/2/2010	Christine	Collins
American Heritage Tour	Philadelphia	PA	6/2/2010	Gene	Custard
American Heritage Tour	Philadelphia	PA	6/2/2010	John	Garden
Bayside Shelling	Captiva	FL	5/1/2010	Christine	Collins
Bayside Shelling	Captiva	FL	5/1/2010	Jim	Wilson
Bayside Shelling	Captiva	FL	5/1/2010	Kori	Yode
Bright Lights Expo	Branson	MO	7/10/2010	Jan	Cabriella
Bright Lights Expo	Branson	MO	7/9/2010	Denise	Camel
Bright Lights Expo	Branson	MO	7/8/2010	Christine	Collins
Bright Lights Expo	Branson	MO	7/10/2010	Gene	Custard

Customer name is duplicated each time the customer purchases a new tour

Each tour name, city, state, and tour start date is duplicated each time a new person purchases that tour

Shared fields primary key in design view field has a key by it - must be unique

FIGURE E-2: Sales data split into three related tables

CustNo	FName	LName	Street	City	State	Zip
1	Mitch	Mayberry	52411 Oakmont Rd	Kansas City	MO	64144
2	Jill	Alman	2505 McGee St	Des Moines	IA	50288
3	Bob	Bouchart	5200 Main St	Kansas City	MO	64105
4	Cynthia	Browning	8206 Marshall Dr	Lenexa	KS	66214
5	Mary	Braven	600 Elm St	Olathe	KS	66031
6	Christine	Collins	520 W 52nd St	Kansas City	KS	64105
7	Denise	Camel	66020 King St	Overland Park	KS	66210
8	Gene	Custard	66900 College Rd	Overland Park	KS	66210
9	Jan	Cabriella	52520 W. 505 Ter	Lenexa	KS	66215
10	Andrea	Eahlie	56 Jackson Rd	Kansas City	MO	64145

Customers Table

One-to-many link (one customer may purchase many tours)

TourNo	TourName	TourStartDate	Duration	City	StateAbbrev
1	Bayside Shelling	7/25/2010	7	Captiva	FL
2	Sunny Days Scuba	7/25/2010	7	Islamadora	FL
3	Cyclone Ski Club	1/21/2010	7	Breckenridge	CO
4	Boy Scout Troop 6	2/1/2010	14	Vail	CO
5	Greenfield Jaycees	3/6/2010	10	Aspen	CO
6	Fullington Family Reunion	3/30/2010	7	Breckenridge	CO
7	Spare Tire Ski Club	4/1/2010	7	Monmouth	WA
8	Wheeler Family Reunion	7/1/2010	7	Osage Beach	MO
9	City High Senior Class Trip	7/9/2010	4	Kimberling City	MO

Tours Table

ID	SaleDate	CustNo	TourID
1	5/1/2010	6	1
2	5/1/2010	32	1
3	5/1/2010	34	1
4	6/2/2010	6	36
5	6/2/2010	4	36
6	6/2/2010	8	36
7	6/2/2010	15	36
8	7/8/2010	6	51
9	7/9/2010	7	51
10	7/10/2010	8	51
11	7/10/2010	9	51
12	7/10/2010	9	36

One-to-many link (one tour may be purchased many times)

Sales Table

Access 2007

TABLE E-1: Common one-to-many relationships

table on "one" side	table on "many" side	linking field	description
Products	Sales	ProductID	A ProductID field must have a unique entry in a Products table, but is listed many times in a Sales table as many copies of that item are sold
Students	Enrollments	StudentID	A StudentID field must have a unique entry in a Students table, but is listed many times in an Enrollments table as multiple classes are recorded for the same student
Employees	Promotions	EmployeeID	An EmployeeID field must have a unique entry in an Employees table, but is listed many times in a Promotions table as the employee is promoted over time

Designing Related Tables

After you develop a valid relational database design, you are ready to define the tables in Access. Using **Table Design View**, you can specify all characteristics of a table including field names, data types, field descriptions, field properties, lookup properties, and primary key field designations. Using the new database design, you are ready to create the Sales table.

STEPS

1. **Start Access, open the Quest-E.accdb database, then enable content if prompted**
   The Customers, States, TourCategories, and Tours tables already exist in the database. You need to create the Sales table.
2. **Click the Create tab on the Ribbon, then click the Table Design button**
   Table Design View opens, allowing you to enter field names and specify data types and field properties for the new table. Field names should be as short as possible, but long enough to be descriptive. The field name you enter in Table Design View is used as the default name for the field in all later queries, forms, and reports.
3. **Type SalesNo, press [Enter], click the Data Type list arrow, click AutoNumber, then press [Enter] twice to move to the next row**
   The AutoNumber data type, which automatically assigns the next available integer in the sequence to each new record, works well for the SalesNo field because each sales number should be unique.
4. **Type the other field names, data types, and descriptions as shown in Figure E-3**
   Field descriptions entered in Table Design View are optional, but are helpful in that they provide further information about the field.
5. **Click SalesNo in the Field Name column, then click the Primary Key button on the Design tab**
   A **key symbol** appears to the left of SalesNo to indicate that this field is defined as the primary key field for this table.
6. **Click the Save button on the Quick Access toolbar, type Sales in the Table Name text box, click OK, then close the table**
   The Sales table is now displayed as a table object in the Quest-E database Navigation Pane, as shown in Figure E-4.

QUICK TIP
When specifying field data types, you can type the first letter of the data type to quickly select it.

TROUBLE
If you set the wrong field as the primary key field, click the Primary Key field button again to toggle it off.

QUICK TIP
To delete or rename an existing table, right-click it in the Navigation Pane, then click Delete or Rename.

FIGURE E-3: Table Design View for the new Sales table

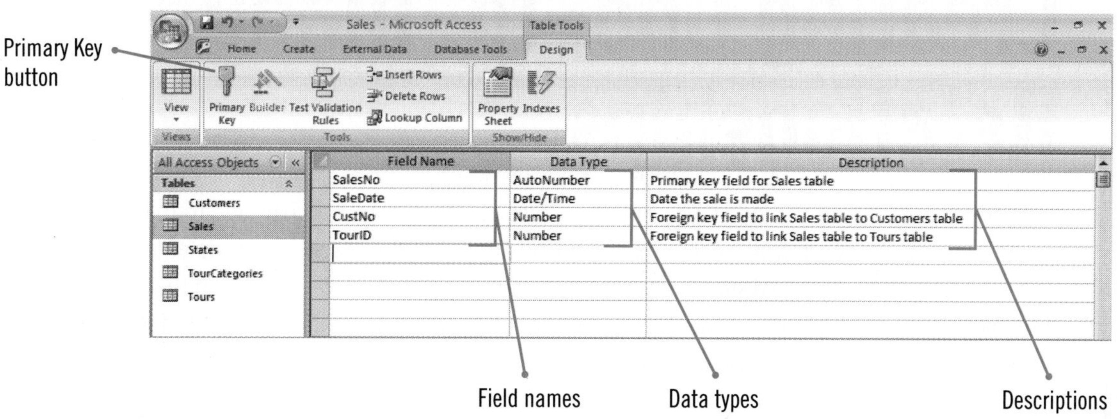

> means it will turn it into uppercase

FIGURE E-4: Sales table in the Quest-E database Navigation Pane

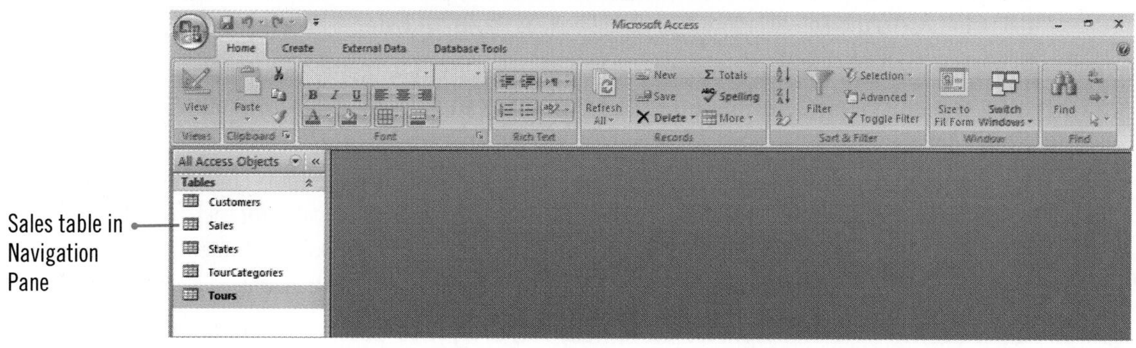

Specifying the foreign key field data type

A foreign key field in the "many" table must have the same data type (Text or Number) as the primary key it is related to in the "one" table. An exception to this rule is when the primary key field in the "one" table has an AutoNumber data type. In this case, the linking foreign key field in the "many" table must have a Number data type. Also note that a Number field used as a foreign key field must have a Long Integer Field Size property to match the Field Size property of the AutoNumber primary key field.

UNIT E

Access 2007

Creating One-to-Many Relationships

After creating the tables you need, you link the tables together in appropriate one-to-many relationships before building queries, forms, or reports using fields from multiple tables. Your database design shows that the common CustNo field should link the Customers table to the Sales table, and that the TourID field should link the Tours table to the Sales table. You are ready to define the one-to-many relationships between the tables of the Quest-E database.

STEPS

1. **Click the Database Tools tab on the Ribbon, then click the Relationships button**

   The States, Tours, and TourCategories table field lists appear in the Relationships window. The primary key fields are identified with a small key symbol to the left of the field name. You need to add the Customers and Sales table field lists to this window.

2. **Click the Show Table button on the Design tab, click Sales, click Add, click Customers, click Add, click Close, then maximize the window**

   With all of the field lists in the Relationships window, you're ready to link the Sales and Customers tables to the rest of the relational database.

3. **Click TourNo in the Tours table field list, then drag it to the TourID field in the Sales table field list**

   Dragging a field from one table to another in the Relationships window links the two tables by the selected fields and opens the Edit Relationships dialog box, as shown in Figure E-5. Recall that referential integrity helps ensure data accuracy.

4. **Click the Enforce Referential Integrity check box in the Edit Relationships dialog box, then click Create**

   The **one-to-many line** shows the linkage between the TourNo field of the Tours table and the TourID field of the Sales table. The "one" side of the relationship is the unique TourNo value for each record in the Tours table. The "many" side of the relationship is identified by an infinity symbol pointing to the TourID field in the Sales table. The CustNo field should link the Customers table to the Sales table.

5. **Click CustNo in the Customers table field list, drag it to CustNo in the Sales table field list, click the Enforce Referential Integrity check box, then click Create**

   The updated Relationships window should look like Figure E-6.

6. **Click the Relationship Report button on the Design tab, click the Print button, then click OK**

   A printout of the Relationships window, called the Relationship report, shows how your relational database is designed and includes table names, field names, primary key fields, and one-to-many relationship lines. This printout is helpful as you later create queries, forms, and reports that use fields from multiple tables.

7. **Click the Close Print Preview button on the Print Preview tab, close the Report Design View window, then click No when prompted to save the report**

8. **Close the Relationships window, then click Yes if prompted to save changes**

QUICK TIP
Drag the table's title bar to move the field list.

QUICK TIP
Drag the bottom border of the field list to display all of the fields.

QUICK TIP
Right-click a relationship line, then click Delete if you need to delete a relationship and start over.

TROUBLE
Click the Landscape button on the Print Preview tab if the report is too wide for portrait orientation.

QUICK TIP
Add your name as a label to the Report Header section in Report Design View and reprint the report if you want your name on the printout.

FIGURE E-5: Edit Relationships dialog box

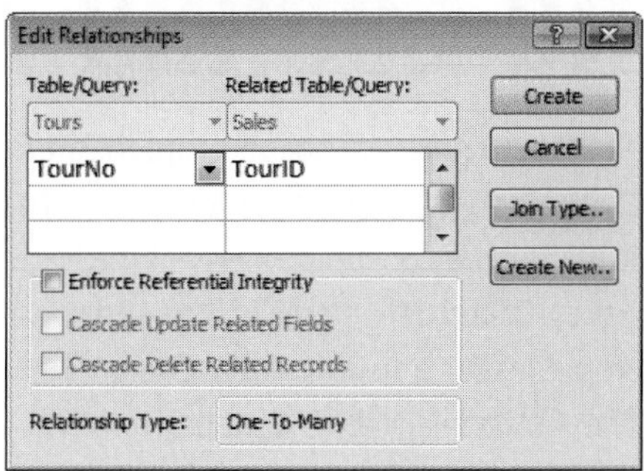

FIGURE E-6: Final Relationships window

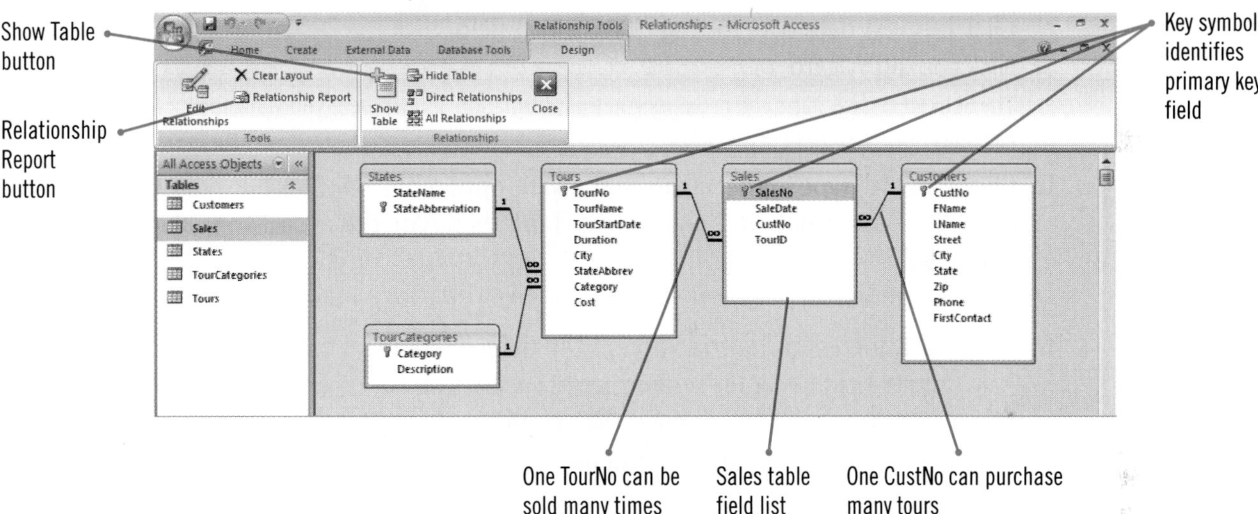

More on enforcing referential integrity

Recall that referential integrity is a set of rules to help ensure that no orphan records are entered or created in the database. An orphan record is a record in the "many" table that doesn't have a matching entry in the linking field of the "one" table. (For example, an orphan record in the Quest database is a record in the Sales table that contains a TourID entry but has no match in the TourNo field of the Tours table, or a record in the Sales table that contains a CustNo entry but no match in the Customers table.) Referential integrity prevents orphan records in multiple ways. By enforcing referential integrity, you cannot allow a **null entry** (nothing) in a foreign key field nor can you make an entry in the foreign key field that does not match a value in the linking field of the "one" table (such as a Sales record with a TourID not included in the Tours table). Referential integrity also prevents you from deleting a record in the "one" table that has a matching entry in the foreign key field of the "many" table (such as a Customer record with a CustNo associated with a Sales record). You should enforce referential integrity on all one-to-many relationships if possible. Unfortunately, if you are working with a database that already contains orphan records, you cannot enforce this powerful set of rules.

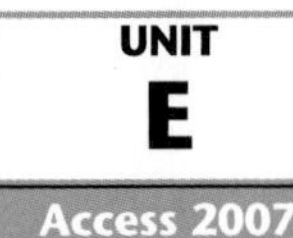

Creating Lookup Fields

A **Lookup field** is a field that contains Lookup properties. **Lookup properties** are field properties that allow you to supply a drop-down list of values for a field. The values can be stored in another table or directly stored in the **Row Source** Lookup property of the field. Fields that are good candidates for Lookup properties are those that contain a defined set of appropriate values such as State, Gender, or Department. You can set Lookup properties for a field in Table Design View using the **Lookup Wizard**. The FirstContact field in the Customers table identifies how the customer first made contact with Quest Specialty Travel such as being referred by a friend, finding the company through the Internet, or responding to a direct mail advertisement. You can use the Lookup Wizard to provide a set of defined values as a drop-down list for the FirstContact field.

STEPS

1. **Right-click the Customers table in the Navigation Pane, click Design View, then maximize Table Design View**

   You access the Lookup Wizard from the Data Type list for the field in which you want to apply Lookup properties.

2. **Click the Text data type for the FirstContact field, click the Data Type list arrow, then click Lookup Wizard**

   The Lookup Wizard starts and prompts you for information about where you want the lookup column to get its values.

3. **Click the I will type in the values that I want option button, click Next, click the first cell in the Col1 column, type Friend, press [Tab], then type the rest of the values as shown in Figure E-7**

   These are the values to populate the lookup value list for the FirstContact field.

4. **Click Next, then click Finish to accept the default label and complete the Lookup Wizard**

   Note that the data type for the FirstContact field is still Text. The Lookup Wizard is a process for setting Lookup property values for a field, not a data type itself.

5. **Click the Lookup tab to observe the new Lookup properties for the FirstContact field as shown in Figure E-8**

   The Lookup Wizard helped you enter the correct Lookup properties for the FirstContact field, but you can always enter or edit them directly if you know what values you want to use for each property. The Row Source property stores the values that are provided in the drop-down list for a Lookup field.

6. **Click the View button on the Design tab, click Yes when prompted to save the table, press [Tab] eight times to move to the FirstContact field, click the FirstContact list arrow as shown in Figure E-9, then click Friend**

   The FirstContact field now provides a list of values that are valid for this field.

7. **Close the Customers table**

QUICK TIP

The **Limit to List** Lookup property determines whether you can enter a new value into a field with other lookup properties, or whether the entries are limited to the drop-down list.

Creating multivalued fields

Multivalued fields allow you to make more than one choice from a drop-down list for a field. As a database designer, multivalued fields allow you to select and store more than one choice without having to create a more advanced database design. To create a multivalued field, use the Lookup Wizard and select the Allow Multiple Values check box for the question that asks "Do you want to store multiple values for this lookup?" This feature is only available for an Access database created or saved in Access 2007 file format.

FIGURE E-7: Entering a Lookup list of values

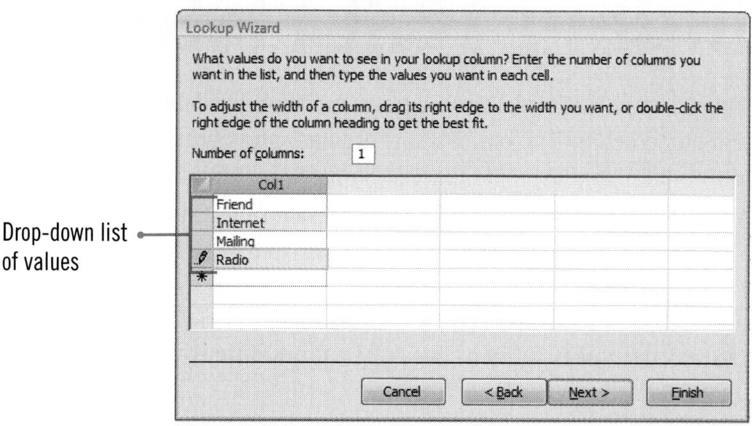

FIGURE E-8: Viewing Lookup properties

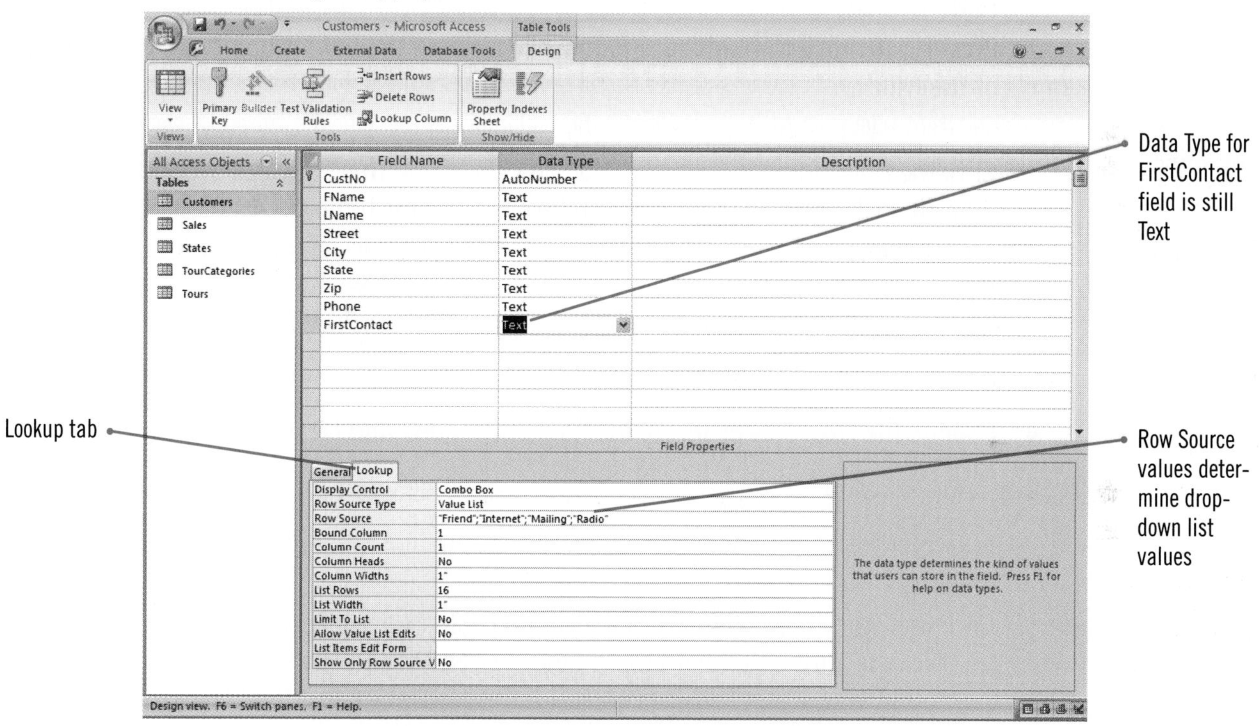

FIGURE E-9: Using a Lookup field in a datasheet

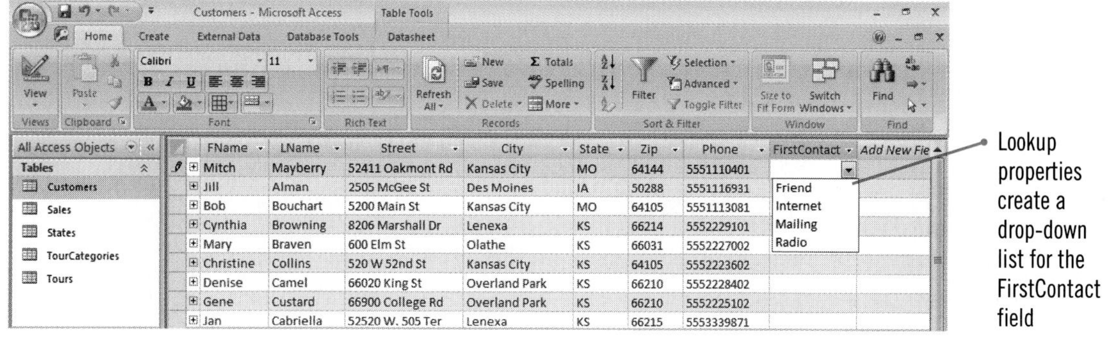

UNIT
E
Access 2007

Modifying Text Fields

Field properties are the characteristics that apply to each field in a table, such as Field Size, Default Value, or Caption. These properties help ensure database accuracy and clarity because they restrict the way data is entered, stored, and displayed. You modify field properties in Table Design View. See Table E-2 for more information on Text field properties. After reviewing the Customers table with Mark Rock, you decide to make field property changes to several Text fields in that table.

STEPS

1. **Right-click the Customers table in the Navigation Pane, then click Design View on the shortcut menu**

   The Customers table opens in Design View. The field properties appear on the General tab of the lower half of the Table Design View window and display the properties of the selected field. Field properties change depending on the field's data type. For example, when you select a field with a Text data type, the Field Size property is visible. However, when you select a field with a Date/Time data type, Access controls the Field Size property, so that property is not displayed. Many field properties are optional, but for those that require an entry, Access provides a default value.

2. **Press [↓] to move through each field while viewing the field properties in the lower half of the window**

   The **field selector button** to the left of the field indicates which field is currently selected.

QUICK TIP

Because no entries in the FirstContact field are greater than 20 characters, you do not lose any data by making this property change.

3. **Click the FirstContact field name, double-click 255 in the Field Size property text box, type 20, click the Save button on the Quick Access toolbar, then click Yes**

   The maximum and the default value for the Field Size property for a Text field is 255. In general, however, you want to make the Field Size property for Text fields only as large as needed to accommodate the longest entry. You can increase the size later if necessary. In some cases, shortening the Field Size property helps prevent typographical errors. For example, you should set the Field Size property for a State field that stores two-letter state abbreviations to 2 to prevent errors such as TXX.

4. **Change the Field Size property to 30 for the FName and LName fields, click , then click Yes**

   No existing entries are greater than 30 characters for either of these fields, so no data is lost. The **Input Mask** property provides a visual guide for users as they enter data. It also helps determine what types of values can be entered into a field.

TROUBLE

If the Input Mask Wizard is not installed on your computer, you can complete this step by typing !(999) 000-0000;;_ directly into the Input Mask property for the Phone field.

5. **Click the Phone field name, click the Input Mask property text box, click the Build button click the Phone Number input mask, click Next, click Next, then click Finish**

   Table Design View of the Customers table should look like Figure E-10, which shows the Input Mask property entered for the Phone field.

6. **Click , click the View button on the Design tab, press [Tab] enough times to move to the Phone field for the first record, type 5554441234, then press [Enter]**

   The Phone Input Mask property creates an easy-to-use visual guide to facilitate accurate data entry.

7. **Close the Customers table**

FIGURE E-10: Changing Text field properties

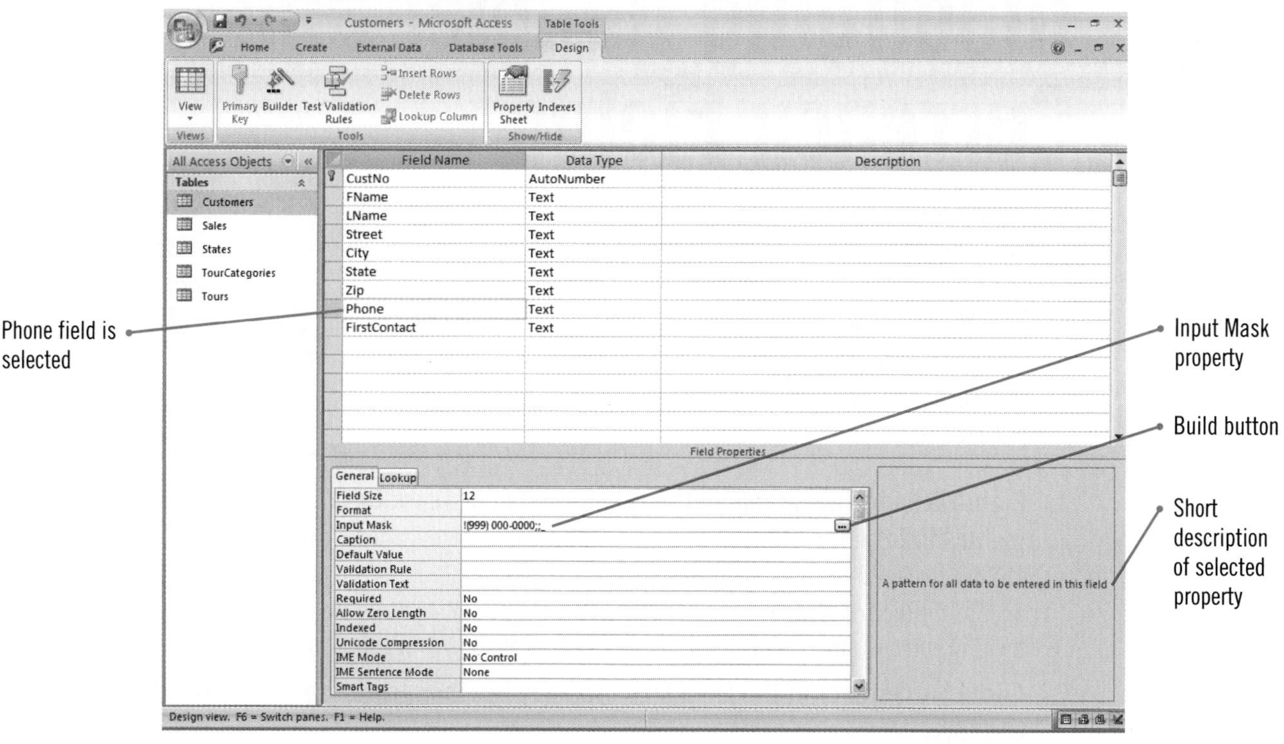

TABLE E-2: Common Text field properties

property	description	sample field	sample property entry
Field Size	Controls how many characters can be entered into the field	State	2
Format	Controls how information will be displayed and printed	State	> (displays all characters in uppercase)
Input Mask	Provides a pattern for data to be entered	Phone	!(999) 000-0000;1;_
Caption	Describes the field in the first row of a datasheet, form, or report; if the Caption property is not entered, the field name itself is used to label the field	Emp#	Employee Number
Default Value	Displays a value that is automatically entered in the given field for new records	City	Kansas City
Required	Determines if an entry is required for this field	LastName	Yes

Exploring the Input Mask property

The Input Mask property provides a pattern for data to be entered, using three parts separated by semicolons. The first part provides a pattern for what type of data can be entered. For example, 9 represents an optional number, 0 a required number, ? an optional letter, and L a required letter. The second part determines whether all displayed characters (such as dashes in a phone number) are stored in the field. For the second part of the input mask, a 0 entry stores all characters such as 555-7722, and a 1 entry stores only the entered data, 5557722. The third part of the input mask determines which character Access uses to guide the user through the mask. Common choices are the asterisk (*), underscore (_), or pound sign (#).

Modifying Number and Currency Fields

Although some properties for Number and Currency fields are the same as the properties of Text fields, each data type has its own list of valid properties. Numeric and Currency fields have similar properties because they both contain numeric values. Currency fields store values that represent money, and Number fields store values that represent values such as quantities, measurements, and scores. The Tours table contains both a Number field (Duration) and a Currency field (Cost). You want to modify the properties of these two fields.

STEPS

1. **Right-click the Tours table in the Navigation Pane, click Design View on the shortcut menu, click the Duration field name, then maximize Table Design View**
   The default Field Size property for a Number field is Long Integer. See Table E-3 for more information on the options for the Field Size property of a Number field. Access controls the size of Currency fields to control the way numbers are rounded in calculations, so the Field Size property isn't available for Currency fields.
2. **Click Long Integer in the Field Size property text box, click the Field Size list arrow, then click Byte**
   Choosing a Byte value for the Field Size property allows entries from 0 to 255, so it greatly restricts the possible values and the storage requirements for the Duration field.
3. **Click the Cost field name, click Auto in the Decimal Places property text box, click the Decimal Places list arrow, then click 0**
   Your Table Design View should look like Figure E-11. Because all of Quest's tours are priced at a round dollar value, you do not need to display cents in the Cost field.

> **QUICK TIP**
> The Property Update Options button allows you to propagate field properties in the queries, forms, and reports that use the Cost field.

4. **Save the table, then view the datasheet**
   Because none of the current entries in the Duration field is greater than 255, which is the maximum value allowed by a Number field with a Byte Field Size, you don't lose any data. You want to test the new property changes.
5. **Press [Tab] three times to move to the Duration field for the first record, type 800, then press [Tab]**
   Because 800 is larger than the Byte Field Size property allows (0-255), an Access error message appears indicating that the value isn't valid for this field.
6. **Press [Esc] twice to remove the inappropriate entry in the Duration field, then press [Tab] four times to move to the Cost field**
   The Cost field is set to display zero digits after the decimal point.
7. **Type 750.25 in the Cost field of the first record, press [↓], then click $750 in the Cost field of the first record**
   Although the Decimal Places property for the Cost field dictates that entries in the field are *formatted* to display zero digits after the decimal point, 750.25 is the actual value stored in the field. Modifying the Decimal Places property does not change the actual data. Rather, the Decimal Places property only changes the way the data is *presented*.
8. **Click the Undo button on the Quick Access toolbar to restore the Cost entry to $750, then close the Tours table**

FIGURE E-11: Changing Currency and Number field properties

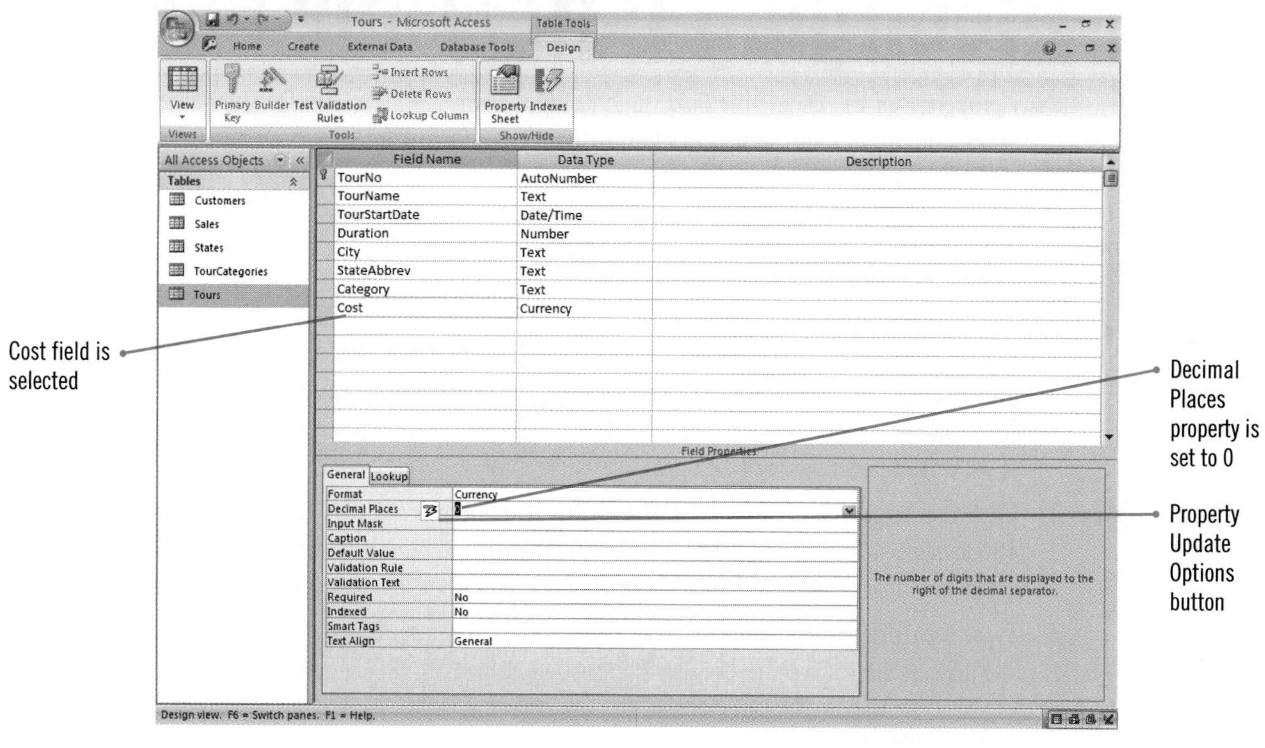

TABLE E-3: Common Number field properties

property	description
Field Size	Determines the largest number that can be entered in the field, as well as the type of data (e.g., integer or fraction)
Byte	Stores numbers from 0 to 255 (no fractions)
Integer	Stores numbers from –32,768 to 32,767 (no fractions)
Long Integer	Stores numbers from –2,147,483,648 to 2,147,483,647 (no fractions)
Single	Stores numbers (including fractions with six digits to the right of the decimal point) times 10 to the –38th to +38th power
Double	Stores numbers (including fractions with over 10 digits to the right of the decimal point) in the range of 10 to the –324th to +324th power
Decimal Places	The number of digits displayed to the right of the decimal point

UNIT
E
Access 2007

Modifying Date/Time Fields

Many properties of the Date/Time field, such as Input Mask, Caption, and Default Value, work the same way as they do in fields with a Text or Number data type. One difference, however, is the **Format** property, which helps you format dates in various ways such as January 25, 2006; 25-Jan-06; or 01/25/2006. You want to change the format of Date/Time fields in the database to display two digits for the month and day values and four digits for the year, as in 05/05/2010.

STEPS

1. **Right-click the Tours table in the Navigation Pane, click Design View on the shortcut menu, click the TourStartDate field name, then maximize Table Design View**

   You want the tour start dates to appear with two digits for the month and day, such as 07/05/2010, instead of the default presentation of dates, 7/5/2010.

2. **Click the Format property box, then click the Format list arrow**

   Although several predefined Date/Time formats are available, none matches the format you want. To define a custom format, enter symbols that represent how you want the date to appear.

> **QUICK TIP**
> Click any property box, then press F1 to open the Microsoft Access Help window to the page that describes that property.

3. **Type mm/dd/yyyy then press [Enter]**

   The updated Format property for the TourStartDate field shown in Figure E-12 sets the date to appear with two digits for the month, two digits for the day, and four digits for the year. The parts of the date are separated by forward slashes.

4. **Save the table, display the datasheet, then click the New (blank) record button on the navigation bar**

   To test the new Format property for the TourStartDate field, you can add a new record to the table.

5. **Press [Tab] to move to the TourName field, type Missouri Eagles, press [Tab], type 9/1/10, press [Tab], type 7, press [Tab], type Hollister, press [Tab], type MO, press [Tab], type a (for Adventure), press [Tab], then type 700**

   Your screen should look like Figure E-13. The new record is entered into the Tours table. The Format property for the TourStartDate field makes the entry appear as 09/01/2010, as desired.

> **QUICK TIP**
> Access assumes that years entered with two digits from 30 to 99 refer to the years 1930 through 1999, and 00 to 29 refers to the years 2000 through 2029. To enter a year before 1930 or after 2029, enter all four digits of the year.

FIGURE E-12: Changing Date/Time field properties

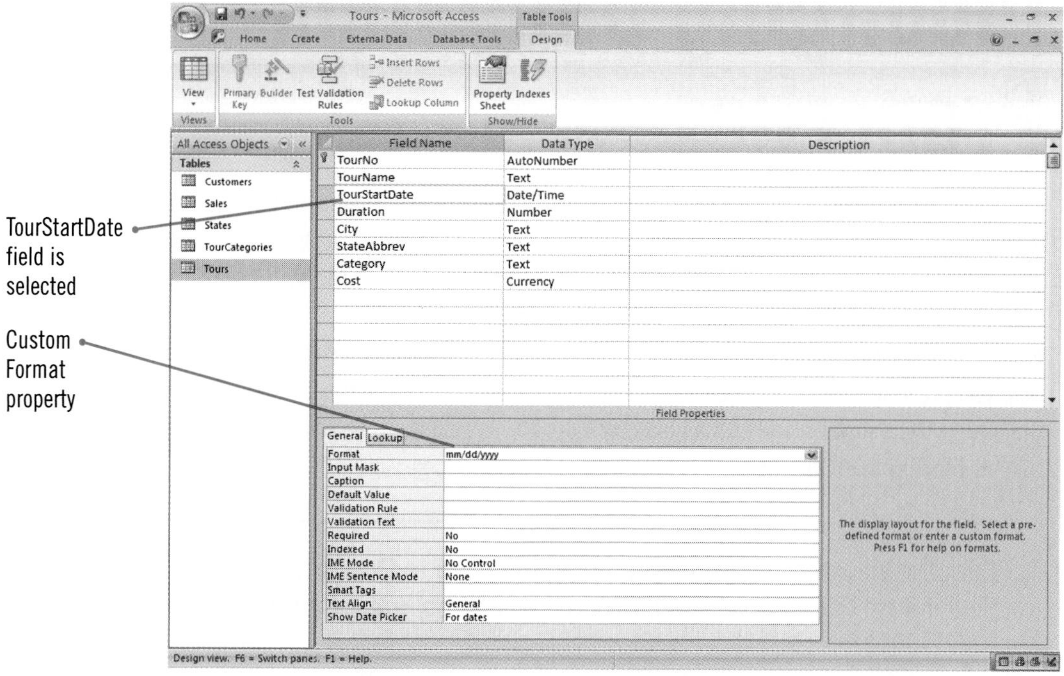

FIGURE E-13: Testing the Format property for the TourStartDate field

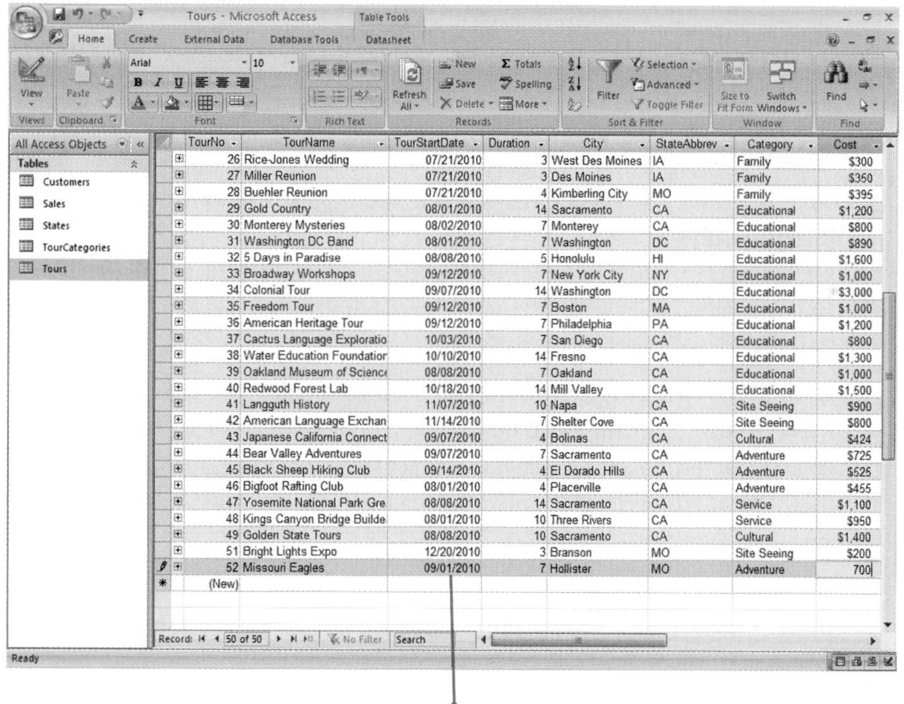

Access 2007

Using Smart Tags

The Property Update Options button is an Access Smart Tag. **Smart Tags** are buttons that appear in certain conditions. They provide a small menu of options to help you work with the task at hand. Access provides the Property Update Options Smart Tag to help you quickly apply property changes to other objects of the database that use the field. The **Error Indicator button** Smart Tag helps identify potential design errors. For example, if you are working in Form Design View and add a text box to the form but do not correctly bind it to an underlying field, the Error Indicator button appears by the text box to alert you to the problem.

Modifying Validation Properties

The **Validation Rule** property determines what entries a field can accept. For example, a Validation Rule for a Date/Time field might require date entries on or after 1/1/2010. A Validation Rule for a Currency field might indicate that valid entries fall between $0 and $1,500. You use the **Validation Text** property to display an explanatory message when a user tries to enter data that doesn't meet the criteria for a valid field entry established by the Validation Rule. Therefore, the Validation Rule and Validation Text field properties help you prevent unreasonable data from being entered into the database. Mark Rock reminds you that Quest tours start no earlier than January 1, 2010. You can use the validation properties to establish this rule for the TourStartDate field.

STEPS

1. **Click the View button on the Home tab to return to Design View, click the TourStartDate field if it isn't already selected, click the Validation Rule property box, then type >=1/1/2010**

   This entry forces all dates in the TourStartDate field to be greater than or equal to 1/1/2010. See Table E-4 for more examples of Validation Rule expressions. The Validation Text property provides a helpful message to the user when the entry in the field breaks the rule entered in the Validation Rule property.

2. **Click the Validation Text box, then type Date must be on or after 1/1/2010**

   The Design View of the Tours table should now look like Figure E-14. Access modifies a property to include additional syntax by changing the entry in the Validation Rule property to >=#1/1/2010#. Pound signs (#) are used to surround date criteria.

3. **Save the table, then click Yes when asked to test the existing data with new data integrity rules**

   Because no dates in the TourStartDate field are earlier than 1/1/2010, Access finds no date errors in the current data and saves the table. You now want to test that the Validation Rule and Validation Text properties work when entering data in the datasheet.

4. **Click the View button on the Design tab to display the datasheet, press [Tab] twice to move to the TourStartDate field, type 1/1/06, then press [Tab]**

   Because you tried to enter a date that was not true for the Validation Rule property for the TourStartDate field, a dialog box opens and displays the Validation Text entry, as shown in Figure E-15.

5. **Click OK to close the validation message**

   You now know that the Validation Rule and Validation Text properties work properly.

6. **Press [Esc] to reject the invalid date entry in the TourStartDate field**

7. **Close the Tours table**

FIGURE E-14: Entering validation properties

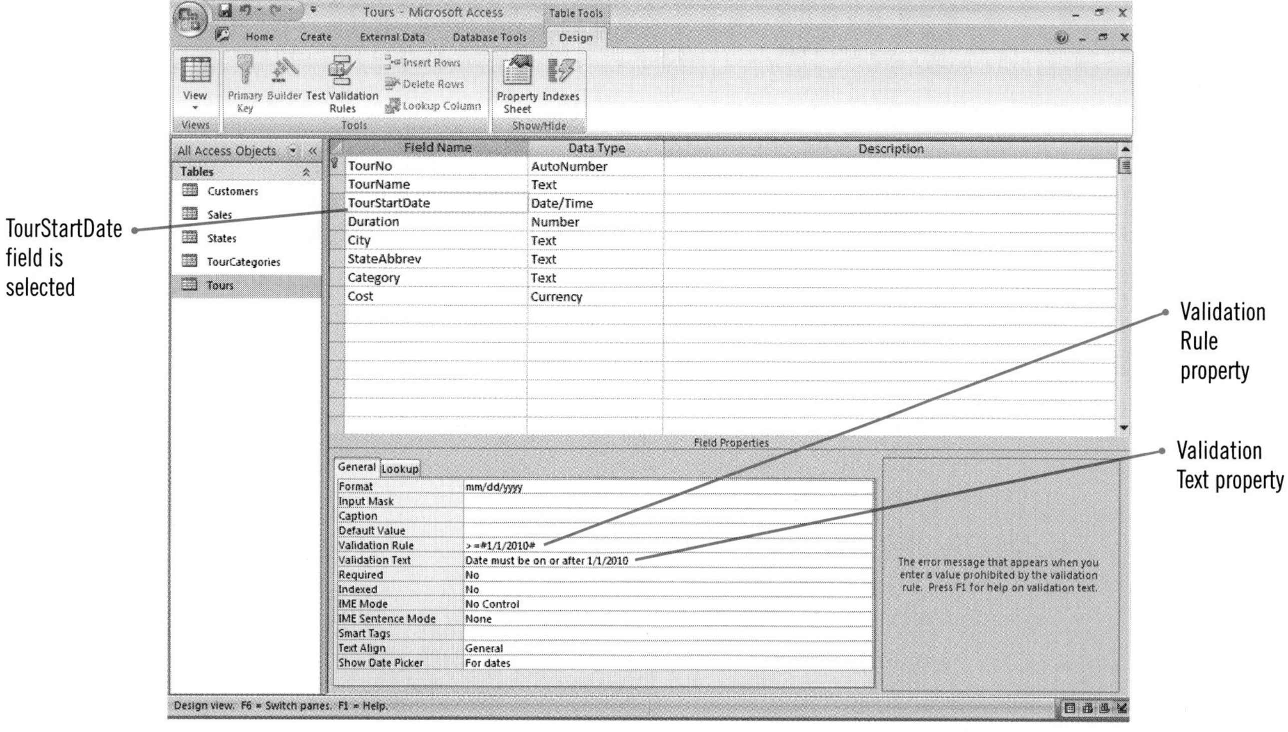

FIGURE E-15: Validation Text message

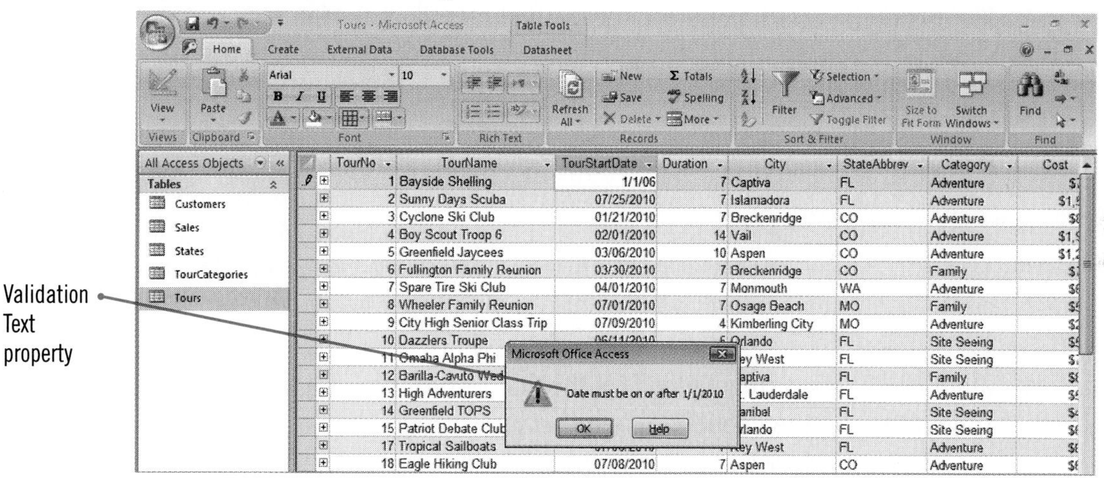

TABLE E-4: Validation Rule expressions

data type	validation rule expression	description
Number or Currency	>0	The number must be positive
Number or Currency	>10 And <100	The number must be between 10 and 100
Number or Currency	10 Or 20 Or 30	The number must be 10, 20, or 30
Text	"IA" Or "NE" Or "MO"	The entry must be IA, NE, or MO
Date/Time	>=#7/1/93#	The date must be on or after 7/1/1993
Date/Time	>#1/1/10# And <#1/1/12#	The date must be between 1/1/2010 and 1/1/2012

Access 2007

STEPS

Creating Attachment Fields

An **Attachment field** allows you to attach an external file such as a Word document, PowerPoint presentation, Excel workbook, or image file to a record. Earlier versions of Access allowed you to link or embed external data using the **OLE** (object linking and embedding) data type. The Attachment data type is superior to OLE because it stores data more efficiently; stores more file formats, such as JPEG images; and requires no additional software to view the files from within Access. Mark Rock asks you to incorporate images on forms and reports to help describe and market each tour. You can use an Attachment field to store JPEG images that help illustrate each tour in the Tours table.

1. **Right-click the Tours table in the Navigation Pane, click Design View, then maximize Table Design View**

   You can add the new field below the Cost field.

2. **Click the Field Name cell below Cost, type Picture, press [Tab], click the Data Type list arrow, then click Attachment**

   Now that you created the new Attachment field, you're ready to add data to it in Datasheet View.

3. **Click the Save button on the Quick Access toolbar, click the View button on the Design tab to switch to Datasheet View, then press [Tab] enough times to move to the new Attachment field**

   The Attachment field cell displays a small paper clip icon with the number of files attached to the field in parentheses, as shown in Figure E-16. You have not attached any files to this field yet, so each record shows zero (0) file attachments. You can attach files to this field directly from Datasheet View.

4. **Right-click the attachment icon for the first record, click Manage Attachments on the shortcut menu, click Add, navigate to the drive and folder where you store your Data Files, double-click Sunset.jpg, then click OK**

   The Sunset.jpg file is now included with the first record, and the datasheet reflects that one (1) file is attached to the Picture field of the first record. You can add more than one file attachment to the same field, but good database practices encourage you to add only one piece of information per field. Therefore, if you want to also attach a Word document listing the trip itinerary to this record, good database practices encourage you to add a second Attachment field to handle this information. You can view all types of file attachments directly from the datasheet. You can also view images from a form or report that displays this information.

5. **Right-click the attachment icon for the first record, click Manage Attachments on the shortcut menu, then double-click Sunset.jpg to open it**

   The image opens in the program that is associated with the .jpg extension on your computer. Figure E-17 shows the Sunset.jpg image as displayed by Windows Photo Gallery, but a different program on your computer might be associated with the .jpg file extension. **JPEG** is an acronym for Joint Photographic Experts Group, which defines the standards for the compression algorithms that allow image files to be stored in an efficient compressed format. Because the size requirements of JPEG images are minimized, the JPEG file format is ideal for storing large numbers of pictures in a database or for transporting images across a network.

6. **Close the window that displays the Sunset.jpg image, click Cancel in the Attachments dialog box, close the Tours table, close the Quest-E.accdb database, then exit Access**

FIGURE E-16: Attachment field in Datasheet View

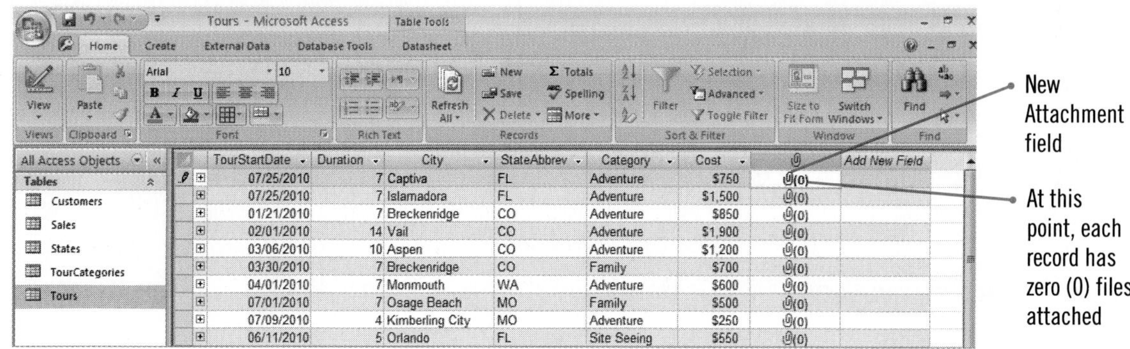
New Attachment field
At this point, each record has zero (0) files attached

FIGURE E-17: Viewing a JPEG image

This image appears in Windows Photo Gallery, but your image might appear in a different program

Recognizing database formats

When you create a new, blank database in Microsoft Office Access 2007, Access gives the file the .accdb extension and formats it as an Access 2007 database. Access 2007 displays the version of the current database file in the title bar when you first open the database. The **.accdb** file extension usually means the database is an Access 2007 format database, but note that Access 2007 format databases are *not* readable by earlier versions of Access such as Access 2000, Access 2002 (XP), or Access 2003. Some features such as multivalued fields and Attachment fields are only available when working on an Access 2007 database. In some cases, you might prefer to use Access 2007, but create or convert database files to an earlier Access format such as Access 2000 or Access 2002-2003. This option is helpful if you share the database with users who are still using earlier versions of Access. In Microsoft Office Access 2007, to save an existing database to a different version, use the Save As command on the Office button menu. Using this feature, Access 2000, 2002-2003 databases are given an **.mdb** file extension.

Practice

If you have a SAM user profile, you may have access to hands-on instruction, practice, and assessment of the skills covered in this unit. Log in to your SAM account (http://sam2007.course.com/) to launch any assigned training activities or exams that relate to the skills covered in this unit.

▼ CONCEPTS REVIEW

Identify each element of Table Design View shown in Figure E-18.

FIGURE E-18

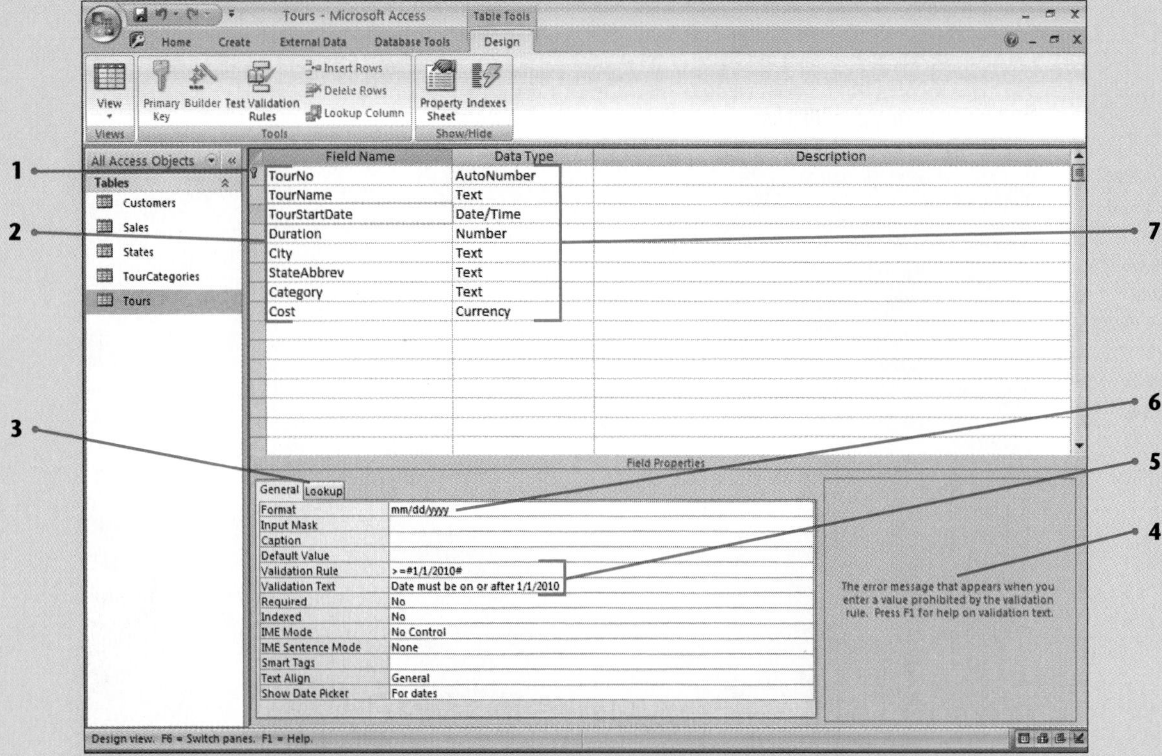

Match each term with the statement that best describes it.

8. **Primary key field**
9. **Validation properties**
10. **Table Design View**
11. **Row Source**
12. **Relational database**
13. **Input Mask**
14. **Lookup properties**
15. **Multivalued field**
16. **Attachment field**

a. Field that allows you to store external files such as a Word document, PowerPoint presentation, Excel workbook, or image files
b. Field that allows you to make more than one choice from a drop-down list for a field
c. Field that holds unique information for each record in the table
d. Several tables linked together in one-to-many relationships
e. Field properties that allow you to supply a drop-down list of values for a field
f. Access window where all characteristics of a table, such as field names and field properties, are defined
g. Field properties that help you prevent unreasonable data entries for a field
h. Field property that provides a visual guide as you enter data
i. Lookup property that determines where the Lookup field gets its list of values

Select the best answer from the list of choices.

17. Which of the following problems most clearly indicates that you need to redesign your database?

- **a.** The Input Mask Wizard has not been used.
- **b.** Referential integrity is enforced on table relationships.
- **c.** Not all fields have Validation Rule properties.
- **d.** There is duplicated data in the field of several records of a table.

18. Which of the following is *not* defined in Table Design View?

- **a.** The primary key field
- **b.** Field Size properties
- **c.** Duplicate data
- **d.** Field data types

19. What is the purpose of enforcing referential integrity?

- **a.** To prevent incorrect entries in the primary key field
- **b.** To prevent orphan records from being entered
- **c.** To require an entry for each field of each record
- **d.** To force the application of meaningful validation rules

20. To create a many-to-many relationship between two tables, you must create:

- **a.** A junction table.
- **b.** Combination primary key fields in each table.
- **c.** A one-to-many relationship between the two tables, with referential integrity enforced.
- **d.** Foreign key fields in each table.

▼ SKILLS REVIEW

1. Examine relational databases.

a. List the fields needed to create an Access relational database to manage membership information for a philanthropic club, community service organization, or international aid group.

b. Identify fields that would contain duplicate values if all of the fields were stored in a single table.

c. Group the fields into subject matter tables, then identify the primary key field for each table.

d. Assume that your database contains two tables: Members and ZipCodes. If you did not identify these two tables earlier, regroup the fields within these two table names, then identify the primary key field for each table, the foreign key field in the Members table, and how the tables would be related using a one-to-many relationship.

2. Design related tables.

a. Start Access 2007, then click the New Blank Database button.

b. Type **Membership-E** in the File Name box, click the Folder icon to navigate to the drive and folder where you store your Data Files, click OK, then click Create.

c. Use Table Design View to create a new table with the name **Members** and the field names and data types shown in Figure E-19.

FIGURE E-19

field name	data type
FirstName	Text
LastName	Text
Street	Text
Zip	Text
Phone	Text
Birthdate	Date/Time
Dues	Currency
MemberNo	Text
MemberType	Text
CharterMember	Yes/No

d. Specify MemberNo as the primary key field, save the Members table, then close it.

e. Use Table Design View to create a new table named **ZipCodes** with the field names and data types shown in Figure E-20.

FIGURE E-20

field name	data type
Zip	Text
City	Text
State	Text

f. Identify Zip as the primary key field, save the ZipCodes table, then close it.

g. Use Table Design View to create a third new table called **Activities** with the field names and data types shown in Figure E-21.

FIGURE E-21

field name	data type
ActivityNo	AutoNumber
MemberNo	Text
ActivityDate	Date/Time
Hours	Number

h. Identify ActivityNo as the primary key field, save the Activities table, then close it.

▼ SKILLS REVIEW (CONTINUED)

3. Create one-to-many relationships.

a. Open the Relationships window, double-click Activities, double-click Members, then double-click ZipCodes to add all three tables to the Relationships window. Close the Show Table dialog box.

b. Resize all field lists as necessary so that all fields are visible, then drag the Zip field from the ZipCodes table to the Zip field in the Members table to create a one-to-many relationship between the ZipCodes table and Members table, using the common Zip field.

c. Enforce referential integrity, and create the one-to-many relationship between ZipCodes and Members.

d. Drag the MemberNo field from the Members table to the MemberNo field in the Activities table to create a one-to-many relationship between the Members table and the Activities table, using the common MemberNo field.

e. Enforce referential integrity, and create the one-to-many relationship between Members and Activities. See Figure E-22.

f. Create a Relationship report for the Membership-E database, add your name as a label to the Report Header section of the report in Report Design View, then print the report.

g. Close the Relationship report without saving the report, then close the Relationships window. Save the changes to the Relationships window if prompted.

FIGURE E-22

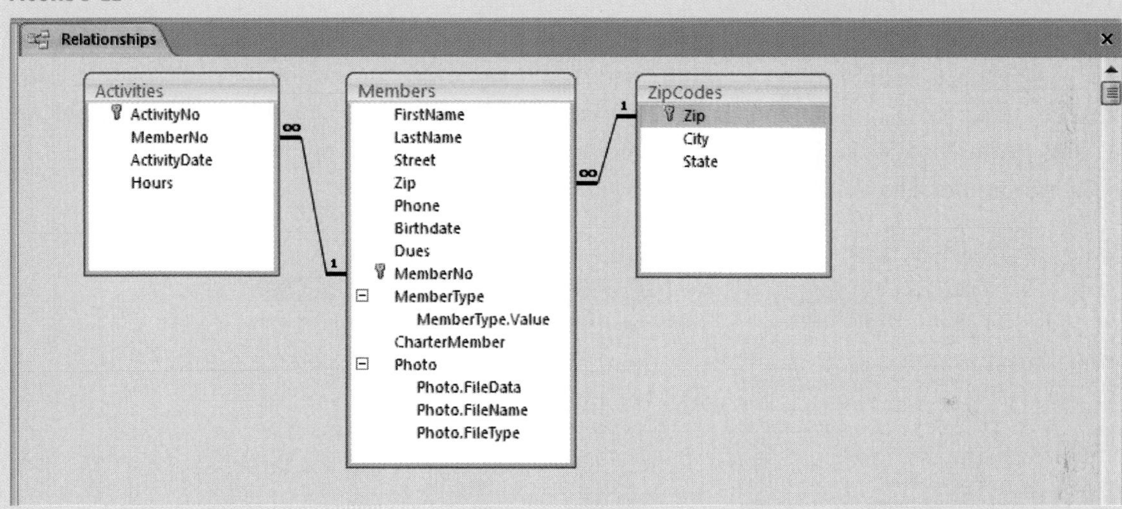

Access 2007

4. **Create Lookup fields.**
   a. Open the Members table in Design View, then start the Lookup Wizard for the MemberType field.
   b. Select the option that allows you to enter your own values, then enter **Active**, **Inactive**, **Teen**, **Adult**, and **Senior** as the values for the lookup column.
   c. Use the default MemberType label, check the Allow Multiple Values check box, finish the Lookup Wizard, and confirm that you want to allow multiple values.
   d. Save and close the Members table.

5. **Modify Text fields.**
   a. Open the ZipCodes table in Design View.
   b. Change the Field Size property of the State field to **2** then save the ZipCodes table and display it in Datasheet View.
   c. Enter a record with the zip code, city, and state for your school. Try to enter more than two characters in the State field, then close the ZipCodes table.
   d. Open the Members table in Design View. Use the Input Mask Wizard to create an Input Mask property for the Phone field. Choose the Phone Number Input Mask. Accept the other default options provided by the Input Mask Wizard. (*Hint*: If the Input Mask Wizard is not installed on your computer, type **!(999) 000-0000;;_** for the Input Mask property for the Phone field.) See Figure E-23.
   e. Change the Field Size property of the FirstName, LastName, and Street fields to **30**. Save the Members table.
   f. Open the Members table in Datasheet View and enter a new record with your name in the FirstName and LastName fields and your school's Street, Zip, and Phone field values. Note the effect of the Input Mask on the Phone field. Enter **1/1/1985** for the Birthdate field, **200** for Dues, and **1** for MemberNo. Choose both Active and Adult for the MemberType field, and do not check the CharterMember field.

FIGURE E-23

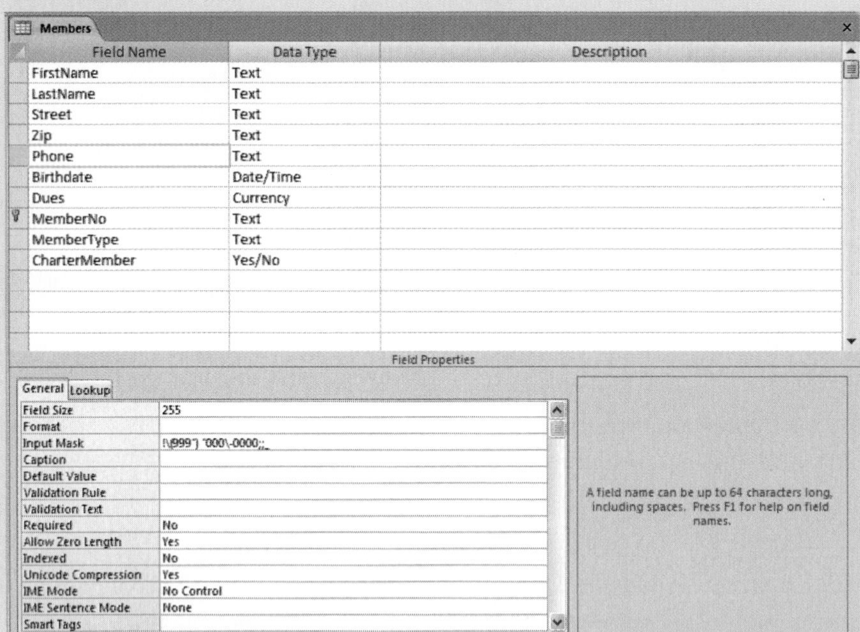

▼ SKILLS REVIEW (CONTINUED)

6. Modify Number and Currency fields.

a. Open the Members table in Design View.

b. Change the Decimal Places property of the Dues field to **0**. Save and close the Members table.

c. Open the Activities table in Design View.

d. Change the Field Size property of the Hours field to **Byte**. Save and close the Activities table.

7. Modify Date/Time fields.

a. Open the Members table in Design View.

b. Change the Format property of the Birthdate field to **mm/dd/yyyy**

c. Save and close the Members table.

d. Open the Activities table in Design View.

e. Change the Format property of the ActivityDate field to **mm/dd/yyyy**

f. Save and close the Activities table

8. Modify field validation properties.

a. Open the Members table in Design View.

b. Click the Birthdate field name, click the Validation Rule text box, then type **<1/1/2000** (Note that Access automatically adds pound signs around date criteria in the Validation Rule property.)

c. Click the Validation Text box, then type **Birthdate must be before 1/1/2000**

d. Save and allow the changes, then open the Members table in Datasheet View.

e. Test the Validation Text and Validation Rule properties by tabbing to the Birthdate field and entering a date after 1/1/2000 such as 1/1/2001. Click OK when prompted with the Validation Text message, press [Esc] to return the Birthdate field value to 01/01/1985, then close the Members table.

▼ SKILLS REVIEW (CONTINUED)

9. **Create Attachment fields.**
   a. Open the Members table in Design View, then add a new field with the field name Photo and an Attachment data type, as shown in Figure E-24. Save the table.
   b. Display the Members table in Datasheet View, then attach the **Member1.jpg** file (provided in the drive and folder where you store your Data Files) to the new Photo field for the first record.
   c. Close the Members table.
   d. Use the Form Wizard to create a form based on all of the fields in the Members table. Use a Columnar layout, a Civic style, and title the form **Members Entry Form**.
   e. Print the first page of the Members Entry Form that shows the picture stored in the Photo field, then close the form.
   f. Close the Membership-E.accdb database, then exit Access.

FIGURE E-24

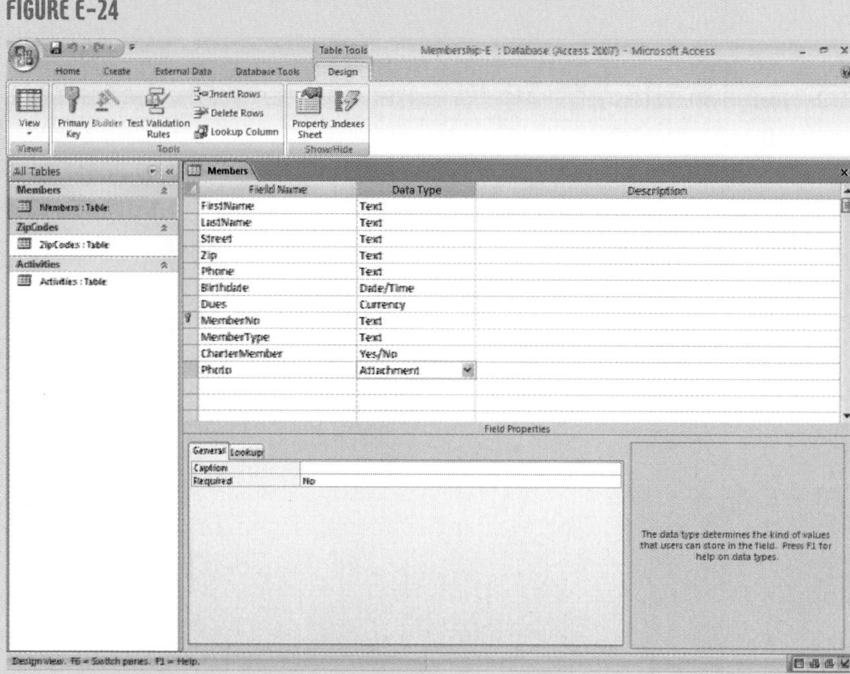

▼ INDEPENDENT CHALLENGE 1

As the manager of a music store's instrument rental program, you decide to create a database to track rentals to schoolchildren. The fields you need to track are organized with four tables: Instruments, Rentals, Customers, and Schools.

a. Start Access, then create a new blank database called **MusicStore-E.accdb** in the folder where you store your Data Files.

b. Use Table Design View to create the four tables in the MusicStore-E database using the information shown in Figure E-25. The primary key field for each table is identified with bold text.

FIGURE E-25

table	field name	data type
Customers	FirstName	Text
	LastName	Text
	Street	Text
	City	Text
	State	Text
	Zip	Text
	CustNo	Text
	SchoolNo	Text
Instruments	Description	Text
	SerialNo	Text
	MonthlyFee	Currency
Schools	SchoolName	Text
	SchoolNo	Text
Rentals	**RentalNo**	AutoNumber
	CustNo	Text
	SerialNo	Text
	RentalDate	Date/Time

c. Enter **>3/1/2010** as the Validation Rule property for the RentalDate field of the Rentals table. This change allows only dates later than 3/1/2010 to be entered into this field.

d. Enter **Dates must be after March 1, 2010** as the Validation Text property to the RentalDate field of the Rentals table. Note that Access adds pound signs (#) to the date criteria entered in the Validation Rule as soon as you enter the Validation Text property.

e. Save and close the Rentals table.

▼ INDEPENDENT CHALLENGE 1 (CONTINUED)

f. Open the Relationships window, add all four tables to the window, as shown in Figure E-26, and create one-to-many relationships as shown. Be sure to enforce referential integrity on each relationship.

g. Preview the Relationship report, add your name as a label to the Report Header section, then print the report, making sure that all fields of each table are visible.

h. Close the Relationship report without saving it. Close the Relationships window, then save the layout if prompted.

i. Close the MusicStore-E.accdb database, then exit Access.

FIGURE E-26

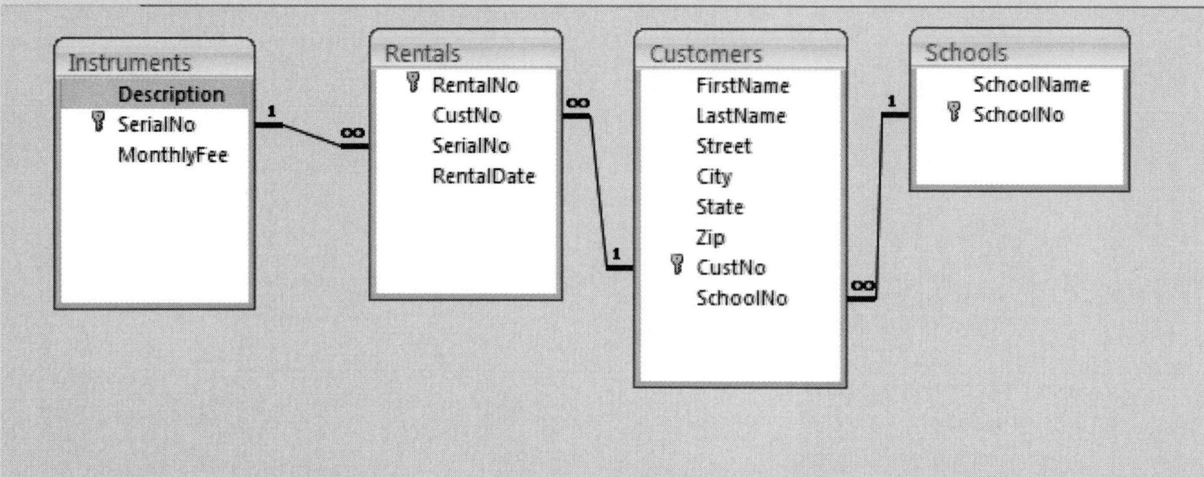

▼ INDEPENDENT CHALLENGE 2

You're a member and manager of a recreational baseball team and decide to create an Access database to manage player information, games, and batting statistics.

This Independent Challenge requires an Internet connection.

a. Start Access, then create a new database called **Baseball-E.accdb** in the drive and folder where you store your Data Files.

b. Create a **Players** table with fields and appropriate data types to record the player first name, last name, and uniform number. Make the uniform number field the primary key field.

c. Create a **Games** table with fields and appropriate data types to record an automatic game number, date of the game, opponent's name, home score, and visitor score. Make the game number field the primary key field.

d. Create an **AtBats** table with fields and appropriate data types to record hits, at bats, the game number, and the uniform number of the player. This table does not need a primary key field.

e. In the Relationships window, create a one-to-many relationship with referential integrity between the Games and AtBats table, using the common game number field.

f. In the Relationships window, create a one-to-many relationship with referential integrity between the Players and AtBats table, using the common uniform number field. The final Relationships window is shown in Figure E-27.

FIGURE E-27

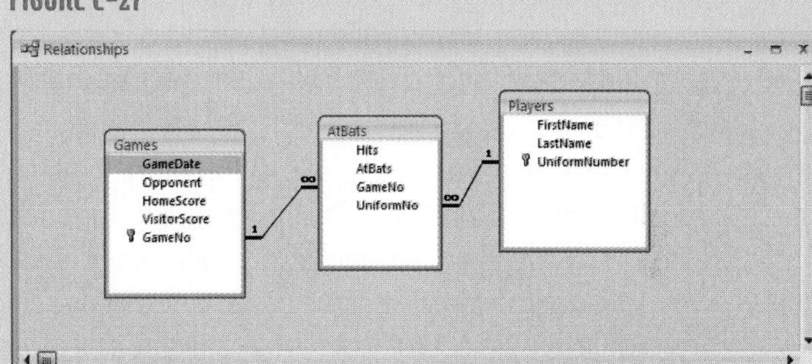

g. Use the Relationship Report button to create a report of the Relationships window, then print it. Close the Relationship report without saving it. Close the Relationships window, saving changes if prompted.

h. Using an Internet search tool, find the roster for a baseball team in your area, and enter nine players into the Players table. One of the players should have your name. Print the Players datasheet.

i. Research the games that this team has previously played, and enter one game record into the Games table.

j. Using the GameNo value of **1** and the UniformNo values from the Players table, enter nine records into the AtBats table to represent the batting statistics for the nine players for that game. Your entries do not need to represent a specific game, but they should be realistic. (*Hint*: Most players bat three or four times per game. A player cannot have more hits in a game than at bats.)

k. Print the AtBats datasheet.

l. Close the Baseball-E.accdb database, then exit Access.

Access 2007

▼ INDEPENDENT CHALLENGE 3

You want to create a database that documents blood bank donations by the employees of your company. Start by designing the database on paper, including the tables, field names, data types, and relationships. You want to track information such as employee name, department, blood type, date of donation, and the hospital that is earmarked to receive the donation. You also want to track basic hospital information, such as the hospital name and address.

a. On paper, create three balanced columns by drawing two vertical lines from the top to the bottom of the paper. Label the columns **Table**, **Field Name**, and **Data Type**, from left to right.
b. In the middle column, list all of the fields that need to be tracked to record the blood donations. When creating your field lists for each table, be sure to separate personal names into at least two fields, FirstName and LastName, so that you can easily sort, filter, and find data based on either part of a person's name.
c. In the first column, identify the table that contains this field. (*Hint*: In this case, you should identify three tables: Employees, Donations, and Hospitals.)
d. Identify the primary key field for each table by circling it. You might have to add a new field to each table if you do not have an existing field that naturally serves as the primary key field. (*Hint*: Each employee is identified with a unique EmployeeID, each hospital with a unique HospitalID, and each donation with a DonationID.)
e. In the third column, identify the appropriate data type for each field.
f. After identifying all field names, table names, and data types for each field, reorder the fields so that the fields for each table are listed together.
g. On a new sheet of paper, sketch the field lists for each table as they would appear in the Access Relationships window. Circle the primary key fields for each table. Include the one-to-many join lines as well as the "one" and "infinity" symbols to identify the "one" and "many" sides of the one-to-many relationship. To help determine how you should create the relationships between the tables, note that one employee can make several blood donations. One hospital can receive many donations. (*Hint*: When building a one-to-many relationship between two tables, one field must be common to both tables. To create a common field, you might need to return to your field lists in Step f and add a foreign key field to the table on the "many" side of the relationship in order to link the tables.)

Advanced Challenge Exercise

- Build the database you designed in Access with the name **BloodDrive-E.accdb**. Don't forget to enforce referential integrity on the two one-to-many relationships in this database.
- Print the Relationship report with your name added as a label to the Report Header section. Close the Relationship report without saving it, then close the Relationships window and save the layout changes.
- Add Lookup properties to the blood type field to provide only valid blood type entries of **A–**, **A+**, **B–**, **B+**, **O–**, **O+**, **AB–**, and **AB+** for this field.
- Close BloodDrive-E.accdb, then exit Access.

▼ REAL LIFE INDEPENDENT CHALLENGE

You want to document the books you've read by creating and storing the information in a relational database. You design the database on paper by identifying the tables, field names, data types, and relationships between the tables.

a. Complete Steps a through g as described in Independent Challenge 3, using the new case information. You like to read multiple books from the same author, so you should separate the author information into a separate table to avoid duplicate author name entries in the Books table. You also want to track information including the book title, category (such as Biography, Mystery, or Science Fiction), rating (a numeric value from 1–10 that indicates how much you liked the book), date you read the book, author's first name, and author's last name. When creating primary key fields, note that each book has an ISBN—International Standard Book Number—that is a unique number assigned to every book. To uniquely identify each author, use an AuthorNo field. Do not use the AuthorLastName field as the primary key field for the Authors table because it does not uniquely identify authors who have the same last names.

Advanced Challenge Exercise

- In Access, build the database you designed. Name the database **Books-E.accdb**, and save it in the drive and folder where you store your Data Files. Don't forget to enforce referential integrity on the one-to-many relationship in this database.
- Print the Relationship report with your name added as a label to the Report Header section. Close the Relationship report without saving it, then close the Relationships window and save the layout changes.
- Add Lookup properties to the field that identifies book categories. Include at least four types of book categories in the list.
- Add at least three records to each table and print them.
- Close Books-E.accdb, then exit Access.

▼ VISUAL WORKSHOP

Open the **Training-E.accdb** database, and create a new table called Vendors using the Table Design View shown in Figure E-28 to determine field names and data types. Make the following property changes: Change the Field Size property of the VState field to **2**, the VZip field to **9**, and VPhone field to **10**. Change the Field Size property of the VendorName, VStreet, and VCity fields to **30**. Apply a Phone Number Input Mask to the VPhone field. Be sure to specify that the VendorID field is the primary key field. Enter one record into the datasheet with your last name in the VendorName field and your school's contact information in the other fields. Print the datasheet in landscape orientation.

FIGURE E-28

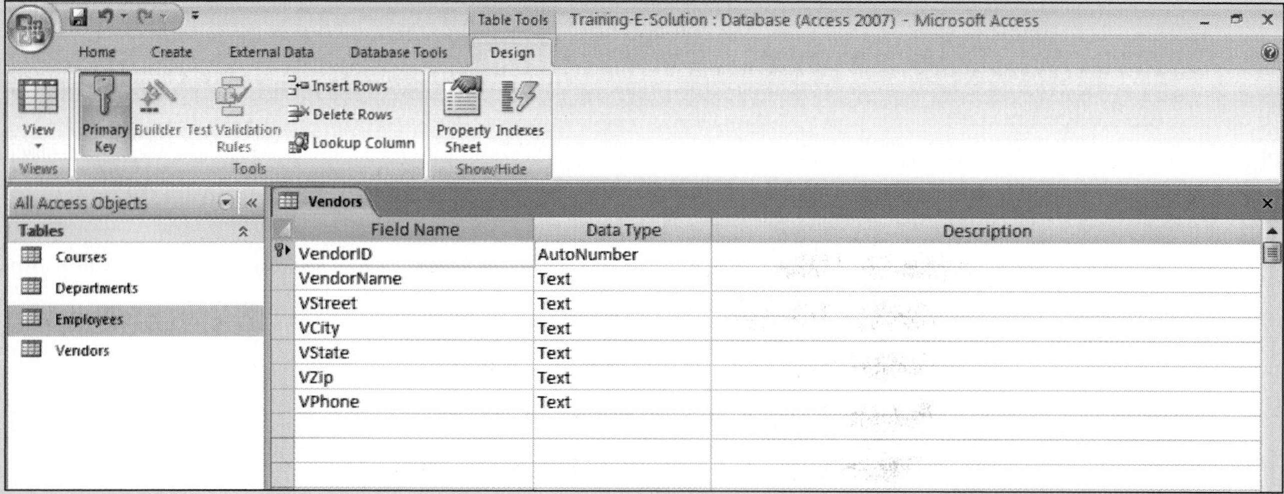

Appendix
A
Appendix

Restoring Defaults in Windows Vista and Disabling and Enabling Windows Aero

Files You Will Need:
No files needed.

Windows Vista is the most recent version of the Windows operating system. An operating system controls the way you work with your computer, supervises running programs, and provides tools for completing your computing tasks. After surveying millions of computer users, Microsoft incorporated their suggestions to make Windows Vista secure, reliable, and easy to use. In fact, Windows Vista is considered the most secure version of Windows yet. Other improvements include a powerful new search feature that lets you quickly search for files and programs from the Start menu and most windows, tools that simplify accessing the Internet, especially with a wireless connection, and multimedia programs that let you enjoy, share, and organize music, photos, and recorded TV. Finally, Windows Vista offers lots of visual appeal with its transparent, three-dimensional design in the Aero experience. This appendix explains how to make sure you are using the Windows Vista default settings for appearance, personalization, security, hardware, and sound and to enable and disable Windows Aero. For more information on Windows Aero, go to *www.microsoft.com/windowsvista/experiences/aero.mspx*.

OBJECTIVES

- Restore the defaults in the Appearance and Personalization section
- Restore the defaults in the Security section
- Restore the defaults in the Hardware and Sound section
- Disable Windows Aero
- Enable Windows Aero

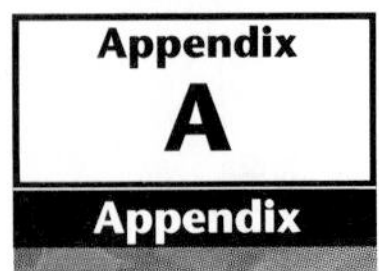

Restoring the Defaults in the Appearance and Personalization Section

The following instructions require a default Windows Vista Ultimate installation and the student logged in with an Administrator account. All of the following settings can be changed by accessing the Control Panel.

STEPS

- To restore the defaults in the Personalization section

1. Click Start, and then click Control Panel. Click Appearance and Personalization, click Personalization, and then compare your screen to Figure A-1
2. In the Personalization window, click Windows Color and Appearance, select the Default color, and then click OK
3. In the Personalization window, click Mouse Pointers. In the Mouse Properties dialog box, on the Pointers tab, select Windows Aero (system scheme) in the Scheme drop-down list, and then click OK
4. In the Personalization window, click Theme. Select Windows Vista from the Theme drop-down list, and then click OK
5. In the Personalization window, click Display Settings. In the Display Settings dialog box, drag the Resolution bar to 1024 by 768 pixels, and then click OK

FIGURE A-1

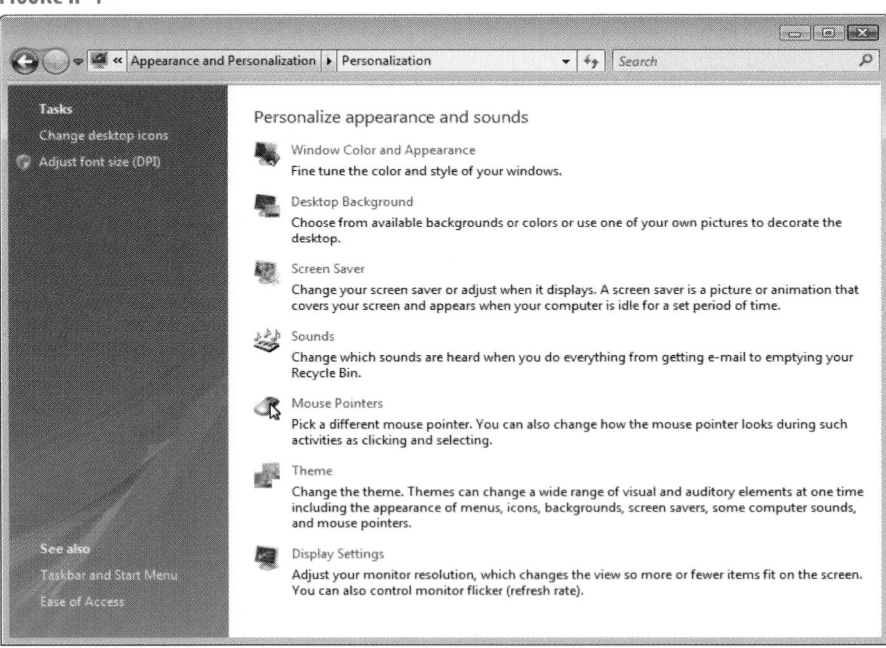

- To restore the defaults in the Taskbar and Start Menu section
  1. Click Start, and then click Control Panel. Click Appearance and Personalization, click Taskbar and Start Menu, and then compare your screen to Figure A-2
  2. In the Taskbar and Start Menu Properties dialog box, on the Taskbar tab, click to select all checkboxes except for "Auto-hide the taskbar"
  3. On the Start Menu tab, click to select the Start menu radio button and check all items in the Privacy section
  4. In the System icons section on the Notification Area tab, click to select all of the checkboxes except for "Power"
  5. On the Toolbars tab, click to select Quick Launch, none of the other items should be checked
  6. Click OK to close the Taskbar and Start Menu Properties dialog box
- To restore the defaults in the Folder Options section
  1. Click Start, and then click Control Panel. Click Appearance and Personalization, click Folder Options, and then compare your screen to Figure A-3
  2. In the Folder Options dialog box, on the General tab, click to select Show preview and filters in the Tasks section, click to select Open each folder in the same window in the Browse folders section, and click to select Double-click to open an item (single-click to select) in the Click items as follows section
  3. On the View tab, click the Reset Folders button, and then click Yes in the Folder views dialog box. Then click the Restore Defaults button
  4. On the Search tab, click the Restore Defaults button
  5. Click OK to close the Folder Options dialog box
- To restore the defaults in the Windows Sidebar Properties section
  1. Click Start, and then click Control Panel. Click Appearance and Personalization, click Windows Sidebar Properties, and then compare your screen to Figure A-4
  2. In the Windows Sidebar Properties dialog box, on the Sidebar tab, click to select Start Sidebar when Windows starts. In the Arrangement section, click to select Right, and then click to select 1 in the Display Sidebar on monitor drop-down list
  3. Click OK to close the Windows Sidebar Properties dialog box

FIGURE A-2

FIGURE A-3

FIGURE A-4

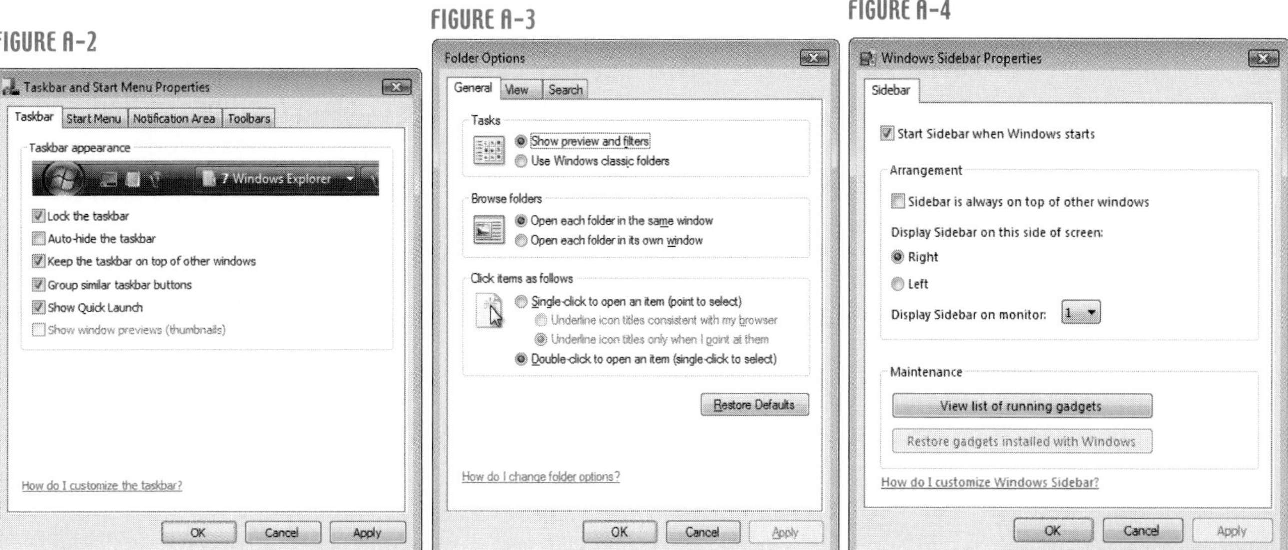

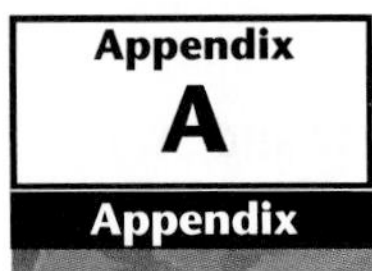

Restoring the Defaults in the Security Section

The following instructions require a default Windows Vista Ultimate installation and the student logged in with an Administrator account. All of the following settings can be changed by accessing the Control Panel.

STEPS

- To restore the defaults in the Windows Firewall section
  1. Click Start, and then click Control Panel. Click Security, click Windows Firewall, and then compare your screen to Figure A-5
  2. In the Windows Firewall dialog box, click Change settings. If the User Account Control dialog box appears, click Continue
  3. In the Windows Firewall Settings dialog box, click the Advanced tab. Click Restore Defaults, then click Yes in the Restore Defaults Confirmation dialog box
  4. Click OK to close the Windows Firewall Settings dialog box, and then close the Windows Firewall window
- To restore the defaults in the Internet Options section
  1. Click Start, and then click Control Panel. Click Security, click Internet Options, and then compare your screen to Figure A-6
  2. In the Internet Properties dialog box, on the General tab, click the Use default button. Click the Settings button in the Tabs section, and then click the Restore defaults button in the Tabbed Browsing Settings dialog box. Click OK to close the Tabbed Browsing Settings dialog box
  3. On the Security tab of the Internet Properties dialog box, click to uncheck the Enable Protected Mode checkbox, if necessary. Click the Default level button in the Security level for this zone section. If possible, click the Reset all zones to default level button
  4. On the Programs tab, click the Make default button in the Default web browser button for Internet Explorer, if possible. If Office is installed, Microsoft Office Word should be selected in the HTML editor drop-down list
  5. On the Advanced tab, click the Restore advanced settings button in the Settings section. Click the Reset button in the Reset Internet Explorer settings section, and then click Reset in the Reset Internet Explorer Settings dialog box
  6. Click Close to close the Reset Internet Explorer Settings dialog box, and then click OK to close the Internet Properties dialog box

FIGURE A-5

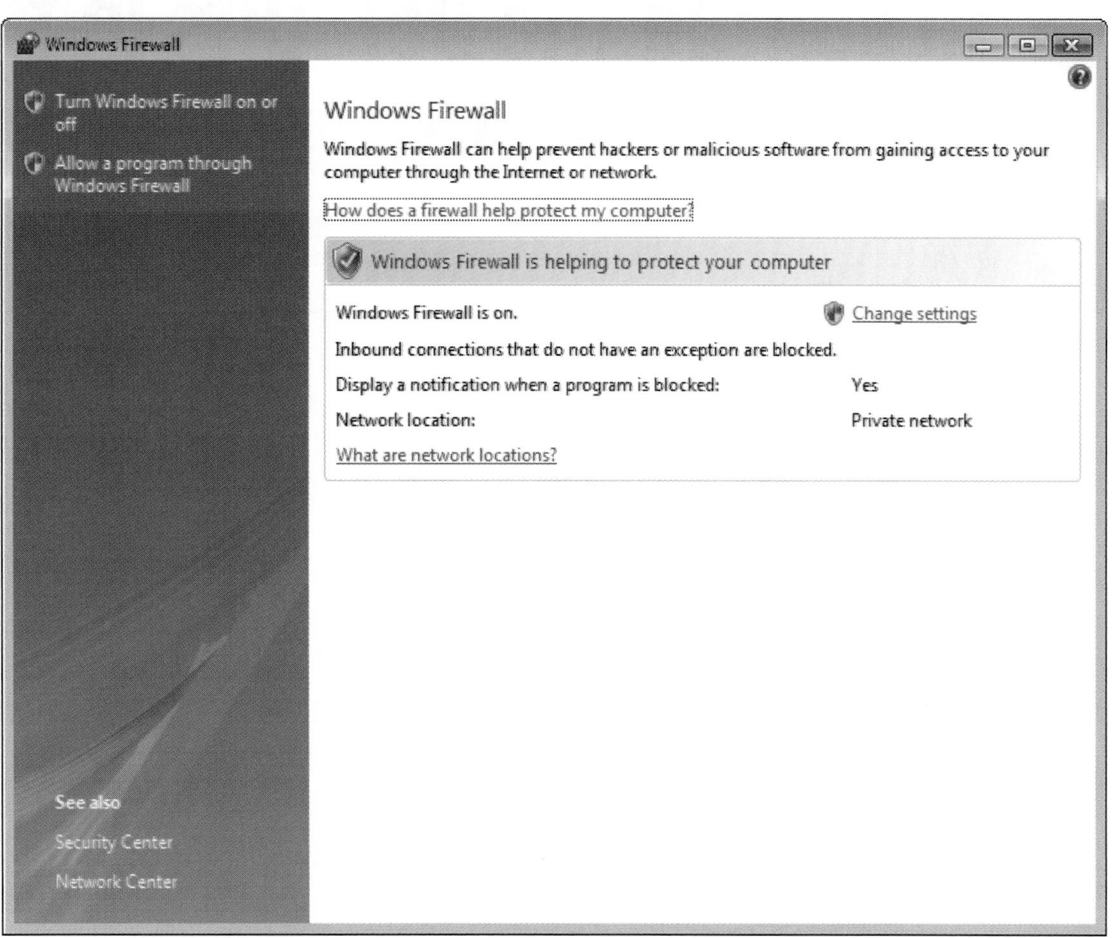

FIGURE A-6

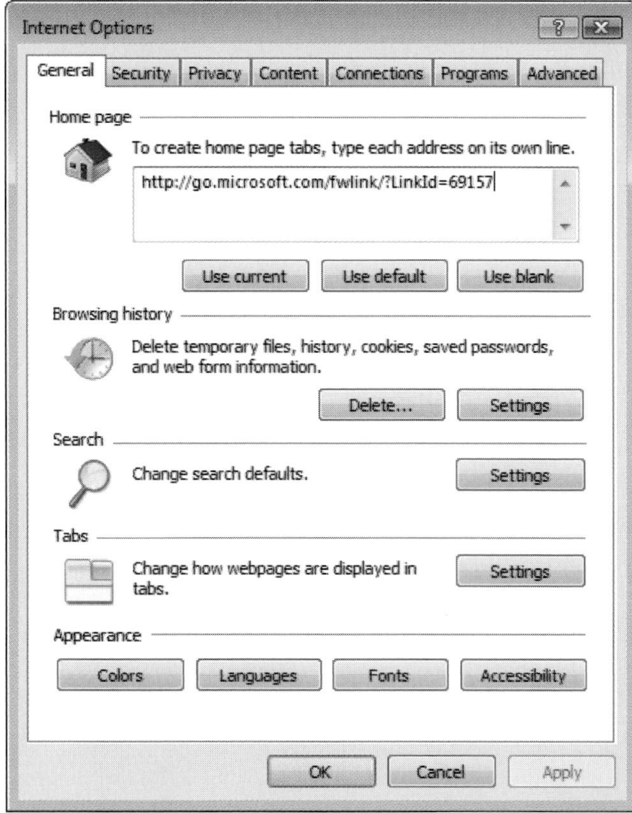

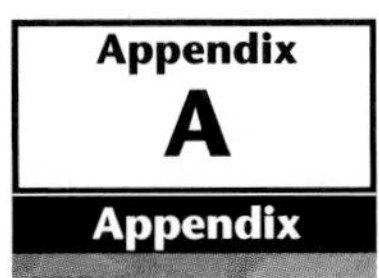

Restoring the Defaults in the Hardware and Sound Section

The following instructions require a default Windows Vista Ultimate installation and the student logged in with an Administrator account. All of the following settings can be changed by accessing the Control Panel.

STEPS

- To restore the defaults in the Autoplay section
  1. Click Start, and then click Control Panel. Click Hardware and Sound, click Autoplay, and then compare your screen to Figure A-7. Scroll down and click the Reset all defaults button in the Devices section at the bottom of the window, and then click Save
- To restore the defaults in the Sound section
  1. Click Start, and then click Control Panel. Click Hardware and Sound, click Sound, and then compare your screen to Figure A-8
  2. In the Sound dialog box, on the Sounds tab, select Windows Default from the Sound Scheme drop-down list, and then click OK
- To restore the defaults in the Mouse section
  1. Click Start, and then click Control Panel. Click Hardware and Sound, click Mouse, and then compare your screen to Figure A-9
  2. In the Mouse Properties dialog box, on the Pointers tab, select Windows Aero (system scheme) from the Scheme drop-down list
  3. Click OK to close the Mouse Properties dialog box

FIGURE A-7

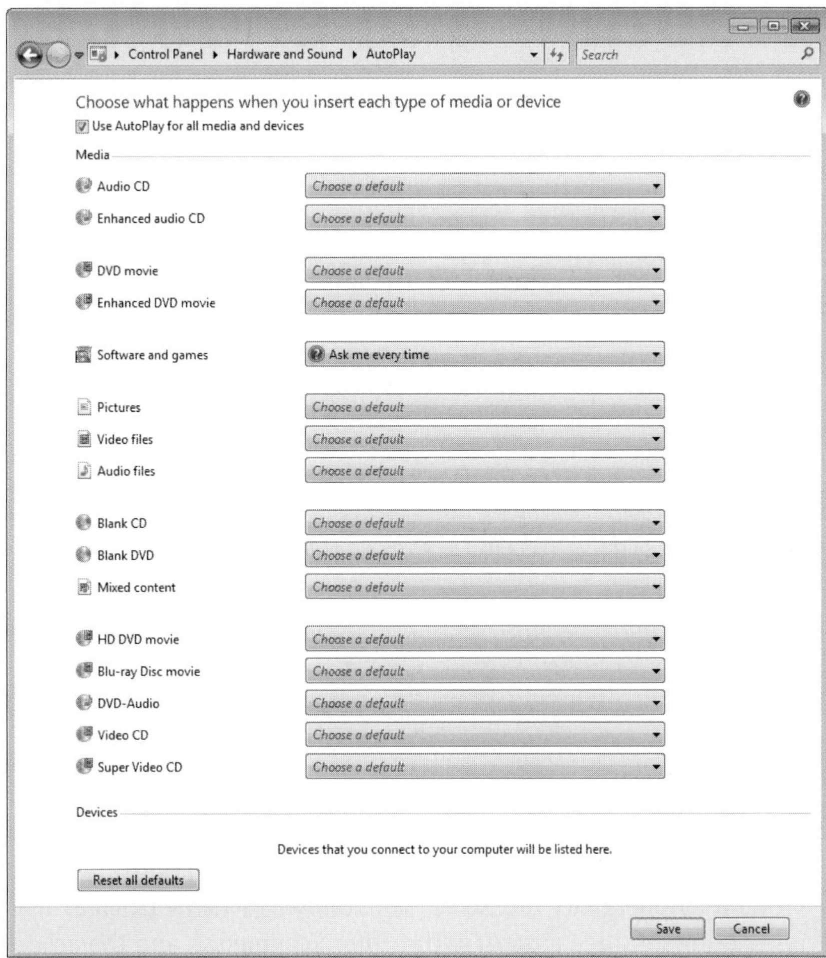

FIGURE A-8

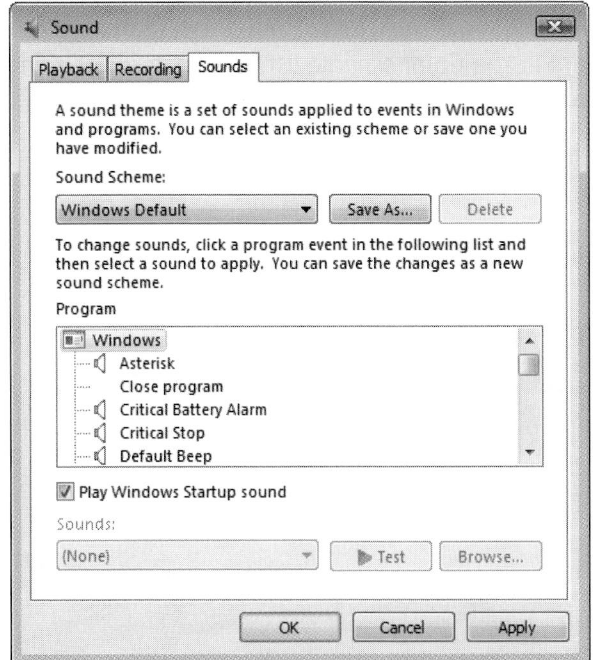

FIGURE A-9

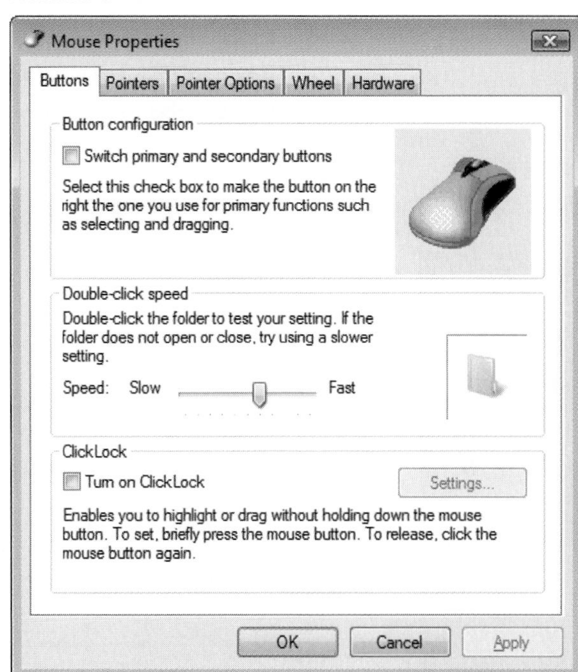

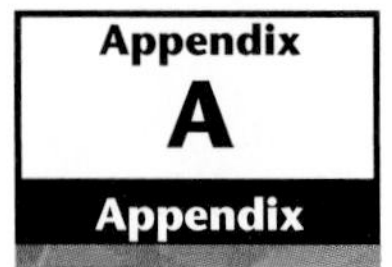

Disabling and Enabling Windows Aero

Unlike prior versions of Windows, Windows Vista provides two distinct user interface experiences: a "basic" experience for entry-level systems and more visually dynamic experience called Windows Aero. Both offer a new and intuitive navigation experience that helps you more easily find and organize your applications and files, but Aero goes further by delivering a truly next-generation desktop experience.

Windows Aero builds on the basic Windows Vista user experience and offers Microsoft's best-designed, highest-performing desktop experience. Using Aero requires a PC with compatible graphics adapter and running a Premium or Business edition of Windows Vista.

The following instructions require a computer capable of running Windows Aero, with a default Windows Vista Ultimate installation and student logged in with an Administrator account.

STEPS

- **To Disable Windows Aero**

We recommend that students using this book disable Windows Aero and restore their operating systems default settings (instructions to follow).

1. **Right-click the desktop, select Personalize, and then compare your screen in Figure A-10. Select Window Color and Appearance, and then select Open classic appeareance properties for more color options. In Appearance Settings dialog box, on the Appearance tab, select any non-Aero scheme (such as Windows Vista Basic or Windows Vista Standard) in the Color Scheme list, and then click OK. Figure A-11 compares Windows Aero to other color schemes. Note that this book uses Windows Vista Basic as the color scheme**

- **To Enable Windows Aero**

1. **Right-click the desktop, and then select Personalize. Select Window Color and Appearance, then select Windows Aero in the Color scheme list, and then click OK in the Appearance Settings dialog box**

FIGURE A-10

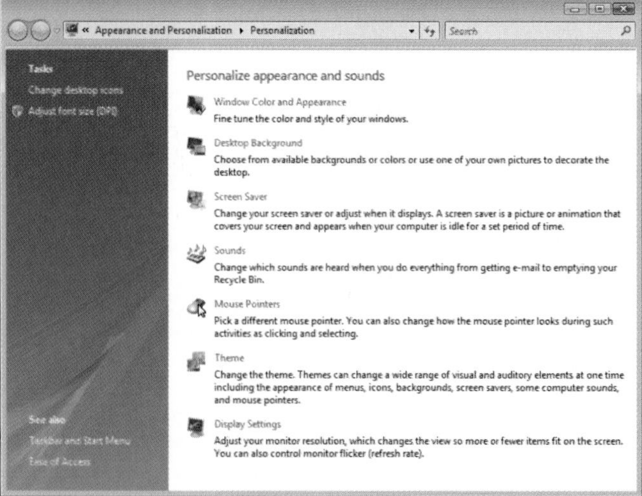

FIGURE A-11

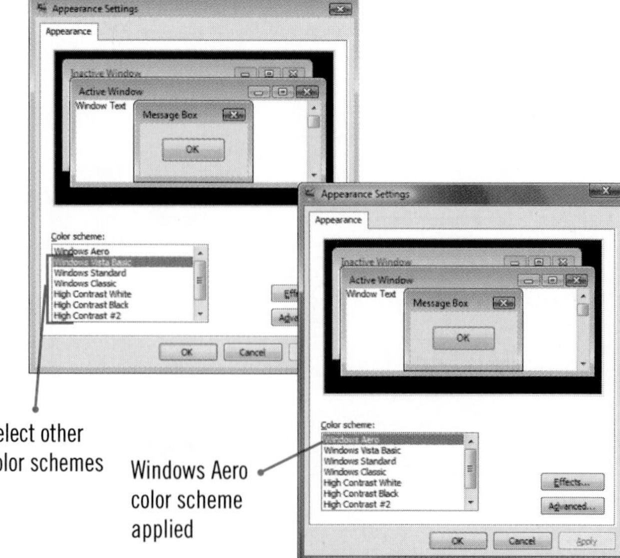

.accdb The file extension that usually means the database is an Access 2007 format database.

.mdb The file extension for Access 2000 and 2002–2003 databases.

Active The currently available document, program, or object; on the taskbar, the button of the active document appears in a darker shade while the buttons of other open documents are dimmed.

Aggregate function A function such as Sum, Avg, and Count used in a summary query to calculate information about a group of records.

Alignment command A command used in Layout or Design View for a form or report to either left-, center-, or right-align a value within its control, or to align the top, bottom, right, or left edge of the control with respect to other controls.

Allow Value List Edits A property you specify to determine whether the Edit List Items button is active in a combo box list.

Alternate Back Color A property that determines the color that alternates with white in the background of a report section.

AND criteria Criteria placed in the same row of the query design grid. All criteria on the same row must be true for a record to appear on the resulting datasheet.

Argument Information that a function uses to create the final answer. Multiple arguments are separated by commas. All of the arguments for a function are surrounded by a single set of parentheses.

Attachment field A field that allows you to attach an external file such as a Word document, PowerPoint presentation, Excel workbook, or image file to a record.

AutoFormat A predefined format that you can apply to a form or report to set the background picture, font, color and alignment formatting choices.

Autonumber A field data type in which Access enters a sequential integer for each record added into the datasheet. Numbers cannot be reused even if the record is deleted.

Avg function Built-in Access function used to calculate the average of the values in a given field.

Back Color property A property that determines the background color of the selected control or section in a form or report.

Backward-compatible Software feature that enables documents saved in an older version of a program to be opened in a newer version of the program.

Binding The field binding determines the field to which a bound control in a form or report is connected.

Bound control A control used in either a form or report to display data from the underlying field; used to edit and enter new data in a form.

Calculated field A field created in Query Design View that results from an expression of existing fields, Access functions, and arithmetic operators. For example, the entry Profit: [RetailPrice]-[WholesalePrice] in the field cell of the query design grid creates a calculated field called Profit that is the difference between the values in the RetailPrice and WholesalePrice fields.

Calculation A new value that is created by entering an expression in a text box on a form or report.

Calendar icon An icon you can click to select a date from a pop-up calendar.

Calendar picker A pop-up calendar from which you can choose dates for a date field.

Category axis On a PivotChart, the horizontal axis. Also called the x-axis. PivotChart.

Chart Field List A list of fields in the underlying record source for a

Clipboard Temporary storage area in Windows.

Column separator The thin line that separates the field names to the left or right.

Combo Box Wizard A bound control used to display a list of possible entries for a field in which you can also type an entry from the keyboard.

Combo box A bound control used to display a list of possible entries for a field in which you can also type an entry from the keyboard. It is a "combination" of the list box and text box controls.

Command button An unbound control used to provide an easy way to initiate an action.

Compatible The capability of different programs to work together and exchange data.

Conditional formatting Formatting that is based on specified criteria. For example, a text box may be conditionally formatted do display its value in red if the value is a negative number.

Contextual tab Tab on the Ribbon that appears when needed to complete a specific task; for example, if you select a chart in an Excel workbook, three contextual Chart Tool tabs (Design, Layout, and Format) appear.

Control Any element on a form or report such as a label, text box, line, or combo box. Controls can be bound, unbound, or calculated.

Control Source property A property of a bound control in a form or report that determines the field to which the control is connected.

Criteria Entries (rules and limiting conditions) that determine which records are displayed when finding or filtering records in a datasheet or form, or when building a query.

Criteria syntax Rules by which criteria need to be entered. For example, text criteria syntax requires that the criteria are surrounded by quotation marks (" "). Date criteria are surrounded by pound signs (#).

Crosstab Query A query that represents data in a cross-tabular layout (fields are used for both column and row headings), similar to PivotTables in other database and spreadsheet products.

Crosstab Query Wizard A wizard used to create crosstab queries and which helps identify fields that will be used for row and column headings, and fields that will be summarized within the datasheet.

Crosstab row A row in the query design grid used to specify the column and row headings and values for the crosstab query.

Current record The record that has the focus or is being edited.

Data type A required property for each field that defines the type of data that can be entered in each field. Valid data types include AutoNumber, Text, Number, Currency, Date/Time, OLE Object, and Memo.

Database designer The person responsible for building and maintaining tables, queries, forms, and reports.

Datasheet A spreadsheet-like grid that displays fields as columns and records as rows.

Datasheet View A view that lists the records of the object in a datasheet. Tables, queries, and most form objects have a Datasheet View.

Date function Built-in Access function used to display the current date on a form or report; enter the Date function as Date().

Default View property A form property that determines whether a subform automatically opens in Datasheet or Continuous Forms view.

Design View A view in which the structure of the object can be manipulated. Every Access object has a Design View.

Dialog box launcher An icon available in many groups on the Ribbon that you can click to open a dialog box or task pane, offering an alternative way to choose commands.

Display When property A control property that determines whether the control appears only on the screen, only when printed, or at all times.

Document window Workspace in the program window that displays the current document.

Domain The recordset (table or query) that contains the field used in a domain function calculation.

Domain function A function used to display a calculation on a form or report using a field that is not included in the Record Source property for the form or report. Also called domain aggregate function.

Drop area A position on a PivotChart or PivotTable where you can drag and place a field. Drop areas on a PivotTable include the Filter field, Row field, Column field, and Totals or Detail field. Drop areas on a PivotChart include the Filter field, Category field, Series field, and Data field.

Edit List Items button A button you click to add items to the combo box list in Form View.

Edit mode The mode in which Access assumes you are trying to edit a particular field, so keystrokes such as [Ctrl][End], [Ctrl][Home], [move the insertion point within the field.

Edit record symbol A pencil-like symbol that appears in the record selector box to the left of the record that is currently being edited in either a datasheet or a form.

Enabled property A control property that determines whether the control can have the focus in Form View.

Error Indicator button A smart tag that helps identify potential design errors in Report or Form Design View.

Expression A combination of values, functions, and operators that calculates to a single value. Access expressions start with an equal sign and are placed in a text box in either Form Design View or Report Design View.

Field list A list of the available fields in the table or query that the field list represents.

Field name The name given to each field in a table.

Field properties Characteristics that further define the field.

Field selector The button to the left of a field in Table Design View that indicates which field is currently selected. Also the thin gray bar above each field in the query grid.

File An electronic collection of stored data that has a unique name, distinguishing it from other files.

Filter By Form A way to filter data that allows two or more criteria to be specified at the same time.

Filter By Selection A way to filter records for an exact match.

Find Duplicates Query Wizard A wizard used to create a query that determines whether a table contains duplicate values in one or more fields.

Find Unmatched Query Wizard A wizard used to create a query that finds records in one table that doesn't have related records in another table.

Focus The property that indicates which field would be edited if you were to start typing.

Foreign key field In a one-to-many relationship between two tables, the foreign key field is the field in the "many" table that links the table to the primary key field in the "one" table.

Form An Access object that provides an easy-to-use data entry screen that generally shows only one record at a time.

Form View View of a form object that displays data from the underlying recordset and allows you to enter and update data.

Form Wizard An Access wizard that helps you create a form.

Format Painter A tool you can use when designing and laying out forms and reports to copy formatting characteristics from one control to another.

Format property A field property that controls how information is displayed and printed.**Formatting** Enhancing the appearance of the information through font, size, and color changes.

Function A special, predefined formula that provides a shortcut for a commonly used calculation, for example, SUM or COUNT.

Gallery A collection of choices you can browse through to make a selection. Often available with Live Preview.

Graphic image *See* Image.

Group On the Ribbon, a set of related commands on a tab.

Group controls To allow you to identify several controls as a group to quickly and easily apply the same formatting properties to them.

Group selection handles Selection handles that surround grouped controls.

Grouping To sort records in a particular order, plus provide a section before and after each group of records.

Hexadecimal Numbers that consist of numbers 0–9 as well as letters A–H.

Image A nontextual piece of information such as a picture, piece of clip art, drawn object, or graph. Because images are graphical (and not numbers or letters), they are sometimes referred to as graphical images.

Infinity symbol The symbol that indicates the "many" side of a one-to-many relationship.

Input Mask property A field property that provides a visual guide for users as they enter data.

Integrate To incorporate a document or parts of a document created in one program into another program; for example, to incorporate an Excel chart into a PowerPoint slide, or an Access table into a Word document.

Interface The look and feel of a program; for example, the appearance of commands and the way they are organized in the program window.

Is Not Null A criterion that finds all records in which any entry has been made in the field.

Is Null A criterion that finds all records in which no entry has been made in the field.

Join line The line identifying which fields establish the relationship between two related tables.

JPEG Acronym for Joint Photographic Experts Group, which defines the standards for the compression algorithms that allow image files to be stored in an efficient compressed format.

Junction table A table created to establish separate one-to-many relationships to two tables that have a many-to-many relationship.

Key field combination Two or more fields that as a group contain unique information for each record.

Landscape orientation A way to print or view a page that is 11 inches wide by 8.5 inches tall.

Layout The general arrangement in which a form displays the fields in the underlying recordset. Layout types include Columnar, Tabular, Datasheet, Chart, and PivotTable. Columnar is most popular for a form, and Datasheet is most popular for a subform.

Layout View An Access view that lets you make some desgin changes to a form or repot while you are browsing.

Like operator An Access comparison operator that allows queries to find records that match criteria that include a wildcard character.

Limit to List A combo box control property that allows you to limit the entries made by that control to those provided by the combo box list.

Link Child Fields A subform property that determines which field serves as the "many" link between the subform and main form.

Link Master Fields A subform property that determines which field serves as the "one" link between the main form and the subform.

List box A bound control that displays a list of possible choices for the user. Used mainly on forms.

Live Preview A feature that lets you point to a choice in a gallery or palette and see the results in the document without actually clicking the choice.

Locked property A control property specifies whether you can edit data in a control on Form View.

Logical view The datasheet of a query is sometimes called a logical view of the data because it is not a copy of the data, but rather, a selected view of data from the underlying tables.

Lookup field A field that has lookup properties. Lookup properties are used to create a drop-down list of values to populate the field.

Lookup properties Field properties that allow you to supply a drop-down list of values for a field.

Lookup Wizard A wizard used in Table Design View that allows one field to "look up" values from another table or entered list. For example, you might use the Lookup Wizard to specify that the Customer Number field in the Sales table display the Customer Name field entry from the Customers table.

Macro An Access object that stores a collection of keystrokes or commands such as those for printing several reports in a row or providing a toolbar when a form opens.

Main form A form that contains a subform control.

Main report A report that contains a subreport control.

Many-to-many relationship The relationship between two tables in an Access database in which one record of one table relates to many records in the other table and vice versa. You cannot directly create a many-to-many relationship between two tables in Access. To relate two tables with such a relationship, you must establish a third table called junction table that creates separate one-to-many relationships with the two original tables.

Module An Access object that stores Visual Basic programming code that extends the functions of automated Access processes.

Multivalued field A field that allows you to make more than one choice from a drop-down list.

Navigation buttons Buttons in the lower-left corner of a datasheet or form that allow you to quickly navigate between the records in the underlying object as well as add a new record.

Navigation mode A mode in which Access assumes that you are trying to move between the fields and records of the datasheet (rather than edit a specific field's contents), so keystrokes such as [Ctrl][Home] and [Ctrl][End] move you to the first and last field of the datasheet.

Navigation Pane A pane in the Access program window that provides a way to move between objects (tables, queries, forms, reports, macros, and modules) in the database.

Null entry The state of "nothingness" in a field. Any entry such as 0 in a numeric field or a space in a text field is not null. It is common to search for empty fields by using the Null criterion in a filter or query. The Is Not Null criterion finds all records where there is an entry of any kind.

OLE object A field data type that stores pointers that tie files, such as pictures, sound clips, or spreadsheets, created in other programs to a record.

One-to-many line The line that appears in the Relationships window and shows which field is duplicated between two tables to serve as the linking field. The one-to-many line displays a "1" next to the field that serves as the "one" side of the relationship and displays an infinity symbol next to the field that serves as the "many" side of the relationship when referential integrity is specified for the relationship. Also called the one-to-many join line.

One-to-many relationship The relationship between two tables in an Access database in which a common field links the tables together. The linking field is called the primary key field in the "one" table of the relationship and the foreign key field in the "many" table of the relationship.

Online collaboration The ability to incorporate feedback or share information across the Internet or a company network or intranet.

Option button A bound control used to display a limited list of mutually exclusive choices for a field, such as "female" or "male" for a gender field in form or report.

Option group A bound control placed on a form that is used to group together several option buttons that provide a limited number of values for a field.

OR criteria Criteria placed on different rows of the query design grid. A record will appear in the resulting datasheet if it is true for any single row.

Orphan record A record in the "many" table of a one-to-many relationship that doesn't have a matching entry in the linking field of the "one" table.

Page orientation Printing or viewing a page of data in either a portrait (8.5 inches wide by 11 inches tall) or landscape (11 inches wide by 8.5 inches tall) direction.

Parameter report A report that prompts you for criteria to determine the records to use for the report.

PivotChart A graphical presentation of the data in a PivotTable.

PivotChart View The view in which you build a PivotChart.

PivotTable An arrangement of data that uses one field as a column heading, another as a row heading, and summarizes a third field, typically a Number field, in the body.

PivotTable View The view in which you build a PivotTable.

Pixel (picture element) One pixel is the measurement of one picture element on the screen.

Portrait orientation A way to print or view a page that is 8.5 inches wide by 11 inches tall.

Previewing Prior to printing, to see onscreen exactly how the printed document will look.

Primary key field A field that contains unique information for each record. A primary key field cannot contain a null entry.

Print Preview An Access view that shows you how a report or other object will print on a sheet of paper.

Program tab Single tab on the Ribbon specific to a particular view, such as Print Preview.

Property A characteristic that further defines a field (if field properties), control (if control properties), section (if section properties), or object (if object properties).

Property sheet A window that displays an exhaustive list of properties for the chosen control, section, or object within the Form Design View or Report Design View.

Query An Access object that provides a spreadsheet-like view of the data, similar to that in tables. It may provide the user with a subset of fields and/or records from one or more tables. Queries are created when the user has a "question" about the data in the database.

Query Datasheet View The view of a query that shows the selected fields and records as a datasheet.

Query design grid The bottom pane of the Query Design View window in which you specify the fields, sort order, and limiting criteria for the query.

Query Design View The window in which you develop queries by specifying the fields, sort order, and limiting criteria that determine which fields and records are displayed in the resulting datasheet.

Quick Access toolbar Customizable toolbar that includes buttons for common Office commands, such as saving a file and undoing an action.

Read-only An object property that indicates whether the object can read and display data, but cannot be used to change (write to) data.

Record Source property In a form or report, the property that determines which table or query object contains the fields and records that the form or report will display. It is the most important property of the form or report object. A bound control on a form or report has Control Source property. In this case, the Control Source property identifies the field to which the control is bound.

Referential integrity A set of Access rules that govern data entry and help ensure data accuracy.

Relational database software Software such as Access that is used to manage data organized in a relational database.

Report An Access object that creates a professional printout of data that may contain such enhancements as headers, footers, and calculations on groups of records.

Report View An Access view that maximizes the amount of data you can see on the screen.

Report Wizard An Access wizard that helps you create a report.

Resize bar A thin gray bar that separates the field lists from the query design grid in Query Design View.

Ribbon Area that displays commands for the current Office program, organized into tabs and groups.

Row selector The small square to the left of a field in Table Design View or the Tab Order dialog box. Called the record selector in Datasheet View and Form View.

Row Source The Lookup property that defines the list of values for the Lookup field.

Ruler A vertical or horizontal guide that both appear in Form and Report Design View to help you position controls.

Run a query To open a query and view the fields and records that you have selected for the query presented as a datasheet.

Screen capture A snapshot of your screen, as if you took a picture of it with a camera, which you can paste into a document.

Section A location of a form or report that contains controls. The section in which a control is placed determines where and how often the control prints.

Section properties Characteristics that define each section in a report.

Select query The most common type of query that retrieves data from one or more linked tables and displays the results in a datasheet.

Simple Query Wizard A wizard used to create a select query.

Sizing handles Small squares at each corner of a selected control in Access. Dragging a handle resizes the control. Also known as handles.

Smart tag A button that provides a small menu of options and automatically appears under certain conditions to help you work with a task, such as correcting errors. For example, the AutoCorrect Options button, which helps you correct typos and update properties, and the Error Indicator button, which helps identify potential design errors in Form and Report Design View, are smart tags.

Sort To reorder records in either ascending or descending order based on the values of a particular field.

Split form A form that shows you two views of the same data at one time: a traditional form and a datasheet view.

SQL (Structured Query Language) A language that provides a standardized way to request information from a relational database system.

Subform A form placed within a form that shows related records from another table or query. A subform generally displays many records at a time in a datasheet arrangement.

Suite A group of programs that are bundled together and share a similar interface, making it easy to transfer skills and program content among them.

Sum function A mathematical function that totals values in a field.

Summary query A query used to calculate and display information about records grouped together.

Summary report A report that calculates and displays information about records grouped together.

Tab A set of commands on the Ribbon related to a common set of tasks or features. Tabs are further organized into groups of related commands.

Tab control An unbound control used to create a three-dimensional aspect to a form so that other controls can be organized and shown in Form View by clicking the "tabs."

Tab order The sequence in which the controls on the form receive the focus when the user presses [Tab] or [Enter] in Form view.

Tab stop In Access, this refers to whether you can tab into a control when entering or editing data; in other words, whether the control can receive the focus.

Table A collection of records for a single subject, such as all of the customer records.

Table Design View The view in which you can add, delete, or modify fields and their associated properties.

Template A sample file, such as a database provided within the Microsoft Access program.

Themes Predesigned combinations of colors, fonts, and formatting attributes that you can apply to a document in any Office program.

Title bar Area at the top of every program window that displays the document and program name.

Total row Row in the query design grid used to specify how records should be grouped and summarized with aggregate functions.

Unbound A group of controls that do not display data.

Unbound control A control that does not change from record to record and exists only to clarify or enhance the appearance of the form, using elements such as labels, lines, and clip art.

User The person primarily interested in entering, editing, and analyzing the data in the database.

User interface A collective term for all the ways you interact with a software program.

Validation Rule A field property that helps eliminate unreasonable entries by establishing criteria for an entry before it is accepted into the database.

Validation Text A field property that determines what message appears if a user attempts to make a field entry that does not pass the validation rule for that field.

Value axis On a PivotChart, the vertical axis. Also called the y-axis.

Value field A numeric field, such as Cost, that can be summed or averaged.

Views Display settings that show or hide selected elements of a document in the document window, to make it easier to focus on a certain task, such as formatting or reading text.

Wildcard A special character used in criteria to find, filter, and query data. The asterisk (*) stands for any group of characters. For example, the criteria I* in a State field criterion cell would find all records where the state entry was IA, ID, IL, IN, or Iowa. The question mark (?) wildcard stands for only one character.

Zooming in A feature that makes a document appear bigger but shows less of it on screen at once; does not affect actual document size.

Zooming out A feature that shows more of a document on screen at once but at a reduced size; does not affect actual document size.

Index

▶S

▶T

▶U

▶V

▶W

▶X

▶Y

▶Z